The Artificial Intelligence Debate

The Artificial Intelligence Debate
False Starts, Real Foundations

edited by
STEPHEN R. GRAUBARD

The MIT Press
Cambridge, Massachusetts
London, England

Second Printing, 1989

First MIT Press edition, 1988

Printed and bound in the United States of America.

Library of Congress Cataloging-in-Publication Data

The Artificial intelligence debate : false starts, real foundations/
  edited by Stephen R. Graubard. — 1st MIT Press ed.

   p.   cm.
  Bibliography: p.
  ISBN 0-262-57074-2 (pbk.)
   1. Artificial intelligence. 2. Machine learning. I. Graubard,
Stephen Richards.
  Q335.5.A783 1988   88-21567
  006.3—dc19   CIP

Contents

Seymour Papert

One AI or Many?

I S THERE ONE AI or are there many? A dramatic shift in the tone
of discussion about artificial intelligence has brought about a
suddenly increased awareness of the presence of divergent ways
of thinking in what has generally been presented as a unified field.
Readers of this issue of *Dædalus* who have not kept abreast of recent
developments may be astonished to see how many of its authors have
chosen to focus on divergences in the field, and particularly on one
trend in AI that has come to be known as connectionism. They would
not be alone in their surprise. Late in 1985 I participated in a
planning meeting to discuss an issue of *Dædalus* on AI. At that time
I knew (and I assume that most people at that meeting knew) that
research activity on "connectionist" themes was growing. But I
would have expressed disbelief had anyone at the meeting suggested
(no one did) that these themes would soon burst out of the technical
journals into such publications as the *New York Times Book
Review*—where connectionism is characterized as cognitive counterrevolution[1]—and become the central talking point wherever AI or
cognitive science is discussed. The contents of this issue of *Dædalus*
reflect this movement more than any deliberate plan: something
intriguing and dramatic had taken place on a larger scale than the
planning of a journal. So when Stephen Graubard invited me to
contribute a piece of my own, I could not resist using the connectionist brouhaha as the occasion to discuss some larger issues about

*Seymour Papert is professor of media technology and director of the Learning and Epistemol-
ogy Group in the Media Laboratory at MIT.*

the nature of artificial intelligence and its appeal to people more interested in the human mind than in building robots.

The field of artificial intelligence is currently divided into what seem to be several competing paradigms. The present contenders differ over the form of mechanisms needed to capture all forms of intelligence. They are each engaged in a search for mechanisms with a universal application. Allen Newell, dean of information processing, believes that he is close, that all knowledge can be formulated as the rules behind a special kind of program known as a "production system." The authors of the current connectionist manifesto, *Parallel Distributed Processing*,[2] do not think they are as close, but speak with confidence that their way—relying not on programs but on networked neuronlike entities—will provide universal mechanisms.

I do not foresee the future in terms of an ultimate victory for any of the present contenders. What I do foresee is a change of frame, away from the search for universal mechanisms. I believe that we have much more to learn from studying the differences, rather than the sameness, of kinds of knowing. And just because knowing takes place in one brain is not a reason to argue, as both connectionists and programmers do, that there is one privileged and universal mechanism on any psychologically relevant level.

An analogy dramatizes what I mean by psychologically relevant. An evolutionary biologist might try to understand how tigers came to have stripes. And a molecular biologist might try to understand the origin of life in some primeval soup. But how life started gives you no information about how a tiger looks. Yet this fallacy pervades the intellectual discourse of connectionists and programmers. The connectionists talk about experiments on the level of small groups of simulated neurons and then, almost in the same breath, talk about how one can walk and think at the same time. Multiprocessing is assumed to be the same kind of enterprise in both cases. Information processing experts display rule systems that match the behavior of people and computers solving logical problems, and jump from there to statements like Allen Newell's: "Psychology has arrived at the possibility of a unified theory of cognition."

There is the same mistake on both sides: the category error of supposing that the existence of a common mechanism provides both an explanation and a unification of all systems, however complex, in which this mechanism might play a central role. My thesis here is that

AI needs to be defined in a way that does not put it in jeopardy of making this category error. As it matures, I see AI developing the conceptual frameworks that will enable us to obtain a rigorous understanding not only of what is the same in such activities as falling in love and playing chess, but of what is different between them. Artificial intelligence should become the methodology for thinking about ways of knowing.

In this essay I use an incident in the development of connectionism to illustrate the current resistance of the field to this way of thinking about its intellectual identity.

I

I do not come to the discussion of connectionism as a neutral observer. In fact, the standard version of its history assigns me a role in a romantic story whose fairytale resonances surely contribute at least a little to connectionism's aura of excitement.

Once upon a time two daughter sciences were born to the new science of cybernetics. One sister was natural, with features inherited from the study of the brain, from the way nature does things. The other was artificial, related from the beginning to the use of computers. Each of the sister sciences tried to build models of intelligence, but from very different materials. The natural sister built models (called neural networks) out of mathematically purified neurones. The artificial sister built her models out of computer programs.

In their first bloom of youth the two were equally successful and equally pursued by suitors from other fields of knowledge. They got on very well together. Their relationship changed in the early sixties when a new monarch appeared, one with the largest coffers ever seen in the kingdom of the sciences: Lord DARPA, the Defense Department's Advanced Research Projects Agency. The artificial sister grew jealous and was determined to keep for herself the access to Lord DARPA's research funds. The natural sister would have to be slain.

The bloody work was attempted by two staunch followers of the artificial sister, Marvin Minsky and Seymour Papert, cast in the role of the huntsman sent to slay Snow White and bring back her heart as proof of the deed. Their weapon was not the dagger but the mightier pen, from which came a book—*Perceptrons*[3]—purporting to prove that neural nets could never fill their promise of building models of mind: *only computer programs could do this.* Victory seemed assured for the artificial sister. And indeed, for the next decade all the rewards of the kingdom came to her progeny, of which the family of expert systems did best in fame and fortune.

But Snow White was not dead. What Minsky and Papert had shown the world as proof was not the heart of the princess; it was the heart of a pig. To be more literal: their book was read as proving that the neural net approach to building models of mind was dead. But a closer look reveals that they really demonstrated something much less than this. The book did indeed point out very serious limitations of a certain class of nets (nowadays known as one-layer perceptrons) but was misleading in its suggestion that this class of nets was the heart of connectionism. *Parallel Distributed Processing,* allowing that the suggestion could have been an honest mistake, lapses into a fairy-tale tone in talking about how things were back in "Minsky and Papert's day." In that far-off time and place, the technical discoveries were still to be made that would open the vision—model connectionism's sustaining myth—of much more powerful neural nets than could then be imagined.

Connectionist writings present the story as having a happy ending. The natural sister was quietly nurtured in the laboratories of a few ardent researchers who kept the faith, even when the world at large let itself be convinced that the enterprise was futile. Who (or what) should be cast in the role of Prince Charming is a problem I shall take up later: Who are the parties to the present-day connectionist love affair? Who woke connectionism? And why now? And what next? But for the moment suffice it to note that the princess has emerged from relative rags and obscurity to win the admiration of all except a few of her sister's disgruntled hangers-on.

II

The story seems to call for a plea of guilty or innocent: Did Minsky and I try to kill connectionism, and how do we feel now about its resurrection? Something more complex than a plea is needed. Yes, there was *some* hostility in the energy behind the research reported in *Perceptrons,* and there is *some* degree of annoyance at the way the new movement has developed; part of our drive came, as we quite plainly acknowledged in our book, from the fact that funding and research energy were being dissipated on what still appear to me (since the story of new, powerful network mechanisms is seriously exaggerated) to be misleading attempts to use connectionist methods in practical applications. But most of the motivation for *Perceptrons* came from more fundamental concerns, many of which cut cleanly across the division between networkers and programmers.

One of these concerns had to do with finding an appropriate balance between romanticism and rigor in the pursuit of artificial intelligence. Many serious endeavors would never get off the ground if pioneers were limited to discussing in public only what they could demonstrate rigorously. Think, for example, of the development of flying machines. The excitement generated when the Wright brothers made their first flight had a large element of the romantic. And rightly so: it is hard to work up respect for those critics who complained that a short hop on a beach did not prove the feasibility of useful air transportation. When final success cannot be taken as a criterion for judging initial steps, the problem of developing a sensible critical methodology is an essential and often delicate part of any very out-of-the-ordinary endeavor. In the case of artificial intelligence, the problem of critical judgment of partial results is compounded by the fact that a little intelligence is not easily recognized as intelligence. Indeed, in English we have a special word for it: although a short flight is still counted as a flight, a little intelligence is counted as stupidity, and in AI's early stages (where it still is), this is all that can be expected. How, then, does one decide whether the latest "stupidity" of a machine should be counted as a step toward intelligence? The methodology Minsky and I used in *Perceptrons* is best explained through an example.

Parallel Distributed Processing reports an experiment in which a simulated machine (I'll call it Exor) learned to tell whether two inputs, each of which must be either a one or a zero, are different.* Exor's learning process consumed 2,232 repetitions of a training cycle; in each repetition the machine was presented with one of the four possible combinations of inputs (one-one, zero-zero, zero-one, one-zero) and a feedback signal to indicate whether it had given the right response ("no" for the first two and "yes" for the others). Smart

---

*XOR, pronounced as if written *exor,* is a computerist abbreviation for "exclusive or" (i.e., "this or that but not both"). This makes it the perfect name for our simulated machine.

or stupid? Should one be more impressed by the fact that the thing "learned" at all, or by the fact that it learned so slowly and laboriously?

There was a time, in the early days of cybernetics, when a machine doing anything at all that resembled learning would have been impressive. Today something more is needed to give significance, and in this case the something more is closely related to our allegory. Exor is a neural net, and the task it learned to perform happens, for all its simplicity, to be one of those things a one-layer net cannot do. Knowing this turns the dilemma of judging Exor into an encapsulation of the larger dilemma of judging connectionism. If you want to believe, Exor allows you to proclaim, "Snow White lives." If you don't, Exor's retarded pace of learning allows you to whisper, "But barely." *Perceptrons* set out on a very different tack: instead of asking whether nets are good, we asked what they are *good for*. The focus of enquiry shifted from generalities about kinds of machines to specifics about kinds of tasks. From this point of view, Exor raises such questions as: Which tasks would be learned faster and which would be learned even more slowly by this machine? Can we make a theory of tasks that will explain why 2,232 repetitions were needed in this particular act of learning? The shift in perspective is sharp: interest has moved from making a judgment of the machine to using the performance of the machine on particular tasks as a way to learn more about the nature of the tasks. This shift is reflected in the subtitle of our book—*Perceptrons: An Introduction to Computational Geometry*. We approached our study of neural networks by looking carefully at the kinds of tasks for which their use was being advocated at the time. Since most of these were in the area of visual pattern recognition, our methodology led us into building theories about such patterns. To our surprise, we found ourselves working a new problem area for geometric research, concerned with understanding why some recognition tasks could easily be performed by a given recognition mechanism, while other computations were extremely costly as measured by the number of repetitions needed for a task or the amount of machinery required. For example, a small single-layer perceptron can easily distinguish triangles from squares, but a very large network is needed to learn whether what is put in front of it is a single connected object or is made up of several parts.

Our surprise at finding ourselves working in geometry was a pleasant one. It reinforced our sense that we were opening a new field, not closing an old one. But although the shift from judging perceptrons abstractly to judging the tasks they perform might seem like plain common sense, it took us a long time to make it. So long, in fact, that we are now only mildly surprised to observe the resistance today's connectionists show to recognizing the nature of our work—and the nature of the problem area into which their own investigations must eventually lead.

III

Artificial intelligence, like any other scientific enterprise, had built a scientific culture. The way of working we used in *Perceptrons* ran against the grain of this culture, in whose development we ourselves had participated.

The quest for universality of mechanism is obscured as a pervasive trait of the AI culture by the circumstance that all successful AI demonstrations, whether by programmers or connectionists, perform quite specific tasks in quite narrow domains. Indeed, AI theorists sometimes claim as an important discovery the theory that domain specificity is not a limitation of machines but a characteristic of intelligence. However, the theoretical energy of AI has not gone into understanding differences between specific domains, but rather into finding general forms for the specific contents.

The universalist trait gains robustness from having numerous roots. Among the deepest may be the mythic nature of AI's original enterprise of mind building mind. The desire for universality was fed also by the legacy of the scientists, largely mathematicians, who created AI. And it was nurtured by the most mundane material circumstances of funding. By 1969, the date of the publication of *Perceptrons*, AI was not operating in an ivory-tower vacuum. Money was at stake. And while this pressured the field into a preference for short-term achievement, it also put a premium on claims that the sponsor's investment would bear fruits beyond the immediate product.

Its universalism made it almost inevitable for AI to appropriate our work as proof that neural nets were universally bad. We did not think of our work as killing Snow White; we saw it as a way to understand her. In fact, more than half of our book is devoted to "properceptron" findings about some very surprising and hitherto unknown things that perceptrons can do. But in a culture set up for global judgment of mechanisms, being understood can be a fate as bad as death. A real understanding of what a mechanism can do carries too much implication about what it can not do.

The same trait of universalism leads the new generation of connectionists to assess their own microlevel experiments, such as Exor, as a projective screen for looking at the largest macroissues in the philosophy of mind. The category error analogous to seeking explanations of the tiger's stripes in the structure of DNA is not an isolated error. It is solidly rooted in AI's culture.

IV

The conceit of using the story of Snow White as a metaphor has allowed me to talk about the connectionist counterrevolution without saying exactly what connectionism is or what it is revolting against. A little more technical detail is needed to situate connectionism in the larger field of sciences of mind.

The actual task of recognizing the sameness of the two binary inputs would be a trivial one for a programmer. The first of several remarkable features possessed by Exor is that no one programmed it; it was "trained" to do its task by a strictly behaviorist process of external association of stimuli with reinforcements. It could have been trained by someone who rigorously followed Watson's strictures against thinking about the innards of a system. But if this was its only merit as a model of mental process, the large number of repetitions would negate its interest: machines specifically designed to simulate conditioned reflexes have done so with a psychologically more plausible number of repetitions.

Exor's claim of universality is a stronger feature. Exor is small and limited in power, but it sustains the vision of larger machines that are built on the same principles and that will learn whatever is learnable with no innate disposition to acquire particular behaviors. The prospect of such performance becomes a vindication of something more than neural nets. It promises a vindication of behaviorism against Jean Piaget, Noam Chomsky, and all those students of mind who criticized the universalism inherent in behaviorism's tabula rasa.

Behaviorism has been beaten down in another version of the Snow White story, but the response of academic psychology to connectionism may turn out to be a classic example of the return of the repressed.

Connectionism does more than bring back old-fashioned behaviorism. It brings it back in a form that offers a reconciliation with biological thinking about the brain. The structure of the machine reflects, albeit in an abstract way, a certain model of how brains might conceivably be built out of neurons. Although the actual Exor experiments are, of course, performed by computer programs, these programs are meant to represent what would happen if one connected together networks of units that are held to be neuronlike in the following sense. Each unit in the network receives signals from the others or from sensor units connected to the outside world; at any given time, each unit has a certain level of activation that depends on the weighted sum of the states of activation of the units sending signals to it, and the signals sent out along the unit's "axon" reflect its state of activation. Learning takes place by a process that adjusts the weights (strengths of connections) between the units; when the weights are different, activation patterns produced by a given input will be different, and finally, the output (response) to an input (stimulus) will change. This feature gives machines in Exor's family a biological flavor that appeals strongly to the spirit of our times and yet takes very little away from the behaviorist simplicity: although one has to refer to the neuronlike structure in order to build the machine, one thinks only in terms of stimulus, response, and a feedback signal to operate it.

V

This presentation of connectionism as behaviorism in computer's clothing helps place *Perceptrons* in perspective: the questions it discusses are a modern form of an old debate originally couched as a humanistic and philosophical discussion of associations and taken up again more recently as a discussion of behaviorism. Such debates often turn around assertions of the form, "*Starting with nothing but* (associations, stimulus and response, or whatever), *you can never get to* (general ideas, language, or whatever)." Discussion of this form has been more or less compelling but seldom anywhere near conclusive to standards of rigor that seemed normal to people trained, as Minsky and I both were, as mathematicians. And indeed, how could the discussion even be formulated with any semblance of rigor in the absence of a tight theory of human thought? And how could one move seriously toward such a tight theory without knowing whether general ideas or whatever can be derived from associations or whatever?

In its narrowest sense, the intention of *Perceptrons* was to avoid for the study of "machine thinking" some of the chicken-and-egg difficulties that have plagued thinking about human thinking. The strategy was to study a class of computational machines that were sufficiently powerful to capture a significant slice of contemporary achievement in AI, yet sufficiently simple to make possible, with the limited analytic tools at our disposal, a rigorous mathematical analysis of their capacities. We chose the class of machines for which the book was named (in honor of Frank Rosenblatt): perceptrons are defined in the book to be a special and especially simple kind of neural net in the same family as Exor. Perceptrons are too simple to be interesting in their own right as models of mental process. But the most promising step toward developing tools powerful enough to analyze more complex systems, including the human mind, seemed to be achieving a thorough understanding of a single case as simple as a perceptron. Many readers, perhaps all except mathematicians, would be shocked to know how simple a machine can be and still elude full understanding of its capabilities. I find it quite awesome to think about how hard it was to confirm or reject our intuitions about the capacities of perceptrons.

Minsky and I both knew perceptrons extremely well. We had worked on them for many years before our joint project of understanding their limits was conceived; indeed, we originally met at a conference where we both coincidentally presented papers with an unlikely degree of overlap in content about what perceptronlike machines could do. With this background we should have been in an exceptional position to formulate strong conjectures about perceptrons. Yet when we challenged ourselves to prove our intuitions it sometimes took years of struggle to pin one down—to prove it true or to discover that it was seriously flawed.

I was left with a deep respect for the extraordinary difficulty of being sure of what a computational system can or cannot do. I wonder at people who seem so secure in their intuitive convictions, or their less-than-rigorous rhetorical arguments, about computers, neural nets, or human minds. One area in which intuition seems particularly in need of rigorous analysis is in dealing with the romantically attractive notion of holistic process.

VI

In the history of psychology, behaviorism and holism (or gestaltism) have been considered polar opposites. Behaviorism fragments the mind into a myriad of separate atoms of a much smaller size than common sense would allow. Holism and gestaltism insist that psychological atoms are bigger than common sense thinks. So it is quite remarkable that connectionism has facets that appeal to each of these schools of thought.

The title of the current bible of connectionism, *Parallel Distributed Processing*, juxtaposes two qualities that are taken in the connectionist movement as prime characteristics certainly of all natural, and probably of effective artificial, embodiments of intelligence. *Parallel* refers to the quality of having many processes go on at the same time: as people walk and talk at the same time, they very likely carry out large numbers of concurrent, mostly unconscious, mental processes. *Distributed* refers to the quality of not being localized: in traditional computers, items of information are stored in particular places, cleanly separated from one another; in neural nets, information is spread out (in principle, a new piece of learning might involve changes everywhere). Much of the sense that deep process is at work in the functioning of nets is related to the suggestion that what ordinary discourse and traditional cognitive theory misleadingly describe as atomistic items of information are holistically represented and yet appropriately evocable.

Parallel plus distributed *feels* right. But work with perceptrons made us acutely aware of ways in which the two qualities are in tension rather than sweet harmony. It is not hard to switch perceptions so as to make the juxtaposition feel intuitively problematic. In ordinary life, customs of separating activities into rooms and offices are founded on experience with the untidy consequences of having everything happening everywhere at the same time. But connection-ism is built on the theory—what Sherry Turkle calls a sustaining myth—that a deeper understanding would reveal the naiveté of such everyday analogies. Just as modern physics teaches us not to project our sense of macroscopic events onto the subatomic world, so too deeper understanding of networks will teach us that our metaphors of macroscopic organization may be equally misleading.

Indeed, one can find analogies in physical science that go very strongly against uninformed intuitions about interference—how pro-cesses disturb one another. The vibrations of all radio and television waves pass through the same space at the same time, and yet tuning circuits can separate them. Even more incomprehensible, if not frankly shocking to common sense, is the hologram, which records a three-dimensional picture in a fully distributed way: if part of the holographic record is destroyed, no particular part of the picture is lost; there is only a uniform degradation of quality.

These examples plainly say that there is precedent in the physical world for distributed superposition. Enough in the universe is holistic so that the concept of distributed neural net cannot be rejected on general intuitive principles. But not everything is holistic, and com-monsense (or even philosophical) opinion is of little use in spotting what is. Specific investigation, sometimes of a subtle and very technical mathematical nature, is needed to find out whether holistic representation is possible in any specific situation and whether (where it can be done) there is an exorbitant price to pay. The Exor machine illustrates, in a simple case, the concept of the cost of holism.

The task that Exor learned can be seen as a superposition of two learnings in the same network: learning to say yes to one-zero and learning to say yes to zero-one. An important fact is that each of these tasks, taken separately, is much easier to learn than the combined task. And this is not an occasional phenomenon: Exor is a very mild case of incurred cost of distribution. One of the research results of *Perceptrons,* and one that required some mathematical labor, shows that in certain situations the degree of difficulty of superposed tasks can exceed the difficulty of each separate task by arbitrary, large factors.

The romantic stance is to make a new network that isn't quite a perceptron and to assume it innocent until proven guilty of the danger of superposition costs. On the whole, connectionist literature does so even when reporting experiments in which the new networks show empirical signs of such costs as those that Exor incurs in its mild way. The rigorous stance assumes the possibility of guilt until innocence can be established: the theorems proved about perceptrons are seen as showing what kind of phenomena need to be precluded before one can make assertions confidently.

VII

I said at the beginning that I would offer some thoughts about Prince Charming. Who woke connectionism? Why this surge of interest and activity? Why now? And I will use my speculations on these themes to comment on the important question, What next?

A purely technical account of Snow White's awakening goes like this: In the olden days of Minsky and Papert, neural networking models were hopelessly limited by the puniness of the computers available at the time and by the lack of ideas about how to make any but the simplest networks learn. Now things have changed. Powerful, massively parallel computers can implement very large nets, and new learning algorithms can make them learn. No romantic Prince Charming is needed for the story.

I don't believe it. The influential recent demonstrations of new networks all run on small computers and could have been done in 1970 with ease. Exor is a "toy problem" run for study and demonstration, but the examples discussed in the literature are still very small. Indeed, Minsky and I, in a more technical discussion of this history (added as a new chapter to a reissue of *Perceptrons*), suggest that the entire structure of recent connectionist theories might be built on quicksand: it is all based on toy-sized problems with no theoretical analysis to show that performance will be maintained when the models are scaled up to realistic size. The connectionist authors fail to read our work as a warning that networks, like "brute force" programs based on search procedures, scale very badly.

A more sociological explanation is needed. Massively parallel supercomputers do play an important role in the connectionist revival. But I see it as a cultural rather than a technical role, another example of a sustaining myth. Connectionism does not use the new computers as physical machines; it derives strength from the "computer in the mind," from its public's largely nontechnical awareness of supercomputers.

I see connectionism's relationship to biology in similar terms. Although its models use biological metaphors, they do not depend on technical findings in biology any more than they do on modern supercomputers. But here too there is a powerful, resonant phenomenon. Biology is increasingly the locus of the greatest excitement. And neurosciences are invading the territory of academic psychology just as psychopharmacology is invading the territory of clinical psychology.

I also see a more subtle, but not less relevant, cultural resonance. This is a generalized turn away from the hard-edged rationalism of the time connectionism last went into eclipse and a resurgent attraction to more holistic ways of thinking. The actual theoretical discussion in the connectionist literature may not be connected in any strict sense to such trends in intellectual fashion. But here again, the concepts of sustaining myth and cultural resonance are pertinent: this time, perhaps, in a two-way process of mutual support.

Voilà Prince Charming: a composite of cultural trends. Reductionist undertones in my discussion do not undermine my good wishes for a happy union with Snow White. The new sense of excitement that is already replacing a certain ho-hum tiredness in cognitive science will ensure the fertility of the union. But the impact of connectionism will come less from the ideas it engenders than from heightened awareness of the problems it avoids.

ENDNOTES

[1] James G. Greeno, "The Cognition Connection," *New York Times Book Review*, 4 Jan. 1987.
[2] David E. Rumelhart, James L. McClelland, and the PDP Research Group, *Parallel Distributed Processing* (Cambridge: MIT Press, 1986).
[3] Marvin Minsky and Seymour Papert, *Perceptrons: An Introduction to Computational Geometry* (Cambridge: MIT Press, 1969).
[4] Rumelhart, McClelland, and the PDP Research Group, *Parallel Distributed Processing*, p. 111.

Hubert L. Dreyfus and Stuart E. Dreyfus

Making a Mind Versus Modeling the Brain: Artificial Intelligence Back at a Branchpoint

[N]othing seems more possible to me than that people some day will come to the definite opinion that there is no copy in the . . . nervous system which corresponds to a particular thought, or a particular idea, or memory.[1]
—*Ludwig Wittgenstein (1948)*

[I]nformation is not stored anywhere in particular. Rather, it is stored everywhere. Information is better thought of as "evoked" than "found."[2]
—*David Rumelhart and Donald Norman (1981)*

IN THE EARLY 1950S, as calculating machines were coming into their own, a few pioneer thinkers began to realize that digital computers could be more than number crunchers. At that point two opposed visions of what computers could be, each with its correlated research program, emerged and struggled for recognition. One faction saw computers as a system for manipulating mental symbols; the other, as a medium for modeling the brain. One sought to use computers to instantiate a formal representation of the world;

Hubert L. Dreyfus is professor of philosophy at the University of California at Berkeley.

Stuart E. Dreyfus is professor of industrial engineering and operations research at the University of California at Berkeley.

the other, to simulate the interactions of neurons. One took problem solving as its paradigm of intelligence; the other, learning. One utilized logic; the other, statistics. One school was the heir to the rationalist, reductionist tradition in philosophy; the other viewed itself as idealized, holistic neuroscience.

The rallying cry of the first group was that both minds and digital computers are physical symbol systems. By 1955 Allen Newell and Herbert Simon, working at the Rand Corporation, had concluded that strings of bits manipulated by a digital computer could stand for anything—numbers, of course, but also features of the real world. Moreover, programs could be used as rules to represent relations between these symbols, so that the system could infer further facts about the represented objects and their relations. As Newell put it recently in his account of the history of issues in AI,

The digital-computer field defined computers as machines that manipulated numbers. The great thing was, adherents said, that everything could be encoded into numbers, even instructions. In contrast, the scientists in AI saw computers as machines that manipulated symbols. The great thing was, they said, that everything could be encoded into symbols, even numbers.[3]

This way of looking at computers became the basis of a way of looking at minds. Newell and Simon hypothesized that the human brain and the digital computer, while totally different in structure and mechanism, had at a certain level of abstraction a common functional description. At this level both the human brain and the appropriately programmed digital computer could be seen as two different instantiations of a single species of device—a device that generated intelligent behavior by manipulating symbols by means of formal rules. Newell and Simon stated their view as a hypothesis:

The Physical Symbol System Hypothesis. A physical symbol system has the necessary and sufficient means for general intelligent action.

By "necessary" we mean that any system that exhibits general intelligence will prove upon analysis to be a physical symbol system. By "sufficient" we mean that any physical symbol system of sufficient size can be organized further to exhibit general intelligence.[4]

Newell and Simon trace the roots of their hypothesis back to Gottlob Frege, Bertrand Russell, and Alfred North Whitehead,[5] but Frege and company were of course themselves heirs to a long, atomistic, rationalist tradition. Descartes had already assumed that all understanding consisted of forming and manipulating appropriate representations, that these representations could be analyzed into primitive elements *(naturas simplices),* and that all phenomena could be understood as complex combinations of these simple elements. Moreover, at the same time, Hobbes had implicitly assumed that the elements were formal components related by purely syntactic operations, so that reasoning could be reduced to calculation. "When a man *reasons,* he does nothing else but conceive a sum total from addition of parcels," Hobbes wrote, "for REASON . . . is nothing but reckoning. . . . "[6] Finally, Leibniz, working out the classical idea of mathesis—the formalization of everything—sought support to develop a universal symbol system so that "we can assign to every object its determined characteristic number."[7] According to Leibniz, in understanding we analyze concepts into more simple elements. In order to avoid a regress to simpler and simpler elements, there must be ultimate simples in terms of which all complex concepts can be understood. Moreover, if concepts are to apply to the world, there must be simple features that these elements represent. Leibniz envisaged "a kind of alphabet of human thoughts"[8] whose "characters must show, when they are used in demonstrations, some kind of connection, grouping and order which are also found in the objects."[9]

Ludwig Wittgenstein, drawing on Frege and Russell, stated in his *Tractatus Logico-Philosophicus* the pure form of this syntactic, representational view of the relation of the mind to reality. He defined the world as the totality of logically independent atomic facts:

1.1. The world is the totality of facts, not of things.

Facts in turn, he held, could be exhaustively analyzed into primitive objects.

2.01. An atomic fact is a combination of objects. . . .

2.0124. If all objects are given, then *thereby* all atomic facts are given.

These facts, their constituents, and their logical relations, Wittgenstein claimed, were represented in the mind.

2.1. We make to ourselves pictures of facts.

2.15. That the elements of the picture are combined with one another in a definite way, represents that the things are so combined with one another.[10]

AI can be thought of as the attempt to find the primitive elements and logical relations in the subject (man or computer) that mirror the primitive objects and their relations that make up the world. Newell and Simon's physical symbol system hypothesis in effect turns the Wittgensteinian vision (which is itself the culmination of the classical rationalist philosophical tradition) into an empirical claim and bases a research program on it.

The opposed intuition, that we should set about creating artificial intelligence by modeling the brain rather than the mind's symbolic representation of the world, drew its inspiration not from philosophy but from what was soon to be called neuroscience. It was directly inspired by the work of D.O. Hebb, who in 1949 suggested that a mass of neurons could learn if when neuron A and neuron B were simultaneously excited, that excitation increased the strength of the connection between them. [11]

This lead was followed by Frank Rosenblatt, who reasoned that since intelligent behavior based on our representation of the world was likely to be hard to formalize, AI should instead attempt to automate the procedures by which a network of neurons learns to discriminate patterns and respond appropriately. As Rosenblatt put it,

The implicit assumption [of the symbol manipulating research program] is that it is relatively easy to specify the behavior that we want the system to perform, and that the challenge is then to design a device or mechanism which will effectively carry out this behavior. . . . [I]t is both easier and more profitable to axiomatize the *physical system* and then investigate this system analytically to determine its behavior, than to axiomatize the *behavior* and then design a physical system by techniques of logical synthesis.[12]

Another way to put the difference between the two research programs is that those seeking symbolic representations were looking for a formal structure that would give the computer the ability to solve a certain class of problems or discriminate certain types of patterns. Rosenblatt, on the other hand, wanted to build a physical device, or to simulate such a device on a digital computer, that could then generate its own abilities:

Many of the models which we have heard discussed are concerned with the question of what logical structure a system must have if it is to exhibit some property, *X*. This is essentially a question about a static system. . . .

An alternative way of looking at the question is: what kind of a system can *evolve* property *X*? I think we can show in a number of interesting cases that the second question can be solved without having an answer to the first.[13]

Both approaches met with immediate and startling success. By 1956 Newell and Simon had succeeded in programming a computer using symbolic representations to solve simple puzzles and prove theorems in the propositional calculus. On the basis of these early impressive results it looked as if the physical symbol system hypothesis was about to be confirmed, and Newell and Simon were understandably euphoric. Simon announced:

It is not my aim to surprise or shock you. . . . But the simplest way I can summarize is to say that there are now in the world machines that think, that learn and that create. Moreover, their ability to do these things is going to increase rapidly until—in a visible future—the range of problems they can handle will be coextensive with the range to which the human mind has been applied.[14]

He and Newell explained:

[W]e now have the elements of a theory of heuristic (as contrasted with algorithmic) problem solving; and we can use this theory both to understand human heuristic processes and to simulate such processes with digital computers. Intuition, insight, and learning are no longer exclusive possessions of humans: any large high-speed computer can be programmed to exhibit them also.[15]

Rosenblatt put his ideas to work in a type of device that he called a perceptron.[16] By 1956 Rosenblatt was able to train a perceptron to classify certain types of patterns as similar and to separate these from other patterns that were dissimilar. By 1959 he too was jubilant and felt his approach had been vindicated:

It seems clear that the . . . perceptron introduces a new kind of information processing automaton: For the first time, we have a machine which is capable of having original ideas. As an analogue of the biological brain, the perceptron, more precisely, the theory of statistical separability, seems to come closer to meeting the requirements of a functional explanation of the nervous system than any system previously proposed. . . . As concept, it would seem that the perceptron has established, beyond doubt, the feasibility and principle of non-human systems which may embody human cognitive functions. . . . The future of information processing devices which operate on statistical, rather than logical, principles seems to be clearly indicated.[17]

In the early sixties both approaches looked equally promising, and both made themselves equally vulnerable by making exaggerated claims. Yet the results of the internal war between the two research programs were surprisingly asymmetrical. By 1970 the brain simulation research, which had its paradigm in the perceptron, was reduced to a few lonely, underfunded efforts, while those who proposed using digital computers as symbol manipulators had undisputed control of the resources, graduate programs, journals, and symposia that constitute a flourishing research program.

Reconstructing how this change came about is complicated by the myth of manifest destiny that any ongoing research program generates. Thus, it looks to the victors as if symbolic information processing won out because it was on the right track, while the neural network or connectionist approach lost because it simply didn't work. But this account of the history of the field is a retrospective illusion. Both research programs had ideas worth exploring, and both had deep, unrecognized problems.

Each position had its detractors, and what they said was essentially the same: each approach had shown that it could solve certain easy problems but that there was no reason to think either group could extrapolate its methods to real-world complexity. Indeed, there was evidence that as problems got more complex, the computation required by both approaches would grow exponentially and so would soon become intractable. In 1969 Marvin Minsky and Seymour Papert said of Rosenblatt's perceptron:

Rosenblatt's schemes quickly took root, and soon there were perhaps as many as a hundred groups, large and small, experimenting with the model. . . .

The results of these hundreds of projects and experiments were generally disappointing, and the explanations inconclusive. The machines usually work quite well on very simple problems but deteriorate very rapidly as the tasks assigned to them get harder.[18]

Three years later, Sir James Lighthill, after reviewing work using heuristic programs such as Simon's and Minsky's, reached a strikingly similar negative conclusion:

Most workers in AI research and in related fields confess to a pronounced feeling of disappointment in what has been achieved in the past 25 years. Workers entered the field around 1950, and even around 1960, with high hopes that are very far from having been realized in 1972. In no part of the field have the discoveries made so far produced the major impact that was then promised. . . .

[O]ne rather general cause for the disappointments that have been experienced: failure to recognize the implications of the 'combinatorial explosion'. This is a general obstacle to the construction of a . . . system on a large knowledge base which results from the explosive growth of any combinatorial expression, representing numbers of possible ways of grouping elements of the knowledge base according to particular rules, as the base's size increases.[19]

As David Rumelhart and David Zipser have succinctly summed it up, "Combinatorial explosion catches you sooner or later, although sometimes in different ways in parallel than in serial."[20] Both sides had, as Jerry Fodor once put it, walked into a game of three-dimensional chess, thinking it was tick-tack-toe. Why then, so early in the game, with so little known and so much to learn, did one team of researchers triumph at the total expense of the other? Why, at this crucial branchpoint, did the symbolic representation project become the only game in town?

Everyone who knows the history of the field will be able to point to the proximal cause. About 1965, Minsky and Papert, who were running a laboratory at MIT dedicated to the symbol-manipulation approach and therefore competing for support with the perceptron projects, began circulating drafts of a book attacking the idea of the perceptron. In the book they made clear their scientific position:

Perceptrons have been widely publicized as "pattern recognition" or "learning" machines and as such have been discussed in a large number of books, journal articles, and voluminous "reports." Most of this writing . . . is without scientific value.[21]

But their attack was also a philosophical crusade. They rightly saw that traditional reliance on reduction to logical primitives was being challenged by a new holism:

Both of the present authors (first independently and later together) became involved with a somewhat therapeutic compulsion: to dispel what we feared to be the first shadows of a "holistic" or "Gestalt" misconception that would threaten to haunt the fields of engineering and artificial intelligence as it had earlier haunted biology and psychology.[22]

They were quite right. Artificial neural nets may, but need not, allow an interpretation of their hidden nodes* in terms of features a human being could recognize and use to solve the problem. While neural network modeling itself is committed to neither view, it can be demonstrated that association does not *require* that the hidden nodes be interpretable. Holists like Rosenblatt happily assumed that individual nodes or patterns of nodes were not picking out fixed features of the domain.

Minsky and Papert were so intent on eliminating all competition, and so secure in the atomistic tradition that runs from Descartes to early Wittgenstein, that their book suggests much more than it actually demonstrates. They set out to analyze the capacity of a one-layer perceptron,† while completely ignoring in the mathematical portion of their book Rosenblatt's chapters on multilayer machines and his proof of the convergence of a probabilistic learning algorithm based on back propagation‡ of errors.[23] According to Rumelhart and McClelland,

Minsky and Papert set out to show which functions can and cannot be computed by [one-layer] machines. They demonstrated, in particular, that such perceptrons are unable to calculate such mathematical functions as parity (whether an odd or even number of points are on in the retina) or the topological function of connectedness (whether all points that are on are connected to all other points that are on either directly or via other points that are also on) without making use of absurdly large numbers of predicates. The analysis is extremely elegant and demonstrates the importance of a mathematical approach to analyzing computational systems.[24]

---

* Hidden nodes are nodes that neither directly detect the input to the net nor constitute its output. They are, however, either directly or indirectly linked by connections with adjustable strengths to the nodes detecting the input and those constituting the output.

† A one-layer network has no hidden nodes, while multilayer networks do contain hidden nodes.

‡ Back propagation of errors requires recursively computing, starting with the output nodes, the effects of changing the strengths of connections on the difference between the desired output and the output produced by an input. The weights are then adjusted during learning to reduce the difference.

But the implications of the analysis are quite limited. Rumelhart and McClelland continue:

Essentially . . . although Minsky and Papert were exactly correct in their analysis of the *one-layer perceptron*, the theorems don't apply to systems which are even a little more complex. In particular, it doesn't apply to multilayer systems nor to systems that allow feedback loops.[25]

Yet in the conclusion to *Perceptrons*, when Minsky and Papert ask themselves the question, Have you considered perceptrons with many layers? they give the impression, while rhetorically leaving the question open, of having settled it:

Well, we have considered Gamba machines, which could be described as "two layers of perceptron." We have not found (by thinking or by studying the literature) any other really interesting class of multilayered machine, at least none whose principles seem to have a significant relation to those of the perceptron. . . . [W]e consider it to be an important research problem to elucidate (or reject) our intuitive judgment that the extension is sterile.[26]

Their attack on gestalt thinking in AI succeeded beyond their wildest dreams. Only an unappreciated few, among them Stephen Grossberg, James A. Anderson, and Teuvo Kohonen, took up the "important research problem." Indeed, almost everyone in AI assumed that neural nets had been laid to rest forever. Rumelhart and McClelland note:

Minsky and Papert's analysis of the limitations of the one-layer perceptron, coupled with some of the early successes of the symbolic processing approach in artificial intelligence, was enough to suggest to a large number of workers in the field that there was no future in perceptron-like computational devices for artificial intelligence and cognitive psychology.[27]

But why was it enough? Both approaches had produced some promising work and some unfounded promises.[28] It was too early to close accounts on either approach. Yet something in Minsky and Papert's book struck a responsive chord. It seemed AI workers shared the quasi-religious philosophical prejudice against holism that motivated the attack. One can see the power of the tradition, for example, in Newell and Simon's article on physical symbol systems. The article begins with the scientific hypothesis that the mind and the computer are intelligent by virtue of manipulating discrete symbols, but it ends with a revelation: "The study of logic and computers has revealed to us that intelligence resides in physical-symbol systems."[29]

Holism could not compete with such intense philosophical convictions. Rosenblatt was discredited along with the hundreds of less responsible network research groups that his work had encouraged. His research money dried up, and he had trouble getting his work published. By 1970, as far as AI was concerned, neural nets were dead. In his history of AI, Newell says the issue of symbols versus numbers "is certainly not alive now and has not been for a long time."[30] Rosenblatt is not even mentioned in John Haugeland's or Margaret Boden's histories of the AI field.[31]

But blaming the rout of the connectionists on an antiholistic prejudice is too simple. There was a deeper way philosophical assumptions influenced intuition and led to an overestimation of the importance of the early symbol-processing results. The way it looked at the time was that the perceptron people had to do an immense amount of mathematical analysis and calculating to solve even the most simple problems of pattern recognition, such as discriminating horizontal from vertical lines in various parts of the receptive field, while the symbol-manipulating approach had relatively effortlessly solved hard problems in cognition, such as proving theorems in logic and solving combinatorial puzzles. Even more important, it seemed that given the computing power available at the time, the neural net researchers could do only speculative neuroscience and psychology, while the simple programs of symbolic representationists were on their way to being useful. Behind this way of sizing up the situation was the assumption that thinking and pattern recognition are two distinct domains and that thinking is the more important of the two. As we shall see later in our discussion of the commonsense knowledge problem, to look at things this way is to ignore both the preeminent role of pattern discrimination in human expertise and also the background of commonsense understanding that is presupposed in everyday real-world thinking. Taking account of this background may well require pattern recognition.

This thought brings us back to the philosophical tradition. It was not just Descartes and his descendants who stood behind symbolic information processing, but all of Western philosophy. According to Heidegger, traditional philosophy is defined from the start by its focusing on facts in the world while "passing over" the world as such.[32] This means that philosophy has from the start systematically ignored or distorted the everyday context of human activity.[33] The branch of the philosophical tradition that descends from Socrates through Plato, Descartes, Leibniz, and Kant to conventional AI takes it for granted, in addition, that understanding a domain consists in having a *theory* of that domain. A theory formulates the relationships among objective, *context-free* elements (simples, primitives, features, attributes, factors, data points, cues, etc.) in terms of abstract principles (covering laws, rules, programs, etc.).

Plato held that in theoretical domains such as mathematics and perhaps ethics, thinkers apply explicit, context-free rules or theories they have learned in another life, outside the everyday world. Once learned, such theories function in this world by controlling the thinker's mind, whether he or she is conscious of them or not. Plato's account did not apply to everyday skills but only to domains in which there is a priori knowledge. The success of theory in the natural sciences, however, reinforced the idea that in any orderly domain there must be some set of context-free elements and some abstract relations among those elements that account for the order of that domain and for man's ability to act intelligently in it. Thus, Leibniz boldly generalized the rationalist account to all forms of intelligent activity, even everyday practice:

[T]he most important observations and turns of skill in all sorts of trades and professions are as yet unwritten. This fact is proved by experience when passing from theory to practice we desire to accomplish something. *Of course, we can also write up this practice, since it is at bottom just another theory more complex and particular. . . .* [italics added][34]

The symbolic information-processing approach gains its assurance from this transfer to all domains of methods that have been developed by philosophers and that are successful in the natural sciences. Since, in this view, any domain must be formalizable, the way to do AI in any area is obviously to find the context-free elements and principles and to base a formal, symbolic representation on this theoretical analysis. In this vein Terry Winograd describes his AI work in terms borrowed from physical science:

We are concerned with developing a formalism, or "representation," with which to describe . . . knowledge. We seek the "atoms" and "particles" of which it is built, and the "forces" that act on it.[35]

No doubt theories about the universe are often built up gradually by modeling relatively simple and isolated systems and then making the model gradually more complex and integrating it with models of other domains. This is possible because all the phenomena are presumably the result of the lawlike relations between what Papert and Minsky call "structural primitives." Since no one *argues* for atomistic reduction in AI, it seems that AI workers just implicitly *assume* that the abstraction of elements from their everyday context, which defines philosophy and works in natural science, must also work in AI. This assumption may well account for the way the physical symbol system hypothesis so quickly turned into a revelation and for the ease with which Papert and Minsky's book triumphed over the holism of the perceptron.

Teaching philosophy at MIT in the mid-sixties, one of us— Hubert—was soon drawn into the debate over the possibility of AI. It was obvious that researchers such as Newell, Simon, and Minsky were the heirs to the philosophical tradition. But given the conclusions of the later Wittgenstein and the early Heidegger, that did not seem to be a good omen for the reductionist research program. Both these thinkers had called into question the very tradition on which symbolic information processing was based. Both were holists, both were struck by the importance of everyday practices, and both held that one could not have a theory of the everyday world.

It is one of the ironies of intellectual history that Wittgenstein's devastating attack on his own *Tractatus,* his *Philosophical Investigations,*[36] was published in 1953, just as AI took over the abstract, atomistic tradition he was attacking. After writing the *Tractatus,* Wittgenstein spent years doing what he called phenomenology[37]—looking in vain for the atomic facts and basic objects his theory required. He ended by abandoning his *Tractatus* and all rationalistic philosophy. He argued that the analysis of everyday situations into facts and rules (which is where most traditional philosophers and AI researchers think theory must begin) is itself only meaningful in some context and for some purpose. Thus, the elements chosen already reflect the goals and purposes for which they are carved out. When we try to find the ultimate context-free, purpose-free elements, as we must if we are going to find the primitive symbols to feed a computer, we are in effect trying to free aspects of our experience of just that pragmatic organization which makes it possible to use them intelligently in coping with everyday problems.

In the *Philosophical Investigations* Wittgenstein directly criticized the logical atomism of the *Tractatus:*

"What lies behind the idea that names really signify simples"?—Socrates says in the *Theaetetus:* "If I make no mistake, I have heard some people say this: there is no definition of the primary elements—so to speak—out of which we and everything else are composed. . . . But just as what consists of these primary elements is itself complex, so the names of the elements become descriptive language by being compounded together." Both Russell's 'individuals' and my 'objects' *(Tractatus Logico-Philosophicus)* were such primary elements. But what are the simple constituent parts of which reality is composed? . . . It makes no sense at all to speak absolutely of the 'simple parts of a chair.'[38]

Already, in the 1920s, Martin Heidegger had reacted in a similar way against his mentor, Edmund Husserl, who regarded himself as the culmination of the Cartesian tradition and was therefore the grandfather of AI.[39] Husserl argued that an act of consciousness, or noesis, does not on its own grasp an object; rather, the act has intentionality (directedness) only by virtue of an "abstract form," or meaning, in the noema correlated with the act.[40]

This meaning, or symbolic representation, as conceived by Husserl, is a complex entity that has a difficult job to perform. In *Ideas Pertaining to a Pure Phenomenology,*[41] Husserl bravely tried to explain how the noema gets the job done. Reference is provided by "predicate-senses," which, like Fregean *Sinne,* just have the remarkable property of picking out objects' atomic properties. These predicates are combined into complex "descriptions" of complex objects, as in Russell's theory of descriptions. For Husserl, who was close to Kant on this point, the noema contains a hierarchy of strict rules. Since Husserl thought of intelligence as a context-determined, goal-directed activity, the mental representation of any type of object had to provide a context, or a "horizon" of expectations or "predelineations" for structuring the incoming data: "a rule governing *possible* other consciousness of [the object] as identical—possible, as exemplifying essentially predelineated types."[42] The noema must contain a rule describing all the features that can be expected with certainty in exploring a certain *type* of object—features that remain "inviolably the same: as long as the objectivity remains intended as *this* one and of this kind."[43] The rule must also prescribe predelineations of properties that are possible, but not necessary, features of this type of object: "Instead of a completely determined sense, there is always, therefore, a *frame of empty sense. . . .* "[44]

In 1973 Marvin Minsky proposed a new data structure, remarkably similar to Husserl's, for representing everyday knowledge:

A *frame* is a data-structure for representing a stereotyped situation, like being in a certain kind of living room, or going to a child's birthday party. . . .

We can think of a frame as a network of nodes and relations. The top levels of a frame are fixed, and represent things that are always true about the supposed situation. The lower levels have many *terminals*—slots that must be filled by specific instances or data. Each terminal can specify conditions its assignments must meet. . . .

Much of the phenomenological power of the theory hinges on the inclusion of expectations and other kinds of presumptions. A *frame's terminals are normally already filled with "default" assignments.*[45]

In Minsky's model of a frame, the "top level" is a developed version of what, in Husserl's terminology, remains "inviolably the same" in the representation, and Husserl's predelineations have become "default assignments"—additional features that can normally be expected. The result is a step forward in AI techniques from a passive model of information processing to one that tries to take account of the interactions between a knower and the world. The task of AI thus converges with the task of transcendental phenomenology. Both must try in everyday domains to find frames constructed from a set of primitive predicates and their formal relations.

Heidegger, before Wittgenstein, carried out, in response to Husserl, a phenomenological description of the everyday world and everyday objects like chairs and hammers. Like Wittgenstein, he found that the everyday world could not be represented by a set of context-free elements. It was Heidegger who forced Husserl to face precisely this problem by pointing out that there are other ways of "encountering" things than relating to them as objects defined by a set of predicates. When we use a piece of equipment like a hammer, Heidegger said, we actualize a skill (which need not be represented in the mind) in the context of a socially organized nexus of equipment, purposes, and human roles (which need not be represented as a set of facts). This context, or world, and our everyday ways of skillful coping in it, which Heidegger called "circumspection," are not something we *think* but part of our socialization, which forms the way we *are*. Heidegger concluded:

> The context . . . can be taken formally in the sense of a system of relations. But . . . [t]he phenomenal content of these 'relations' and 'relata' . . . is such that they resist any sort of mathematical functionalization; nor are they merely something thought, first posited in an 'act of thinking'. They are rather relationships in which concernful circumspection as such already dwells.[46]

This defines the splitting of the ways between Husserl and AI on the one hand and Heidegger and the later Wittgenstein on the other. The crucial question becomes, Can there be a theory of the everyday world as rationalist philosophers have always held? Or is the commonsense background rather a combination of skills, practices, discriminations, and so on, which are not intentional states and so, *a fortiori*, do not have any representational content to be explicated in terms of elements and rules?

By making a move that was soon to become familiar in AI circles, Husserl tried to avoid the problem Heidegger posed. Husserl claimed that the world, the background of significance, the everyday context, was merely a very complex system of facts correlated with a complex system of beliefs, which, since they have truth conditions, he called validities. One could, in principle, he held, suspend one's dwelling in the world and achieve a detached description of the human belief system. One could thus complete the task that had been implicit in philosophy since Socrates: one could make explicit the beliefs and principles underlying all intelligent behavior. As Husserl put it,

> [E]ven the background . . . of which we are always concurrently conscious but which is momentarily irrelevant and remains completely unnoticed, still functions according to its implicit validities.[47]

Since he firmly believed that the shared background could be made explicit as a belief system, Husserl was ahead of his time in raising the question of the possibility of AI. After discussing the possibility that a formal axiomatic system might describe experience and pointing out that such a system of axioms and primitives—at least as we know it in geometry—could not describe everyday shapes such as "scalloped" and "lens-shaped," Husserl left open the question whether these everyday concepts could nonetheless be formalized. (This was like raising and leaving open the AI question whether one can axiomatize commonsense physics.) Taking up Leibniz's dream of a mathesis of all experience, Husserl added:

The pressing question is . . . whether there could not be . . . an idealizing procedure that substitutes pure and strict ideals for intuited data and that would . . . serve . . . as the basic medium for a mathesis of experience.[48]

But, as Heidegger predicted, the task of writing out a complete theoretical account of everyday life turned out to be much harder than initially expected. Husserl's project ran into serious trouble, and there are signs that Minsky's has too. During twenty-five years of trying to spell out the components of the subject's representation of everyday objects, Husserl found that he had to include more and more of the subject's commonsense understanding of the everyday world:

To be sure, even the tasks that present themselves when we take single types of objects as restricted clues prove to be extremely complicated and always lead to extensive disciplines when we penetrate more deeply. That is the case, for example, with . . . spatial objects (to say nothing of a Nature) as such, of psycho-physical being and humanity as such, culture as such.[49]

He spoke of the noema's "huge concreteness"[50] and of its "tremendous complication,"[51] and he sadly concluded at the age of seventy-five that he was a perpetual beginner and that phenomenology was an "infinite task."[52]

There are hints in his paper "A Framework for Representing Knowledge" that Minsky has embarked on the same "infinite task" that eventually overwhelmed Husserl:

Just constructing a knowledge base is a major intellectual research problem. . . . We still know far too little about the contents and structure of common-sense knowledge. A "minimal" common-sense system must "know" something about cause-effect, time, purpose, locality, process, and types of knowledge. . . . We need a serious epistemological research effort in this area.[53]

To a student of contemporary philosophy, Minsky's naiveté and faith are astonishing. Husserl's phenomenology *was* just such a research effort. Indeed, philosophers from Socrates through Leibniz to early Wittgenstein carried on serious epistemological research in this area for two thousand years without notable success.

In the light of Wittgenstein's reversal and Heidegger's devastating critique of Husserl, one of us—Hubert—predicted trouble for symbolic information processing. As Newell notes in his history of AI, this warning was ignored:

> Dreyfus's central intellectual objection . . . is that the analysis of the context of human action into discrete elements is doomed to failure. This objection is grounded in phenomenological philosophy. Unfortunately, this appears to be a nonissue as far as AI is concerned. The answers, refutations, and analyses that have been forthcoming to Dreyfus's writings have simply not engaged this issue—which indeed would be a novel issue if it were to come to the fore.[54]

The trouble was, indeed, not long in coming to the fore, as the everyday world took its revenge on AI as it had on traditional philosophy. As we see it, the research program launched by Newell and Simon has gone through three ten-year stages. From 1955 to 1965 two research themes, representation and search, dominated the field then called "cognitive simulation." Newell and Simon showed, for example, how a computer could solve a class of problems with the general heuristic search principle known as means-end analysis— namely, to use any available operation that reduces the distance between the description of the current situation and the description of the goal. They then abstracted this heuristic technique and incorporated it into their General Problem Solver (GPS).

The second stage (1965–75), led by Marvin Minsky and Seymour Papert at MIT, was concerned with what facts and rules to represent. The idea was to develop methods for dealing systematically with knowledge in isolated domains called "microworlds." Famous programs written around 1970 at MIT include Terry Winograd's SHRDLU, which could obey commands given in a subset of natural language about a simplified "blocks-world," Thomas Evan's analogy problem program, David Waltz's scene analysis program, and Patrick Winston's program, which could learn concepts from examples.

The hope was that the restricted and isolated microworlds could be gradually made more realistic and combined so as to approach real-world understanding. But researchers confused two domains, which, following Heidegger, we shall distinguish as "universe" and "world." A set of interrelated facts may constitute a *universe,* like the physical universe, but it does not constitute a *world.* The latter, like the world of business, the world of theater, or the world of the physicist, is an organized body of objects, purposes, skills, and practices on the basis of which human activities have meaning or make sense. To see the difference, one can contrast the *meaningless* physical universe with the *meaningful* world of the discipline of physics. The world of physics, the business world, and the theater world make sense only against a background of common human concerns. They are local elaborations of the one commonsense world we all share. That is, subworlds are not related like isolable physical systems to the larger systems they *compose* but rather are local elaborations of a whole that they *presuppose.* Microworlds are not worlds but isolated meaningless domains, and it has gradually become clear that there is no way they could be combined and extended to arrive at the world of everyday life.

In its third stage, roughly from 1975 to the present, AI has been wrestling with what has come to be called the commonsense knowledge problem. The representation of knowledge was always a central problem for work in AI, but the two earlier periods—cognitive simulation and microworlds—were characterized by an attempt to avoid the problem of commonsense knowledge by seeing how much could be done with as little knowledge as possible. By the middle 1970s, however, the issue had to be faced. Various data structures, such as Minsky's frames and Roger Schank's scripts, have been tried without success. The commonsense knowledge problem has kept AI from even beginning to fulfill Simon's prediction of twenty years ago that "within twenty years machines will be capable of doing any work a man can do."[55]

Indeed, the commonsense knowledge problem has blocked all progress in theoretical AI for the past decade. Winograd was one of the first to see the limitations of SHRDLU and all script and frame attempts to extend the microworlds approach. Having "lost faith" in AI, he now teaches Heidegger in his computer science course at Stanford and points out "the difficulty of formalizing the commonsense background that determines which scripts, goals and strategies are relevant and how they interact."[56]

What sustains AI in this impasse is the conviction that the commonsense knowledge problem must be solvable, since human beings have obviously solved it. But human beings may not normally use commonsense *knowledge* at all. As Heidegger and Wittgenstein pointed out, what commonsense *understanding* amounts to might well be *everyday know-how*. By "know-how" we do not mean procedural rules but knowing what to do in a vast number of special cases.[57] For example, commonsense physics has turned out to be extremely hard to spell out in a set of facts and rules. When one tries, one either requires more common sense to understand the facts and rules one finds or else one produces formulas of such complexity that it seems highly unlikely they are in a child's mind.

Doing theoretical physics also requires background skills that may not be formalizable, but the domain itself can be described by abstract laws that make no reference to these background skills. AI researchers mistakenly conclude that commonsense physics too must be expressible as a set of abstract principles. But it just may be that the problem of finding a *theory* of commonsense physics is insoluble because the domain has no theoretical structure. By playing with all sorts of liquids and solids every day for several years, a child may simply learn to discriminate prototypical cases of solids, liquids, and so on and learn typical skilled responses to their typical behavior in typical circumstances. The same might well be the case for the social world. If background understanding is indeed a skill and if skills are based on whole patterns and not on rules, we would expect symbolic representations to fail to capture our commonsense understanding.

In the light of this impasse, classical, symbol-based AI appears more and more to be a perfect example of what Imre Lakatos has called a degenerating research program.[58] As we have seen, AI began auspiciously with Newell and Simon's work at Rand and by the late 1960s turned into a flourishing research program. Minsky predicted that "within a generation the problem of creating 'artificial intelligence' will be substantially solved."[59] Then, rather suddenly, the field ran into unexpected difficulties. It turned out to be much harder than one expected to formulate a theory of common sense. It was not, as Minsky had hoped, just a question of cataloguing a few hundred thousand facts. The commonsense knowledge problem became the center of concern. Minsky's mood changed completely in five years.

He told a reporter that "the AI problem is one of the hardest science has ever undertaken."[60]

The rationalist tradition had finally been put to an empirical test, and it had failed. The idea of producing a formal, atomistic theory of the everyday commonsense world and of representing that theory in a symbol manipulator had run into just the difficulties Heidegger and Wittgenstein had discovered. Frank Rosenblatt's intuition that it would be hopelessly difficult to formalize the world and thus to give a formal specification of intelligent behavior had been vindicated. His repressed research program (using the computer to instantiate a holistic model of an idealized brain), which had never really been refuted, became again a live option.

In journalistic accounts of the history of AI, Rosenblatt is vilified by anonymous detractors as a snake-oil salesman:

Present-day researchers remember that Rosenblatt was given to steady and extravagant statements about the performance of his machine. "He was a press agent's dream," one scientist says, "a real medicine man. To hear him tell it, the Perceptron was capable of fantastic things. And maybe it was. But you couldn't prove it by the work Frank did."[61]

In fact, he was much clearer about the capacities and limitations of the various types of perceptrons than Simon and Minsky were about their symbolic programs.[62] Now he is being rehabilitated. David Rumelhart, Geoffrey Hinton, and James McClelland reflect this new appreciation of his pioneering work:

Rosenblatt's work was very controversial at the time, and the specific models he proposed were not up to all the hopes he had for them. But his vision of the human information processing system as a dynamic, interactive, self-organizing system lies at the core of the PDP approach.[63]

The studies of perceptrons . . . clearly anticipated many of the results in use today. The critique of perceptrons by Minsky and Papert was widely misinterpreted as destroying their credibility, whereas the work simply showed limitations on the power of the most limited class of perceptron-like mechanisms, and said nothing about more powerful, multiple layer models.[64]

Frustrated AI researchers, tired of clinging to a research program that Jerry Lettvin characterized in the early 1980s as "the only straw afloat," flocked to the new paradigm. Rumelhart and McClelland's book *Parallel Distributed Processing* sold six thousand copies the day it went onto the market, and thirty thousand are now in print. As Paul Smolensky put it,

In the past half-decade the connectionist approach to cognitive modeling has grown from an obscure cult claiming a few true believers to a movement so vigorous that recent meetings of the Cognitive Science Society have begun to look like connectionist pep rallies.[65]

If multilayered networks succeed in fulfilling their promise, researchers will have to give up the conviction of Descartes, Husserl, and early Wittgenstein that the only way to produce intelligent behavior is to mirror the world with a formal theory in the mind. Worse, one may have to give up the more basic intuition at the source of philosophy that there must be a theory of every aspect of reality— that is, there must be elements and principles in terms of which one can account for the intelligibility of any domain. Neural networks may show that Heidegger, later Wittgenstein, and Rosenblatt were right in thinking that we behave intelligently in the world without having a theory of that world. If a theory is not *necessary* to explain intelligent behavior, we have to be prepared to raise the question whether in everyday domains such a theoretical explanation is even *possible*.

Neural net modelers, influenced by symbol-manipulating AI, are expending considerable effort, once their nets have been trained to perform a task, in trying to find the features represented by individual nodes and sets of nodes. Results thus far are equivocal. Consider Hinton's network for learning concepts by means of distributed representations.[66] The network can be trained to encode relationships in a domain that human beings conceptualize in terms of features, without the network being given the features that human beings use. Hinton produces examples of cases in which some nodes in the trained network can be interpreted as corresponding to the features that human beings pick out, although these nodes only roughly correspond to those features. Most nodes, however, cannot be interpreted semantically at all. A feature used in a symbolic representation is either present or not. In the net, however, although certain nodes are more active when a certain feature is present in the domain, the amount of activity not only varies with the presence or absence of this feature but is affected by the presence or absence of other features as well.

Hinton has picked a domain—family relationships—that is constructed by human beings precisely in terms of the features that human beings normally notice, such as generation and nationality. Hinton then analyzes those cases in which, starting with certain random initial-connection strengths, some nodes can, after learning, be interpreted as representing those features. Calculations using Hinton's model show, however, that even his net seems to learn its associations for some random initial-connection strengths without any obvious use of these everyday features.

In one very limited sense, any successfully trained multilayer net can be interpreted in terms of features—not everyday features but what we shall call highly abstract features. Consider the simple case of layers of binary units activated by feed-forward, but not lateral or feedback, connections. To construct such an account from a network that has learned certain associations, each node one level above the input nodes could, on the basis of the connections to it, be interpreted as detecting when one of a certain set of input patterns is present. (Some of the patterns will be the ones used in training, and some will never have been used.) If the set of input patterns that a particular node detects is given an invented name (it almost certainly won't have a name in our vocabulary), the node could be interpreted as detecting the highly abstract feature so named. Hence, every node one level above the input level could be characterized as a feature detector. Similarly, every node a level above those nodes could be interpreted as detecting a higher-order feature, defined as the presence of one of a specified set of patterns among the first level of feature detectors. And so on up the hierarchy.

The fact that intelligence, defined as the knowledge of a certain set of associations appropriate to a domain, can always be accounted for in terms of relations among a number of highly abstract features of a skill domain does not, however, preserve the rationalist intuition that these explanatory features must capture the essential structure of the domain so that one could base a theory on them. If the net were taught one more association of an input-output pair (where the input prior to training produced an output different from the one to be learned), the interpretation of at least some of the nodes would have to be changed. So the features that some of the nodes picked out before the last instance of training would turn out not to have been invariant structural features of the domain.

Once one has abandoned the philosophical approach of classical AI and accepted the atheoretical claim of neural net modeling, one question remains: How much of everyday intelligence can such a network be expected to capture? Classical AI researchers are quick to point out—as Rosenblatt already noted—that neural net modelers have so far had difficulty dealing with stepwise problem solving. Connectionists respond that they are confident that they will solve that problem in time. This response, however, reminds one too much of the way that the symbol manipulators in the sixties responded to the criticism that their programs were poor at the perception of patterns. The old struggle continues between intellectualists, who think that because they can do context-free logic they have a handle on everyday cognition but are poor at understanding perception, and gestaltists, who have the rudiments of an account of perception but no account of everyday cognition.[67] One might think, using the metaphor of the right and the left brain, that perhaps the brain or the mind uses each strategy when appropriate. The problem would then be how to combine the strategies. One cannot just switch back and forth, for as Heidegger and the gestaltists saw, the pragmatic background plays a crucial role in determining relevance, even in everyday logic and problem solving, and experts in any field, even logic, grasp operations in terms of their functional similarities.

It is even premature to consider combining the two approaches, since so far neither has accomplished enough to be on solid ground. Neural network modeling may simply be getting a deserved chance to fail, as did the symbolic approach.

Still, there is an important difference to bear in mind as each research program struggles on. The physical symbol system approach seems to be failing because it is simply false to assume that there must be a theory of every domain. Neural network modeling, however, is not committed to this or any other philosophical assumption. Nevertheless, building an interactive net sufficiently similar to the one our brain has evolved may be just too hard. Indeed, the commonsense knowledge problem, which has blocked the progress of symbolic representation techniques for fifteen years, may be looming on the neural net horizon, although researchers may not yet recognize it. All neural net modelers agree that for a net to be intelligent it must be able to generalize; that is, given sufficient examples of inputs associated with one particular output, it should associate further inputs of the same type with that same output. The question arises, however: What counts as the same type? The designer of the net has in mind a specific definition of the type required for a reasonable generalization and counts it a success if the net generalizes to other instances of this type. But when the net produces an unexpected association, can one say it has failed to generalize? One could equally well say that the net has all along been acting on a different definition of the type in question and that that difference has just been revealed. (All the "continue this sequence" questions found on intelligence tests really have more than one possible answer, but most human beings share a sense of what is simple and reasonable and therefore acceptable.)

Neural network modelers attempt to avoid this ambiguity and make the net produce "reasonable" generalizations by considering only a prespecified allowable family of generalizations—that is, allowable transformations that will count as acceptable generalizations (the hypothesis space). These modelers then attempt to design the architecture of their nets so that they transform inputs into outputs only in ways that are in the hypothesis space. Generalization will then be possible only on the designer's terms. While a few examples will be insufficient to identify uniquely the appropriate member of the hypothesis space, after enough examples only one hypothesis will account for all the examples. The net will then have learned the appropriate generalization principle. That is, all further input will produce what, from the designer's point of view, is the appropriate output.

The problem here is that the designer has determined, by means of the architecture of the net, that certain possible generalizations will never be found. All this is well and good for toy problems in which there is no question of what constitutes a reasonable generalization, but in real-world situations a large part of human intelligence consists in generalizing in ways that are appropriate to a context. If the designer restricts the net to a predefined class of appropriate responses, the net will be exhibiting the intelligence built into it by the designer for that context but will not have the common sense that would enable it to adapt to other contexts, as a truly human intelligence would.

Perhaps a net must share size, architecture, and initial-connection configuration with the human brain if it is to share our sense of appropriate generalization. If it is to learn from its own "experiences" to make associations that are humanlike rather than be taught to make associations that have been specified by its trainer, a net must also share our sense of appropriateness of output, and this means it must share our needs, desires, and emotions and have a humanlike body with appropriate physical movements, abilities, and vulnerability to injury.

If Heidegger and Wittgenstein are right, human beings are much more holistic than neural nets. Intelligence has to be motivated by purposes in the organism and goals picked up by the organism from an ongoing culture. If the minimum unit of analysis is that of a whole organism geared into a whole cultural world, neural nets as well as symbolically programmed computers still have a very long way to go.

ENDNOTES

[1] Ludwig Wittgenstein, *Last Writings on the Philosophy of Psychology* (Chicago: Chicago University Press, 1982), vol. 1, 504 (66e). (Translation corrected.)

[2] David E. Rumelhart and Donald A. Norman, "A Comparison of Models," *Parallel Models of Associative Memory,* ed. Geoffrey Hinton and James Anderson (Hillsdale, N.J.: Lawrence Erlbaum Associates, 1981), 3.

[3] Allen Newell, "Intellectual Issues in the History of Artificial Intelligence," in *The Study of Information: Interdisciplinary Messages,* ed. F. Machlup and U. Mansfield (New York: Wiley, 1983), 196.

[4] Allen Newell and Herbert Simon, "Computer Science as Empirical Inquiry: Symbols and Search," reprinted in *Mind Design,* ed. John Haugeland (Cambridge: MIT Press, 1981), 41.

[5] Ibid., 42.

[6] Thomas Hobbes, *Loviathan* (New York: Library of Liberal Arts, 1958), 45.

[7] Leibniz, *Selections,* ed. Philip Wiener (New York: Scribner, 1951), 18.

[8] Ibid., 20.

[9] Ibid., 10.

[10] Ludwig Wittgenstein, *Tractatus Logico-Philosophicus* (London: Routledge and Kegan Paul, 1960).

[11] D. O. Hebb, *The Organization of Behavior* (New York: Wiley, 1949).

[12] Frank Rosenblatt, "Strategic Approaches to the Study of Brain Models," *Principles of Self-Organization,* ed. H. von Foerster (Elmsford, N.Y.: Pergamon Press, 1962), 386.

[13] Ibid., 387.

[14] Herbert Simon and Allen Newell, "Heuristic Problem Solving: The Next Advance in Operations Research," *Operations Research* 6 (January–February 1958):6.

[15] Ibid. Heuristic rules are rules that when used by human beings are said to be based on experience or judgment. Such rules frequently lead to plausible solutions to problems or increase the efficiency of a problem-solving procedure. Whereas algorithms guarantee a correct solution (if there is one) in a finite time, heuristics only increase the likelihood of finding a plausible solution.

[16]David E. Rumelhart, James L. McClelland, and the PDP Research Group in their recent collection of papers, *Parallel Distributed Processing: Explorations in the Microstructure of Cognition*, vol. 1 (Cambridge: MIT Press, 1986), describe the perceptron as follows:

> Such machines consist of what is generally called a *retina*, an array of binary inputs sometimes taken to be arranged in a two-dimensional spatial layout; a set of *predicates*, a set of binary threshold units with fixed connections to a subset of units in the retina such that each predicate computes some local function over the subset of units to which it is connected; and one or more decision units, with modifiable connections to the predicates. (p. 111)

They contrast the way a parallel distributed processing (PDP) model like the perceptron stores information with the way information is stored by symbolic representation:

> In most models, knowledge is stored as a static copy of a pattern. Retrieval amounts to finding the pattern in long-term memory and copying it into a buffer or working memory. There is no real difference between the stored representation in long-term memory and the active representation in working memory. In PDP models, though, this is not the case. In these models, the patterns themselves are not stored. Rather, what is stored is the *connection strengths* between units that allow these patterns to be re-created. (p. 31)
>
> [K]nowledge about any individual pattern is not stored in the connections of a special unit reserved for that pattern, but is distributed over the connections among a large number of processing units. (p. 33)

This new notion of representation led directly to Rosenblatt's idea that such machines should be able to acquire their ability through learning rather than by being programmed with features and rules:

> [I]f the knowledge is [in] the strengths of the connections, learning must be a matter of finding the right connection strengths so that the right patterns of activation will be produced under the right circumstances. This is an extremely important property of this class of models, for it opens up the possibility that an information processing mechanism could learn, as a result of tuning its connections, to capture the interdependencies between activations that it is exposed to in the course of processing. (p. 32)

[17]Frank Rosenblatt, *Mechanisation of Thought Processes: Proceedings of a Symposium held at the National Physical Laboratory* (London: Her Majesty's Stationery Office, 1958), vol. 1, 449.

[18]Marvin Minsky and Seymour Papert, *Perceptrons: An Introduction to Computational Geometry* (Cambridge: MIT Press, 1969), 19.

[19]Sir James Lighthill, "Artificial Intelligence: A General Survey" in *Artificial Intelligence: A Paper Symposium* (London: Science Research Council, 1973).

[20]Rumelhart and McClelland, *Parallel Distributed Processing*, 158.

[21]Minsky and Papert, *Perceptrons*, 4.

[22]Ibid., 19.

[23]Frank Rosenblatt, *Principles of Neurodynamics, Perceptrons and the Theory of Brain Mechanisms* (Washington, D.C.: Spartan Books, 1962), 292. See also:

> The addition of a fourth layer of signal transmission units, or cross-coupling the A-units of a three-layer perceptron, permits the solution of generalization problems, over arbitrary transformation groups. (p. 576)
>
> In back-coupled perceptrons, selective attention to familiar objects in a complex field can occur. It is also possible for such a perceptron to attend selectively to objects which move differentially relative to their background. (p. 576)

[24]Rumelhart and McClelland, *Parallel Distributed Processing*, 111.

[25]Ibid., 112.

[26]Minsky and Papert, *Perceptrons*, 231–32.

[27]Rumelhart and McClelland, *Parallel Distributed Processing*, 112.

[28]For an evaluation of the symbolic representation approach's actual successes up to 1978, see Hubert Dreyfus, *What Computers Can't Do*, 2d ed. (New York: Harper and Row, 1979).

[29]Newell and Simon, "Computer Science and Empirical Inquiry," 197.

[30]Newell, "Intellectual Issues," 10.

[31]John Haugeland, *Artificial Intelligence: The Very Idea* (Cambridge: MIT Press, 1985); and Margaret Boden, *Artificial Intelligence and Natural Man* (New York: Basic Books, 1977). Work on neural nets was continued in a marginal way in psychology and neuroscience. James A. Anderson at Brown University continued to defend a net model in psychology, although he had to live off other researchers' grants, and Stephen Grossberg worked out an elegant mathematical implementation of elementary cognitive capacities. For Anderson's position see "Neural Models with Cognitive Implications" in *Basic Processing in Reading*, ed. D. LaBerse and S. J. Samuels (Hillsdale, N.J.: Lawrence Erlbaum Associates, 1978). For examples of Grossberg's work during the dark ages, see his book *Studies of Mind and Brain: Neural Principles of Learning, Perception, Development, Cognition and Motor Control* (Boston: Reidel Press, 1982). Kohonen's early work is reported in *Associative Memory—A System-Theoretical Approach* (Berlin: Springer-Verlag, 1977).

 At MIT Minsky continued to lecture on neural nets and to assign theses investigating their logical properties. But according to Papert, Minsky did so only because nets had interesting mathematical properties, whereas nothing interesting could be proved concerning the properties of symbol systems. Moreover, many AI researchers assumed that since Turing machines were symbol manipulators and Turing had proved that Turing machines could compute anything, he had proved that all intelligibility could be captured by logic. On this view a holistic (and in those days statistical) approach needed justification, while the symbolic AI approach did not. This confidence, however, was based on confusing the uninterpreted symbols of a Turing machine (zeros and ones) with the semantically interpreted symbols of AI.

[32]Martin Heidegger, *Being and Time* (New York: Harper and Row, 1962), sec. 14–21; Hubert Dreyfus, *Being-in-the-World: A Commentary on Division I of Being and Time* (Cambridge: MIT Press, forthcoming, 1988).

[33]According to Heidegger, Aristotle came closer than any other philosopher to understanding the importance of everyday activity, but even he succumbed to the distortion of the phenomenon of the everyday world implicit in common sense.

[34]Leibniz, *Selections*, 48.

[35]Terry Winograd, "Artificial Intelligence and Language Comprehension," in *Artificial Intelligence and Language Comprehension* (Washington, D.C.: National Institute of Education, 1976), 9.

[36]Ludwig Wittgenstein, *Philosophical Investigations* (Oxford: Basil Blackwell, 1953).

[37]Ludwig Wittgenstein, *Philosophical Remarks* (Chicago: University of Chicago Press, 1975).

[38]Wittgenstein, *Philosophical Investigations*, 21.

[39]See *Husserl, Intentionality and Cognitive Science,* ed. Hubert Dreyfus (Cambridge: MIT Press, 1982).

[40]"Der Sinn . . . so wie wir ihn bestimmt haben, ist nicht ein konkretes Wesen im Gesamtbestande des Noema, sondern eine Art ihm einwohnender abstrackter Form." See Edmund Husserl, *Ideen Zu Einer Reinen Phänomenologie und Phänomenologischen Philosophie* (The Hague: Nijhoff, 1950). For evidence that Husserl held that the noema accounts for the intentionality of mental activity, see Hubert Dreyfus, "Husserl's Perceptual Noema," in *Husserl, Intentionality and Cognitive Science.*

[41]Edmund Husserl, *Ideas Pertaining to a Pure Phenomenology and to a Phenomenological Philosophy,* trans. F. Kersten (The Hague: Nijhoff, 1982).

[42]Edmund Husserl, *Cartesian Meditations,* trans. D. Cairns (The Hague: Nijhoff, 1960), 45.

[43]Ibid., 53.

[44]Ibid., 51.

[45]Marvin Minsky, "A Framework for Representing Knowledge," in *Mind Design,* ed. John Haugeland (Cambridge: MIT Press, 1981), 96.

[46]Heidegger, 121–22.

[47]Edmund Husserl, *Crisis of European Sciences and Transcendental Phenomenology,* trans. D. Carr (Evanston: Northwestern University Press, 1970), 149.

[48]Edmund Husserl, *Ideen zu einer reinen Phänomenologie und phenomenologischen Philosophie,* bk. 3 in vol. 5, *Husserliana* (The Hague: Nijoff, 1952), 134.

[49]Husserl, *Cartesian Meditations,* 54–55.

[50]Husserl, *Formal and Transcendental Logic,* trans. D. Cairns (The Hague: Nijhoff, 1969), 244.

[51]Ibid., 246.

[52]Husserl, *Crisis,* 291.

[53]Minsky, "A Framework," 124.

[54]Newell, "Intellectual Issues," 222–23.

[55]Herbert Simon, *The Shape of Automation for Men and Management* (New York: Harper and Row, 1965), 96.

[56]Terry Winograd, "Computer Software for Working with Language," *Scientific American* (September 1984):142.

[57]This account of skill is spelled out and defended in Hubert Dreyfus and Stuart Dreyfus, *Mind Over Machine* (New York: Macmillan, 1986).

[58]Imre Lakatos, *Philosophical Papers,* ed. J. Worrall (Cambridge: Cambridge University Press, 1978).

[59]Marvin Minsky, *Computation: Finite and Infinite Machines* (New York: Prentice-Hall, 1977), 2.

[60]Gina Kolata, "How Can Computers Get Common Sense?" *Science* 217 (24 September 1982):1237.

[61]Pamela McCorduck, *Machines Who Think* (San Francisco: W. H. Freeman, 1979), 87.

[62]Some typical quotations from Rosenblatt's *Principles of Neurodynamics:*

> In a learning experiment, a perceptron is typically exposed to a sequence of patterns containing representatives of each type or class which is to be distinguished, and the appropriate choice of a response is "reinforced" according to some rule for memory modification. The perceptron is then presented with a test stimulus, and the probability of giving the appropriate response for the class of the stimulus is ascertained. . . . If the test stimulus activates a set of sensory elements which are entirely distinct from those which

were activated in previous exposures to stimuli of the same class, the experiment is a test of "pure generalization." The simplest of perceptrons ... have no capability for pure generalization, but can be shown to perform quite respectably in discrimination experiments particularly if the test stimulus is nearly identical to one of the patterns previously experienced. (p. 68)

Perceptrons considered to date show little resemblance to human subjects in their figure-detection capabilities, and gestalt-organizing tendencies. (p. 71)

The recognition of sequences in rudimentary form is well within the capability of suitably organized perceptrons, but the problem of figural organization and segmentation presents problems which are just as serious here as in the case of static pattern perception. (p. 72)

In a simple perceptron, patterns are recognized before "relations"; indeed, abstract relations, such as "A is above B" or "the triangle is inside the circle" are never abstracted as such, but can only be acquired by means of a sort of exhaustive rote-learning procedure, in which every case in which the relation holds is taught to the perceptron individually. (p. 73)

A network consisting of less than three layers of signal transmission units, or a network consisting exclusively of linear elements connected in series, is incapable of learning to discriminate classes of patterns in an isotropic environment (where any pattern can occur in all possible retinal locations, without boundary effects). (p. 575)

A number of speculative models which are likely to be capable of learning sequential programs, analysis of speech into phonemes, and learning substantive "meanings" for nouns and verbs with simple sensory referents have been presented in the preceding chapters. Such systems represent the upper limits of abstract behavior in perceptrons considered to date. They are handicapped by a lack of a satisfactory "temporary memory," by an inability to perceive abstract topological relations in a simple fashion, and by an inability to isolate meaningful figural entities, or objects, except under special conditions. (p. 577)

The applications most likely to be realizable with the kinds of perceptrons described in this volume include character recognition and "reading machines," speech recognition (for distinct, clearly separated words), and extremely limited capabilities for pictorial recognition, or the recognition of objects against simple backgrounds. "Perception" in a broader sense may be potentially within the grasp of the descendants of our present models, but a great deal of fundamental knowledge must be obtained before a sufficiently sophisticated design can be prescribed to permit a perceptron to compete with a man under normal environmental conditions. (p. 583)

[63]Rumelhart and McClelland, *Parallel Distributed Processing*, vol. 1, 45.

[64]Ibid., vol. 2, 535.

[65]Paul Smolensky, "On the Proper Treatment of Connectionism," *Behavioral and Brain Sciences*, forthcoming.

[66]Geoffrey Hinton, "Learning Distributed Representations of Concepts," in *Proceedings of the Eighth Annual Conference of the Cognitive Science Society* (Amherst, Mass.: Cognitive Science Society, August 1986).

[67]For a recent influential account of perception that denies the need for mental representation, see James J. Gibson, *The Ecological Approach to Visual Perception* (Boston: Houghton Mifflin, 1979). Gibson and Rosenblatt collaborated on a research paper for the U.S. Air Force in 1955; see J. J. Gibson, P. Olum, and F. Rosenblatt, "Parallax and Perspective During Aircraft Landing," *American Journal of Psychology* 68 (1955):372–85.

Robert Sokolowski

Natural and Artificial Intelligence

IN THIS ESSAY we will not attempt to decide whether artificial intelligence is the same as natural intelligence. Instead we will examine some of the issues and terms that must be clarified before that question can be resolved. We will discuss how the question about the relationship between natural and artificial intelligence can be formulated.

One of the first things that must be clarified is the ambiguous word *artificial*. This adjective can be used in two senses, and it is important to determine which one applies in the term *artificial intelligence*. The word *artificial* is used in one sense when it is applied, say, to flowers, and in another sense when it is applied to light. In both cases something is called artificial because it is fabricated. But in the first usage artificial means that the thing seems to be, but really is not, what it looks like. The artificial is the merely apparent; it just shows how something else looks. Artificial flowers are only paper, not flowers at all; anyone who takes them to be flowers is mistaken. But artificial light is light and it does illuminate. It is fabricated as a substitute for natural light, but once fabricated it is what it seems to be. In this sense the artificial is not the merely apparent, not simply an imitation of something else. The appearance of the thing reveals what it is, not how something else looks.

The movement of an automobile is another example of something that is artificial in the second sense of the word. An automobile

Robert Sokolowski is professor of philosophy at The Catholic University of America.

moves artificially; it moves only because human beings have constructed it to move and have made it go by the release of stored
energy. But it really does move—it does not only seem to be moving.
In contrast, the artificial wood paneling in the car only seems to be
wood; it burns, bends, breaks, and decays as plastic, not wood. It also
smells, sounds, and feels like plastic, not wood. It seems to be wood
only to vision and only from a certain angle and in certain kinds of
light.

In which sense do we use the word *artificial* when we speak of
artificial intelligence? Critics of artificial intelligence, those who
disparage the idea and say it has been overblown and oversold,
would claim that the term is used in the first sense, to mean the merely
apparent. They would say that artificial intelligence is really nothing
but complex mechanical structures and electrical processes that
present an illusion (to the gullible) of some sort of thinking. Support-
ers of the idea of artificial intelligence, those who claim that the term
names something genuine and not merely apparent, would say that
the word *artificial* is used in the second of the senses we have
distinguished. Obviously, they would say, thinking machines are
artifacts; obviously they are run by human beings; but once made
and set in motion, the machines do think. Their thinking may be
different from that of human beings in some ways, just as the
movement of a car is different from that of a rabbit and the flight of
an airplane is different from that of a bird, but it is a kind of genuine
thinking, just as there is genuine motion in the car and genuine flight
in the plane.

Suppose we were to claim that artificial intelligence is a genuine,
though constructed, intelligence. Must we then prove the truth of that
claim? Are we obliged to show that the machines really think, that
they do not only seem to possess intelligence? Perhaps not; no one
has to prove the fact that artificial light illuminates and that airplanes
really fly. We just see that they do. If thinking machines display the
activity of thinking, why should we not admit that they truly are
intelligent?

The problem is that thinking is not as visible and palpable as are
illumination, motion, and flight; it is not as easy to say whether
thinking is present or not. Even when we talk with another human
being, we cannot always be sure if that person is speaking and acting
thoughtfully or merely reciting by rote, behaving automatically. And

there are cases in which machines only seem to think but really do not: the electronic calculator can do remarkable things, but only someone who is deceived by it—someone like the person who takes artificial flowers for real ones—would say that the calculator possesses its own intelligence. The calculator may reveal the intelligence of those who built and programmed it, but it does not originate its own thinking.

How is artificial intelligence different from the calculator? How is it different from numeric computing? What does it do that we can call its own machine thinking, its own activity that cannot be dissolved into the thinking of the people who made and programmed the machine? If we are to claim that the thinking machine, though an artifact, does exhibit intelligence, we must clarify what we mean by the "thinking" it is said to execute. This may not be a proof, but it is an explanation, and some such justification seems to be required to support our claim that machines think.

Alan Turing set down the principle that if a machine behaves intelligently, we must credit it with intelligence.[1] The behavior is the key. But the Turing test cannot stand by itself as the criterion for the intelligence of machines. Machine thinking will always reproduce only part of natural thinking; it may be limited, for instance, to the responses that are produced on a screen. In this respect our experience of the machine's thinking is like talking to someone on the telephone, not like being with that person and seeing him act, speak, and respond to new situations. How do we know that our partial view of the machine's intelligence is not like that angle of vision from which artificial flowers look real to us? How can we know that we are not being deceived if we are caught in the perspective from which a merely apparent intelligence looks very much like real intelligence? Some sort of argument has to be added to the Turing test to show that artificial intelligence is artificial in the second sense of the word and not in the first—that although it is constructed and partial, it is still genuine and not merely apparent. We need to say more about intelligence to show whether it really is there or not, and we need to clarify the difference between its natural and artificial forms.

I

In discussing the distinction between natural and artificial intelligence, we must be careful not to establish divisions that are abrupt and naive. If we formulate our question in terms of stark alternatives we may put our argument into a straitjacket and deprive it of the flexibility it needs. With this rigid approach we might set the computer in opposition to the brain, considering natural intelligence an activity carried on in the brain, artificial intelligence an activity carried on in computers. Here the brain, there the computer; here the natural intelligence, there the artificial intelligence. The activity is defined by the material in which it takes place.

This approach is blunt and naive because it neglects something that bridges natural and artificial intelligence: the written word. Artificial intelligence does not simply mimic the brain and nervous system; it transforms, codifies, and manipulates written discourse. And natural intelligence is not just an organic activity that occurs in a functioning brain; it also is embodied in the words that are written on paper, inscribed in clay, painted on a billboard. Writing comes between the brain and the computer.

When thinking is embodied in the written word, there is something artificial about it. Consider a flashing neon sign that says Hotel. People do not react to the sign as they would to a rock or a tree. They both read the sign and answer it. They behave toward it in a manner analogous to the way they would react to someone who told them that the building was a hotel and that they could get a room there. Furthermore, the person who put the sign where it is—the one who is stating something in the sign and can be held responsible for saying what the sign says—does not have to remain near it for the sign to have its effect. He can let the sign go; it works without him. It is an artifice, and one that manifests and communicates something to someone, inviting both an interpretation and a response.

Of course, artificial intelligence promises to do more than writing can do, but it has a foothold in writing: it puts into motion the thinking that is embodied in writing. Our philosophical challenge is to clarify what sort of motion thinking is.[2] The continuity between writing and artificial intelligence should make us less apprehensive about being somehow replaced by thinking machines. In a way, we are already replaced by the written word. If I leave written instructions behind me, I do not have to be around for the instructions to take effect. But this does not cancel my thinking; it enhances it. If we find written records in the ruins of an ancient city, we do not think that the speakers in that city were obliterated as speakers by the documents or that their subjectivity was destroyed by them; we think that their speech was more vividly appreciated as speech in contrast with the written word. We also believe that their thinking was amplified by their writing, not muffled by it, because through the written word they are able to "speak" to us. Likewise, the codification of writing in artificial intelligence does not mean that we no longer have to think. Rather, our own thinking can be more vividly appreciated in contrast with what can be done by machines; the fact that some dimensions of thinking can be carried out mechanically makes us more vividly aware of those dimensions that we alone can perform. If artificial thinking can substitute for some of our thinking as artificial light can take over some of the functions of natural light, then the kinds of thinking for which no substitute is possible will surface more clearly as our own.

The gradual diffusion of writing into human affairs can serve as a historical analogue for the seepage of artificial intelligence into human exchanges. Writing did not simply replace the linguistic activities that people carried out before there was writing; its major impact was to make new kinds of activity possible and to give a new shape to old kinds. It enlarged and differentiated economic, legal, political, and aesthetic activities, and it made history possible. It even allowed religion to take on a new form: it permitted the emergence of religions involving a book, with all the attendant issues of text, interpretation, and commentary. Writing did all this by amplifying intelligence. Printing accelerated the spread of the written word, but it did not change the nature of writing.

The question that can be put to artificial intelligence is whether it is merely an extension of printing or a readjustment in the human enterprise that began when writing entered into human affairs. Word processing is clearly just a refinement of printing, a kind of glorified typing, but artificial intelligence appears to be more than that. It seems able to reform the embodiment of thought that was achieved in and by writing. What will artificial intelligence prove to be? Will it be just a postscript to writing, or will writing turn out to be a four-thousand-year prelude to artificial intelligence? Will writing's full impact lie in its being a preparation for mechanical thinking?

If artificial intelligence is indeed a transformation of writing, then it is more like artificial light and less like artificial flowers: a genuine substitute for some forms of thought, not merely a superficial imitation. Thinking is shaped by writing; intelligence is modified when it takes on the written form; writing permits us to identify and differentiate things in ways that were not possible when we could speak but not write. If artificial intelligence can in turn transform writing, it may be able to embody a kind of intelligence that cannot occur in any other way, just as the automobile provides a kind of motion that was not available before the car was invented.

In the case of any new technology, the new is first understood within the horizon set by the old. The earliest automobiles, for instance, looked very much like carriages. It takes time for truly new possibilities to assert themselves, to shape both themselves and the environment within which they must find their place. It took time for the automobile to generate highways and garages. The expert systems developed in the early stages of artificial intelligence are following this pattern.[3] They attempt to replace a rather prosaic form of thinking, a kind that seems ripe for replacement: the kind exercised by the man in the information booth or the pharmacist—the person who knows a lot of facts and can coordinate them and draw out some of their implications. Expert systems are the horseless carriages of artificial intelligence. They are analogous to the early writings that just recorded the contents of the royal treasury or the distribution of the grain supply.

This is not to belittle expert systems. The initial, small, obvious replacements for the old ways of doing things must settle in before the more distinctive accomplishments of a new intellectual form can take place—in this case, before the Dantes, Shakespeares, and Newtons, or the Jaguars, highways, and service stations of artificial intelligence can arise. And just as the people who experienced the beginning of writing could hardly imagine what Borges and Bohr could do, or what a national library or a medical research center or an insurance contract could be, so we—if artificial intelligence is indeed a renovation of writing—will find it hard to conceive what form the flowering of machine thinking may take.

Furthermore, there is a lot of human thinking that is rather mechanical. It demands only that we be well informed and that we be able to register relationships and draw inferences within what we know. The extent to which such routine thinking permeates our intellectual activity may only be realized when artificial thinking succeeds in doing most of this work for us.[4] Large tracts of scientific data-gathering, measuring, and correlation, of planning strategies in taxation or insurance, of working out acceptable combinations of antibiotics and matching them with infections, of constructing networks and schedules for airline travel, of figuring out how to cope with laws and regulations, are tasks that can be codified and organized according to specifiable rules. Artificial intelligence will most readily be able to relieve us of such laborious thinking. But, since there are few unmixed blessings, it is also likely to introduce new routines and drudgeries and unwelcome complexities that would not have arisen if computers had not come into being.

We are quite properly astonished at how machines can store knowledge and information, and at how they even seem to "think" with this knowledge and information. But these capabilities of machines should not blind us to something that is simpler but perhaps even more startling: the uncanny storage and representation that occurs when meaning is embodied in the written word. In artificial intelligence the embodiment changes, but the major difference is in the new kind of embodying material, not in embodiment as such. The neon light flashing the word Hotel engages many of the features found in thinking machines: a meaning is available, a course of behavior is indicated, inferences are legitimated. There seems to be no one who speaks or owns the meaning—the meaning seems to float—and yet it is somehow there in the sign. The meaning is available for everyone and seems to outlast any particular human speaker.

In artificial intelligence such meanings get embodied in materials that permit extremely complex manipulations of a syntactic kind. Hence the machine seems to reason, whereas the sign does not seem to reason but only to state. Instead of simply comparing computers and brains, we should also compare the "reasoning" of the machine with the "stating" of the sign, and examine storage and representation as they occur in the machine and in writing.

It is true that artificial intelligence may go beyond printouts into artificially voiced speech. It may move beyond printing to the more subtle embodiment of meaning that occurs in sounds. If it succeeds in doing so, its "speech" will have been a transformation of its writing and will bear the imprint of writing. Artificial intelligence will have moved in a direction that is the reverse of that followed by natural thinking, which went from voiced speech to the written word.

II

The written word can serve as a broker between natural and artificial intelligence. It straddles the two: natural intelligence is embodied and modified in writing, yet writing is somewhat artificial, something of an artifact. Let us investigate this mediating role of writing more closely. How can writing serve as a bridge to artificial intelligence?

We will circle into this issue by asking a more general question about the conditions necessary for the emergence of artificial intelligence: What things are required to allow artificial intelligence to come into being? An obvious answer is that certain computer languages, such as LISP and Prolog, are necessary. Another is that the computers themselves, with the appropriate hardware, architecture, and memory, are also required. Still another answer is that the mathematical logic devised during the past hundred years or so by Gottlob Frege, Giuseppe Peano, Bertrand Russell, and others was necessary as a condition for both the software and the hardware we now have. It is interesting that these advances in mathematics and logic were carried on for purely theoretical reasons—to show, for example, that arithmetic is a part of pure logic (Frege's goal)—and not to prepare a language for thinking machines.[5] The technological application took advantage of the opening provided by the theoretical achievement: "The opportunity created the appetite, the supply the demand."[6]

All these prerequisites for artificial intelligence—computer languages, computer hardware, and formalized logics—have been made by identifiable persons at definite times. We can give names and dates for their invention. But there is another enabling condition that is of still another nature. It is of much greater philosophical interest, and it is also much more elusive; it is hard to say when it appeared on the scene and who was responsible for bringing it about. But without it, neither artificial intelligence nor any of its other prerequisites could have arisen. The condition in question is that we are able to take a linguistic sign in two ways. We can think about what the sign expresses, or we can think about the sign and the way it is composed.

To illustrate the distinction, consider two ways of translating.[7] Consider first the translator who works at international meetings and who translates speeches as they are being given. Such a translator thinks about the topic being discussed. If the speech is about ocean shipping, the translator thinks about ships, cargoes, laws, coastlines, and ocean currents. He talks along with the original speaker; he may anticipate some of the speaker's phrases or words, and might even sometimes speak ahead of the speaker. The translator can do this because he is guided by the things that are spoken about and presented in the speech; he does not focus on analyzing the speaker's words.

In contrast, consider someone who is learning Greek and trying to translate a Greek text. He inspects each word, notices the word endings, picks out which word must be the verb and which the subject, tries to figure out how this word results from certain elisions and contractions, tries to determine what it means and how it fits with the other words. Gradually he figures out a possible sense for the sentence. In this case what is expressed in the words does not guide the translation; rather, the thing meant comes last, only after the words have been the direct concern for quite some time. This translator could not anticipate the speaker's words because the translator is not being guided by the subjects discussed. In this case the things expressed are on the margin of attention while the words are the focus of thought, whereas in the first case the words are on the margin while the subject expressed is in focus.

We can shift from a focus on what is expressed to a focus on words, we can move back to the things expressed, and we can move back and forth again and again. When we are in one focus, the other always remains on the margin as a focus we can enter. And the two foci are not merely annexed to each other; each is what it is only in conjunction with the other. The focus on words as words is possible because it is played off against the focus on what the words express; the focus on the subject is what it is (for us as speakers) only as played off against a focus on what the subject is called or what it could be called. There are no words except as drawn into this double perspective; there are no words just "lying around."

Now artificial intelligence is possible because we can turn our attention quite decisively toward the word, and instead of analyzing its grammatical or phonemic composition, we can begin to codify the word—to replace its letters by a series of binary digits and its syntactical possibilities by computerized operations. We can alphabetize and grammatize the word in a new way. We can reduce it to strings of ones and zeros and rules of manipulation. But in doing so, we never cancel our appreciation that this is a word we are dealing with, and that it expresses a certain thing; we never cut away the margin in which the meaning is expressed. For this reason the final result of our codification and transformation continues to express something. For this reason we call the outcome of what we and the machine do an artificial *intelligence*—an understanding of something, not just a rearrangement of marks.

This is where the "intentionality" of computer programs should be explored and understood: not by asking how the computer is like a brain, but by asking how the outputs of the computer are like written words, and how our shift of focus, between thinking about expressions and thinking about what is expressed, can still take place in regard to the "speech" that is delivered up to us by the processes going on in the thinking machine.[8]

It can even be misleading to say that the word must have a meaning, because the meaning might then appear to be an entity of some sort that comes between the word and the thing it represents. In some theories about cognition, such a substantialized meaning gets located in the brain or in the mind, and an argument may follow as to whether this meaning is also to be found as some sort of representation in the computer and its program.[9] There is no need for such an entity. All we need to do is acknowledge the capacity that is in us to focus on the word while the thing it represents is in the margin, or to focus on the thing while the word that symbolizes it is in the margin. Nothing more is needed. The meaning is simply the thing as meant by the word.

We know that Frege devised his new logical notation in the years prior to 1879, when his *Begriffsschrift* was published. But when did somebody realize that we can focus on words as words and that we can take words apart even while keeping in mind what they mean?

There is no date for this; this goes way back. And who was the somebody who appreciated this? Artificial intelligence is greatly indebted to him, and so are we all, since we can hardly imagine ourselves without this ability. We could turn toward the word even if we were limited to voiced speech, but we can turn toward it much more explicitly and decisively and analytically once we have begun to write. But the ability we have to shift our focus precedes writing and makes writing possible, and it also precedes and enables the further codification of writing that occurs in artificial intelligence.

Our ability to shift our focus from, say, a tree to the word *tree,* helps us explain how words are established as symbols and how things are established as being named by words or signified by symbols. But this ability to shift focus can also help us approach one of the most vexing problems associated with artificial and natural intelligence—the problem of how physiological events in the brain can present something that occurs in the world, the problem of how we are to describe mental representations or mental images or mental symbols. When I perceive this lamp, something occurs in my brain. Neural networks are activated. How is it that these activations are more than just an electrical storm or a chemical process in the brain? How is it that they serve to present or represent something beyond themselves and beyond the brain? How is it that they serve to present this lamp? How are we to describe the "brain-word," or the "brain-image," of the lamp?

Most writers who discuss this issue simply say that there is a mental symbol or representation that does the job, but they do not differentiate the "brain-symbol" from the kinds of symbols we normally deal with—those we find in sound, on paper, on canvas, in wood, in stone. A crucial difference between the brain-symbol and the normal, "public" symbol seems to be the following. In the case of the public symbol, we can focus either on the symbol or the thing it symbolizes: on *this lamp* or the lamp itself. But in the case of the brain-symbol, the individual cannot focus on the neural activation in his brain; he can only attend to the object presented, the lamp. The brain-symbol is essentially and necessarily transparent to him. But one who does focus on the brain-word—the neurologist, say, who examines the neural activations involved in seeing this lamp—cannot see these activations as a presentation of the lamp; he cannot intend the lamp through them (as he might marginally intend the lamp while focusing on the term *this lamp*). For the neurologist, the cerebral activations are essentially and necessarily opaque; they are a biological phenomenon in their own right. For him they are not symbolic, not even marginally so. He has to be told by the person he is examining that a lamp is being seen.

Thus the brain-word is not like the spoken word, but reflection on how we constitute the spoken word can help us clarify the perplexing nature of the brain-word. A person, in the case of the public symbol, can shift from the symbol to the thing; but in the case of the brain-symbol, he is fragmented into two persons: the one who sees the thing but not the brain-symbol, and the one who sees the brain-event but not the thing. These remarks, of course, are only the beginning of an analysis of mental representations, but they do indicate that one of the best ways we have of adapting our language to describe the brain properly is to contrast the brain-symbol with the public symbol and work out this contrast in all its details. Earlier in this essay we used the embodiment of meaning that occurs in writing as an aid in describing artificial intelligence; here we use the embodiment of meaning found in public symbols as an aid in understanding the representation that occurs in natural intelligence.

Let us leave the issue of mental representation and turn once again to the written word. We have taken it for granted that the writing in question is alphabetic writing, the kind familiar to speakers of English. But there is also ideogrammatic writing, and it would be interesting to compare alphabetic and ideogrammatic writing in regard to the shift of focus we have described—the shift between attending to the thing and attending to the word.

An ideograph, since it is something like a picture of the thing meant, keeps that thing vividly in the mind even when one turns to the written word.[10] An alphabetic word, on the other hand, lets go of any image of the object and symbolizes the sounds of the spoken word. Ideogrammatic writing pulls us toward the thing, alphabetic writing pulls us toward the word, but neither can cut away the other of the two foci. It would no longer be writing if it did.

Artificial intelligence has worked primarily with alphabetic symbolism. It is interesting to speculate whether some features of ideogrammatic script could find a place in artificial intelligence, to complement the alphabetic in some way. Ideogrammatic writing does away with inflections and brings the deep grammatical structures of sentences close to the surface[11]; these qualities might simplify the grammar and logic of narration and make narratives easier to codify. Ideogrammatic expression might not be useful for creating programming languages, but could be used to modify what programs print out for users of computers to read and interpret. An ideogrammatic influence on the language at the user-machine interface would make this language different from the one we normally speak—it might produce a kind of pidgin English, for example—but we should expect that.[12] Our natural language has developed quite apart from any involvement with thinking machines and is not adapted to them. It has served other purposes in other circumstances. Why should artificial intelligence be forced into all the constraints that would be required to make its output look like a speech in ordinary English? The thinking machine is a new presence, as writing once was. Our natural language, with its exuberant adaptability, will find ways to curl around it and into it, even if it has to stretch beyond its alphabetic form to do so.

III

The kind of thinking that artificial intelligence is supposed to be able to emulate is deductive inferential reasoning—drawing out conclusions once axioms and rules of derivation have been set down. Making deductions means reaching new truths on the basis of those we already know. It was this sort of reasoning that Frege wanted to formalize in his new logical notation, the forerunner of computer languages. Frege wanted to secure the accuracy of deductions by making each step in the deduction explicit and formally justified, and by keeping the derivations clear of any hidden premises. His notation was supposed to make such purity of reasoning possible.[13] The subsequent outcome of Frege's efforts have been logics and programs that make the deductions so explicit that they can be carried out mechanically; indeed, the part of an artificial intelligence program that draws out conclusions is sometimes called by the colorful name of "the inference engine."

But drawing inferences is not the only kind of intelligence; there are other kinds as well. We will discuss quotation and making distinctions as two forms of intellectual activity that are not reducible to making inferences. We will also discuss the desire that moves us to think. These forms and aspects of natural intelligence—quotation, distinguishing, desire—are of interest to artificial intelligence in two ways. If artificial intelligence can somehow embody them, it will prove itself all the more successful in replacing natural intelligence. But if it becomes apparent that artificial intelligence cannot imitate these powers and activities, we will have discovered some of the borders of artificial thinking and will better understand the difference between natural and artificial intelligence.

Artificial intelligence depends on both engineering and phenomenology. The engineering is the development of hardware and programs; the phenomenology is the analysis of natural cognition, the description of the forms of thinking that the engineering may either try to imitate and replace, or try to complement if it cannot replace them. Our present discussion is a contribution to the phenomenology of natural intelligence, carried out in the context set by the purposes and possibilities of artificial intelligence.

QUOTATION

One of the essential characteristics of natural intelligence is that we as speakers can quote one another. This does not just mean that we can repeat the words that someone else has said; it means that we can appreciate and state how things look to someone else. Our citation of someone else's words is merely the way we present to ourselves and others how the world seems to someone different from ourselves.[14] The ability to quote allows us to add perspectives to the things we experience and express. I see things not only from my own point of view, but as they seem to someone from another point of view, as they seem to someone who has a history different from mine, as they seem to someone with interests different from mine. It is a mark of greater intelligence to be able to appreciate things as they are experienced by others, a mark of lesser intelligence to be unable to do so: we are obtuse if we see things only one way, only our way.

We do not describe this ability properly if we call it the power to put ourselves in someone else's place, as though the important thing were to share that person's moods and feelings, to sympathize with his subjective states. Even the feelings and moods we may want to share are a response to the way things look, and the way things look to someone can be captured in a quotation. Furthermore, there can be complex layers of quotation. I can, for example, cite not only how something seems to John, but also how its seeming to John seems to Mary. But no matter how complex the citation, I remain the one doing the quotations; I remain the citational center.

When we speak we always play off the way things seem to us against the way they seem to others. The way things seem to others influences the way they seem to us. This supplement of alternative viewpoints is neglected when we concentrate on straight-line deductive inferences. The logic of deduction is a logic for monologues—a cyclopic, one-eyed logic. All diversity of points of view is filtered out. Only what follows from our premises is admitted. And even in the formal logics that try to handle cases that are not covered by a specific set of axioms—even in nonmonotonic logics, which try to cope with situations and facts that do not follow from the premises that are set down in the system—we still remain limited to inferences executed from a single point of view. As Raymond Reiter has written, "All current nonmonotonic formalisms deal with single agent reasoners. However, it is clear that frequently agents must ascribe nonmonotonic inferences to other agents, for example, in cooperative planning or speech acts. Such multi-agent settings require appropriate formal theories which currently we are lacking."[15]

The restriction of logic to a single point of view is a legitimate and useful abstraction, but it should be seen as limited, as not providing a full picture of human thinking. In our natural thinking, the opinions of others exercise an influence on the opinions we hold. We do not derive our positions only from the axioms we accept as true. If artificial intelligence is to emulate natural thinking, it must develop programs that can handle alternative viewpoints and not just straight-line inferential reasoning. It must develop a logic that will somehow take the expectations and statements of an interlocutor into account and formalize a conversational argument, not just a monological one. Such an expansion of artificial thinking would certainly help in the simulation of strategies and competitive situations. On the other hand, if quotation is beyond artificial intelligence, then perhaps we alone can be the final citational centers in thinking; perhaps our thinking machines will always just be quoted by us, never able to quote us in return.

MAKING DISTINCTIONS

Another kind of thinking different from inferential reasoning is the activity of making distinctions.[16] A computer program can make a distinction in the sense that it can select one item instead of another, but such an activity assumes that the terms of the distinction have been programmed into the machine. A more elementary issue is whether a distinction can "dawn" on a machine. Can a machine originally establish the terms of a distinction?

In our natural thinking we do not infer distinctions. To recognize that there are two distinct aspects to a situation is a more rudimentary act of thinking than is inference. It is also a mark of great intelligence, especially if the two terms of the distinction have not been previously established in the common notions stored in our language. For example, to appreciate that in a difficult situation there is something threatening and also something insidiously desirable, and to have a sense of the special flavor of both the threat and the attraction, is a raw act of insight. It is not derived from premises. This sort of thinking, this dawning of distinctions, is at the origin of the categories that make up our common knowledge. It is prior to the axioms from which our inferences are derived.

Similarly, the stock of rules and representations that make up a computer program, a data base, and a knowledge base presumes that the various stored representations have been distinguished, one from the other. This store of distinctions has to have been built up by natural intelligence. And each representation, each idea in natural intelligence, is not just soaked up by the mind as a liquid is soaked up by a blotter; each idea must also be distinguished from its appropriate others.[17] Some thinking, some distinguishing, goes into every notion we have. The thoughtful installation of an idea always involves distinction. Is there any way that artificial intelligence can generate a distinction between kinds of things? Can distinctions dawn on a machine? Or is the thinking machine like a household pet, fed only what we choose to give it?

DESIRE

Desire is involved with thinking in two ways. There is first the desire to know more: the curiosity to learn more facts or the urge to understand more fully. But there is also the desire for other satisfactions such as nourishment, exercise, repose, and the like. Let us call these desires the passions. How is thinking related to passion?

A common way of expressing this relationship is to say that reason is the slave of the passions.[18] In this view, the passions we are born with establish the ends we want to pursue, the satisfactions we seek; reason then comes into play to figure out how we can attain what the passions make us want. Desires provide the ends, thinking provides the means. In this view there is little room for rational discussion of goals because the goals are not established by reason.

Such an understanding of the relation between desire and reason fits well with some presuppositions of artificial intelligence. It is easy to see that the computer might help us determine how to get to a goal—perhaps by using the General Problem Solver techniques initiated by Allen Newell, Cliff Shaw, and Herbert A. Simon—but the computer has to have the goals set down for it in advance, just as it needs to have its axioms set down.[19] The computer helps us reach our goals by working out inferences appropriate to the problem we face and the resources we have. Thus, if natural intelligence is indeed the slave of the passions, artificial intelligence may go far in replacing it.

But natural reason is not completely external to our desires. It is true that as agents we begin with passions that precede thought, but before long our thinking enters into our desires and articulates what we want, so that we want in a thoughtful way. We desire not just nourishment but to eat a dinner; we want not just shelter but a home. Our passions become penetrated by intelligence. Furthermore, new kinds of desire arise that only a thoughtful being could have. We can desire honor, retribution, justice, forgiveness, valor, security against future dangers, political society. Our "rational desire" involves not only curiosity and the thoughtful articulation of the passions but also the establishment of ways of wanting that could not occur if we did not think.

Artificial intelligence might be able to do something with goals that are set in advance, but can it emulate the mixture of desire and intelligence that makes up so much of what we think and do? Can it emulate curiosity? The thinking machine is moved by electrical energy, but can there be any way of giving it the kind of origin of motion that we call desire? Can its reasoning become a thoughtful desire? Or will all the wanting be always our own?

*   *   *

Drawing inferences is an intellectual activity that is less radically our own than are the three activities we have just examined. Once axioms and rules of derivation have been set down, anyone can infer conclusions. Even if we happen to be the ones who carry out the deductions, we need not believe what we conclude. We need only say that these conclusions follow from those premises. Inference can remain largely syntactic. But in quotation we stand out more vividly on our own, since we distinguish our point of view from that of someone else. In making a distinction we also think more authentically, more independently, since we get behind any axioms and premises that someone might set down for us and simply allow one thing to distinguish itself from another. In thoughtful desire we express the character we have developed and the way our emotions have been formed by thinking. Quotation, distinction, and desire are more genuine forms of thinking than inference. And although these forms of thinking are more thoroughly our own, they do not become merely subjective or relativistic. They express an objectivity and a truth appropriate to the dimensions of thinking and being in which they are involved, dimensions that are neglected in inferential reasoning.[20]

If artificial intelligence were able to embody such forms of thinking as quotation, distinction, and desire, it would seem much more like a genuine replacement for natural intelligence than a mere simulacrum of it. It would seem, in its artificiality, to be similar to artificial light. It would seem somehow capable of originating its own thinking, of doing something not resolvable into the reasoning and responsibility of those who make and use the thinking machines. But even if artificial intelligence cannot fully embody such activities, it can at least complement them, and precisely by complementing them it can help us to understand what they are. We can learn a lot about quotation, distinction, and desire by coming to see why they cannot be mechanically reproduced, if that does turn out to be the case. We can learn a lot about natural intelligence by distinguishing it from artificial intelligence. And if artificial intelligence helps us understand what thinking is—whether by emulation or by contrast—it will succeed in being not just a technology but part of the science of nature.

ENDNOTES

[1] Alan Turing, "Computing Machinery and Intelligence," *Mind* 59 (1950):434–60.

[2] Frege speaks of a *Gedankenbewegung* as the process his notation is supposed to express. See "On the Scientific Justification of a Conceptual Notation," in *Conceptual Notation and Related Articles,* ed. T. Bynum (Oxford: Claredon, 1972), 85.

[3] See Paul Harmon and David King, *Expert Systems in Business* (New York: John Wiley & Sons, 1985).

[4] Jacques Arsac asks, "How many semantic activities of man can be represented by signs in an appropriate language, and treated 'informatically' [i.e., coded and syntactically manipulated]? Who, at this point in time, can determine the borders that this science will not be able to cross?" Arsac, *La science informatique* (Paris: Dunod, 1970), 45.

[5] See G. P. Baker and P. M. S. Hacker, *Frege: Logical Excavations* (New York: Oxford University Press, 1984), 8: "Frege's avowed primary goal was to substantiate the logicist thesis that arithmetic is part of pure logic. Everything else he did was peripheral. Consequently *he* viewed what we judge to be his greatest achievement, i.e., his invention of concept-script, as altogether instrumental."

[6] The phrase is from J. J. Scarisbrick, *The Reformation and The English People* (New York: Blackwell, 1984), 74.

[7] I adapt these examples from Arsac, *La science informatique,* 34–47.

[8] For a recent statement and survey of the problem of intentionality and computer science, see Kenneth M. Sayre, "Intentionality and Information Processing: An Alternative Model for Cognitive Science," *Behavioral and Brain Sciences* 9 (1986):121–65. On the importance of "intentionality" or "representation," see the conclusion of Howard Gardner, *The Mind's New Science: A History of the Cognitive Revolution* (New York: Basic Books, 1985), 381–92.

[9] In my opinion this "substantializing" of a "sense" occurs in some interpretations of Husserl's doctrine of the noema—those that take the noema as a mental representation that accounts for the intentional character of mental activity. I have commented on this issue, and given references to various positions and participants in this controversy, in "Intentional Analysis and The Noema," *Dialectica* 38 (1984):113–29, and in "Husserl and Frege," *The Journal of Philosophy* 84 (1987) (forthcoming). For an attempt to explain what meaning is without appealing to mental representations, or, as they are sometimes called, "abstract entities," see my essay "Exorcising Concepts," *Review of Metaphysics* 40 (1987):451–63.

[10] See Ernest Fenollosa, *The Chinese Written Character as a Medium for Poetry,* ed. E. Pound (San Francisco: City Lights Books, 1936), esp. p. 9: "In reading Chinese we do not seem to be juggling mental counters, but to be watching *things* work out their own fate."

[11] As David Diringer says about Chinese, "There is an extreme paucity of grammatical structure in Chinese; strictly speaking, there is no Chinese grammar, and hardly any syntax." *The Alphabet,* 3d ed. (New York: Funk and Wagnalls, 1968), vol. 1, 63.

[12] If we tried to read aloud some of the formulas devised by C. A. R. Hoare we would find ourselves speaking something very much like pidgin English. See the formulas in *Communicating Sequential Processes* (Englewood Cliffs, NJ: Prentice-Hall,

1985), 27–30, 43, 47–49. Ideograms tend to express events rather than predicates, and Hoare's formalism is an attempt to capture events in a process; see p. 25. And Hoare is quite aware that he is symbolizing not words or names, but things and events. He begins his book as follows (p. 23): "Forget for a while about computers and computer programming, and think instead about objects in the world around us, which act and interact with us and with each other in accordance with some characteristic pattern of behavior. Think of clocks and counters and telephones and board games and vending machines. To describe their patterns of behavior, first decide what kinds of event or action will be of interest, and choose a different name for each kind."

[13]See Baker and Hacker, *Frege: Logical Excavations,* p. 35: Frege's concept-script "was designed to give a perspicuous representation of inferences, to ensure that no tacit presuppositions remain hidden. . . . The heart of *Begriffsschrift* is then the elaboration of a notation for presenting inferences and the setting up of a formal system for rigorously testing their cogency. . . . He foreswore expressing in concept-script anything 'which is without importance for the chain of inference.' "

[14]See Robert Sokolowski, "Quotation," *Review of Metaphysics* 37 (1984):699–723.

[15]Raymond Reiter, "Nonmonotonic Reasoning," *Annual Reviews of Computer Science* 2 (1987):183. I am grateful to John McCarthy for bringing this article to my attention.

[16]See Robert Sokolowski, "Making Distinctions," *Review of Metaphysics* 32 (1979):639–76.

[17]An interesting example of how one term can rest on several distinctions, and how the "activation" of one or another of the distinctions can modify the sense of an actual use of the term, is found in Pierre Jacob, "Remarks on the Language of Thought," in *The Mind and the Machine: Philosophical Aspects of Artificial Intelligence,* ed. S. Torrance (New York: John Wiley, 1984), 74: "For Bob's use of the predicate [black], something will count as black if it is not perceived as dark blue or any other color but black, whether or not it is dyed. For Joe's use of the predicate, something will count as black not only if it looks black but also if it turns out not to be dyed." The incident sense of "not black" makes a difference in the current sense of "black."

[18]The phrase is, of course, from David Hume: "Reason is, and ought only to be the slave of the passions, and can never pretend to any other office than to serve and obey them." *A Treatise of Human Nature,* ed. L. A. Selby-Bigge (New York: Oxford University Press, 1960), vol. 3, 415.

[19]For a summary of the General Problem Solver (GPS) and means-ends analysis, see John Haugeland, *Artificial Intelligence* (Cambridge: MIT Press, 1985), 178–83.

[20]In *Artificial Intelligence,* Haugeland contrasts two models of thinking: the "Aristotelian," in which the mind is said to think by absorbing resemblances of things, and the "Hobbesian," in which thinking is said to be computation carried out on mental symbols. Haugeland calls Hobbes "the grandfather of AI" because of his computational understanding of reason (p. 23), but he concludes that we may need to invoke a theory of meaning that involves both resemblance and computation (p. 222). It seems to me that rich resources for such a theory can be found in the philosophy of Husserl, for whom all presentations are articulated and all mental articulations are presentational. For Husserl, syntax and semantics are essentially parts of a larger whole. As against Haugeland I would say, however, that the mind should not be conceived as absorbing resemblances of things but simply as presenting things in many different ways.

Pamela McCorduck

Artificial Intelligence: An Aperçu

AN IMAGINED PARADISE: thick-trunked trees with densely fronded crowns; sinuous vines; enormous flowers. Within this paradise, the eternal couple—his extended arm pointing ahead as he looks over his shoulder, perhaps to urge on his mate, hair flying as she catches up.

Another scene: the trees taller, weighted by a recent rain; an utter absence of breeze, the undergrowth sparer now, but even so he tries to hide—from her, not us, for we can see his legs beneath a gigantic flowering shrub—while she seeks him, shading her eyes for a better view. More scenes: she's gone, then he's gone too; the artist now focuses completely on details of the vegetation (Figs. 1–3).

The artist has never seen what is only imagined, has joined in the long tradition, from Cro-Magnon cave walls to Egyptian funerary art to Henri Rousseau, of expressing what might be—as significant to the human imagination as what is.

Except the artist is a computer program. Equipped—shall I say endowed?—with ideas about plant growth, about the size and shape of human beings and plausible poses they might take, equipped too with some ideas about art (closure, occlusion, spatial balance, symmetries pleasing and boring), the program goes on its autonomous way, doing drawings by the thousands. It remembers what it has already done, and won't repeat itself unless explicitly asked to do so. Its name is AARON. A little joke about Aaron's rod there, I once supposed, but I supposed wrong: AARON was intended to be the

Pamela McCorduck, a lecturer in the writing program at Columbia University, is author of Machines Who Think *(1979) and* The Universal Machine *(1985).*

Fig. 1.

first of a series of programs, to be named alphabetically. Instead AARON has persisted, evolving into greater complexity and maturity. Aaron is the Hebrew name of Harold Cohen, the artist who created the program, endowed it with its essence, and who watches, amazed as anyone, while AARON draws. AARON is artificial intelligence.

The drawings of Aaron raise puzzling questions. To be sure, some of the same questions are also raised by other works of art—questions regarding the nature and meaning of art itself, within a culture and outside it; questions about the role of the viewer (I see a paradise, but another might see a horticultural nightmare—or, if unacquainted with the conventions of Western line drawing, nothing at all. Still others cannot forget or forgive AARON's genesis, and so deprecate what they see). AARON's work also joins a much smaller set of art objects that ask the artist's identity (AARON? Harold Cohen?).

AARON is only a semi-intelligent machine. That is, it draws its pictures but doesn't then quarrel with critics, gallery owners, or even Harold Cohen. It has no perceptual apparatus to "see" what it

Fig. 2.

imagines (though we now know that what humans perceive is very much a function of our internal symbolic structures, shaped by a long acculturation process). Another question arises: Lacking eyes, lacking interests beyond its own drawings, can AARON pretend to intelligence at all? In other words, is intelligence all-or-none?

To confuse matters further, I've interpreted the pictures my own way, but is perception only in the eye of the beholder? Suppose, instead of Eden, what's pictured is a tropical Black Forest, the couple a Hansel and Gretel trying hopelessly to find their way back from abandonment. Is this equally legitimate (or equally illegitimate, given AARON's lack of interest in either interpretation)?

To these questions presently. For now, the point is this: AARON is artificial intelligence, intelligence *in vitro*—not the whole complex of intelligent behavior as we have come to recognize it in humans. Instead, artificial intelligence is certain significant parts of intelligent behavior, cultured in silicon for the same reasons cells are cultured and studied: to understand the parts as a step toward understanding the whole. This may be the most problematic issue for those who

Fig. 3.

believe that intelligent behavior, once separated from a fully functioning general intelligence such as the human mind, can no longer be considered truly intelligent.

Embryonic as they are, the findings of AI do more than serve to expand our knowledge. They are already being applied to assist us in a variety of tasks, practical and whimsical. Perhaps most important, AI has begun to redefine our sense of ourselves and our place in the world. A syncretic discipline as significant to art as to science, to emotion as to reason, AI is a compelling part of our human past and an inevitable part of our human (and, some would say, extra-human) future. There's nothing else like it.

For the past thirty years AI research has taken two general approaches, though they exist in fluid reciprocity with each other. The first general approach has been to mimic human intelligence in a computer program—in particular, to find functional models that elucidate human cognition. The second approach has aimed to attack and solve problems without necessarily referring to models of human intelligence, with the aim of exhibiting intelligent behavior of a high order outside the human cranium.

As a science, AI has evolved into a search for the principles, perhaps the laws, of intelligent behavior in general, whether exhibited by a human or a computer. The first such principles have been proposed; one present task of AI research is to verify them and to articulate more.

BESTOWING THE ESSENCE

Within the last few years a fascinating goal has captured imaginations across scientific disciplines. Joining the computer scientists, engineers, psychologists, and linguists who have pursued the goal for nearly thirty years, physicists and biologists have also taken up the question of how, in a scientific way, mind can arise from matter.

For nearly as long as we have records, human beings have imagined bestowing their essence upon artifacts—idols, automata, robots, simulacra, unpredictable deities, obedient slaves—animated, artificial intelligences, every one of them. What comprises this human essence has, of course, changed over time, both in content and expression, but a theme recurs: to be human is to think—to reason, cogitate, associate, create.

The first instances of this imaginative impulse are rhetorical structures, and given the centrality of language, the form persists to this day: stories, myths, even philosophical arguments. They are found, for example, in Homer's *Iliad:* the attendants to Hephaestus are "golden, and in appearance like living young women. / There is intelligence in their hearts, and there is speech in them / and strength, and from the immortal gods they have learned how to do things."[1]

Contemporary and similar tales appear in China: the intellectually (and physically) adventurous King Mu of the Chou Dynasty is said to have an immortal robot that is "very near to artificial flesh and blood," all part of the great Chinese fascination with life generated by chemical means. This idea finds new life among the Arabs, nine or ten centuries later, in *Ilm al-takwin*, the "science of artificial generation," which will eventually lend the idea of the *al-iksir*, or elixir of life, to medieval European alchemists.[2]

Those Arab heirs to the Hellenes may have been the first to state formally that a distinction exists between natural and artificial substances. The distinction the Arabs made did not imply that the natural was superior to the artificial, only that it was different. But not very different: they asserted that one excellent means of knowing the natural was to study the artificial. Though that premise underlies the whole Western idea of scientific modeling, it would not have made much sense to the traditional Chinese, who were inclined to view everything—animate and inanimate, natural and artificial—as indissolubly connected. Such an easygoing, inclusive world view permeated both Shintoism and Buddhism, and subsequently spared the modern Japanese from debates about whether artificial intelligence is real or fake. On that score they watch us with wonder.

But I return to Western history. Medieval Europe seems obsessed by artificial intelligences: they appear everywhere the intellect is exercised. Pope Sylvester II, Albertus Magnus, Roger Bacon, and others were of the company said to have fashioned talking heads of brass that foretold the future and solved knotty problems, "brazen heads" both proof and source of wisdom. The Spanish mystic Ramon Lull lifted wholesale an Arab contraption, a thinking machine called the *zairja,* and recast it along more Christian lines, calling it, with no undue modesty, the *Ars Magna.* It consisted of a series of concentric disks that could be spun and matched by categories and other criteria, the idea being to bring reason to bear on all subjects. The *Ars Magna* and its Arab forerunner, the *zairja,* were each modeled on the assumption that thinking could be carried on outside the human mind—indeed, mechanized.

THE PHILOSOPHERS APPROACH MIND

If mind is an essential human property (or process), its nature is elusive. Heated disputes developed in the seventeenth century about mind and body, whether they were different or the same. Descartes concluded that they were different; Spinoza rejected that dualism, believing the human mind and body to be aspects of the same thing, two attributes of God. In 1650, the year Descartes died, Bishop Ussher published his famous calculation of the world's beginning: he set it at 4004 B.C. Protoscience and pseudoscience coexisted uneasily. Leibniz also pondered the mind-body issue and eventually decided that mind and body were indeed separate, but exactly matched, monads. Under the influence of Newton's elegant mechanics, philosophers such as Locke and Hume applied themselves to searching for a rational understanding of mind, trying to divine laws analogous to Newton's, not of matter but of thought.

This had its risks. The Church, for example, with its strong ideas about a proper dualistic Christian attitude toward mind and body, did not welcome dissent, as Julien Offray de la Mettrie discovered a century after Descartes. La Mettrie studied the philosophers and scoffed: Words without substance, he snorted, speculation without knowledge. In short, mere rhetoric.

In 1747 la Mettrie published a book called *L'Homme Machine,* based on his practice as a physician. He proposed a comprehensive theory of the mind and cited evidence that physical substances affected thinking; diet, pregnancy, drugs, fatigue, disease all figured in his analysis. Rude and contentious, he intended his theories (and his language) to shock. He made enemies, not only among the authorities, who hounded him first out of Paris and then the Netherlands, but also among the philosophers who finally received him at the court of Frederick the Great in Berlin. After his death there, they discarded his ideas and refused even to mention his name.

La Mettrie is important because he is the first to offer empirical evidence in behalf of theory: the revolutions in the physical sciences touch him differently from the way they touched the philosophers. His work marks the beginning of the end of amateurism in understanding human thought.

THE COMPUTER

To be reminded of early attempts to fashion artificial intelligences— to capture the mind outside the human cranium—is not to say that there is nothing new under the sun. The computer, the first instrument able to process symbols in a general-purpose way, began awkwardly, then somewhat more smoothly, to capture certain essential qualities of human thought.

Patrick Winston of MIT has observed that the computer is an ideal experimental subject, requires little care and feeding, is endlessly patient, and does not bite.[3] The computer allows intelligent performance to be rigorously defined, built, and tested, and provides the rapid feedback necessary for progress in experimentation. Thus, for example, the notion of *symbol* takes on precise meaning and is shown to be essential to intelligent behavior.

The computer has made explicit the fundamental division between the two components of intelligent behavior, hardware and software, finally demystifying the mind-body conundrum. The computer not only provides an instance of symbolic functioning arising out of matter; it also reveals how this can happen.

In 1948 the MIT mathematician Norbert Wiener published a brief but seminal work entitled *Cybernetics*. It recorded the switch from one dominant paradigm, energy, to a new one, information. One major advantage of the new paradigm to explain thinking was that it dealt with open systems, systems coupled to the outside world both for the reception of impressions and the performance of actions; the older paradigm of energy dealt only with closed, conservative systems. Another, perhaps even more important, advantage of the new paradigm was that it dealt with the behavior of symbols, soon to emerge as central to the study of intelligent action. Wiener's small book made scarcely any mention of the computer in its first edition (an unsurprising lapse, given the awkwardness and unreliability of these machines at the time).

That the computer was potentially an all-purpose symbolic manipulator and that it could be used as such was precisely the opinion shared by all early AI researchers. During the summer of 1956 all ten of them came together, for shorter or longer periods of time, on the campus of Dartmouth College. As they told their benign foundation patron, they proceeded on the basis of the conjecture that every aspect of learning or any other feature of intelligence can in principle be so precisely described that a machine can be made to simulate it.[4]

By the time of the Dartmouth conference a landmark program existed. The work of a team from Carnegie Mellon University (then Carnegie Tech) and the Rand Corporation (including Allen Newell, J. C. Shaw, and Herbert Simon), the program was brought to the conference by Newell and Simon. Called the Logic Theorist, it proved certain theorems in Whitehead and Russell's *Principia Mathematica*. The Logic Theorist discovered a shorter and more satisfying proof to theorem 2.85 than that used by Whitehead and Russell. Simon wrote the news to Lord Russell, who responded with delight. But *The Journal of Symbolic Logic* declined to publish an article—coauthored by the Logic Theorist—that described the proof.

The Logic Theorist, created in an intellectual milieu very different from that shared by others at Dartmouth that summer, was invented by men not much taken with logic, mathematical formalisms, neural nets, or any of the earlier attempts to make machines think. Instead, the Logic Theorist rested upon the so-called information-processing view, which held that complex systems of processing information, built up out of relatively small and simple components, could exhibit intelligent behavior. How to make those processes work required an intimate knowledge of the computer; Newell, Simon, and their first AI students were as handy and inventive with programming languages as they were with electronics. They designed a higher-level programming language called IPL-V (Information Processing Language Five) that reflected what cognitive psychology had previously demonstrated about human associative memory.

John McCarthy, one of the original Dartmouth conference organizers and inventor of the phrase *artificial intelligence,* liked the general idea of list processing but was offended by the untidiness of IPL V. McCarthy created his own language, LISP (for List Processing). In its many dialects, LISP became the unchallenged *lingua franca* of AI research and applications in the next twenty-five years. Not only did AI researchers begin to produce programs that would perform certain tasks considered to require intelligence, but they began to articulate a set of ideas about intelligence that were more revolutionary in their implications than any specific chess-playing or theorem-proving program.

In 1975, on the occasion of receiving the Turing Award (the most prestigious prize in computer sciences), Allen Newell and Herbert Simon articulated, in the form of a scientific hypothesis, an assumption that they believed underlay all work in AI. They spoke of a physical symbol system hypothesis.[5]

All science, they explained, characterizes the essential nature of the systems it studies. These characterizations are qualitative—the cell doctrine in biology, plate tectonics in geology, atomism in chemistry—and establish a frame within which more detailed, often quantitative, studies can be pursued. In computing, the qualitative description that forms and defines the science is a physical symbol system.

Physical clearly denotes that such systems obey the laws of physics—they are realizable by engineered systems made of engineered components. A *symbol system* is a collection of patterns and processes, the processes capable of producing, destroying, and modifying the symbols. The most important property of patterns is that they are able to designate objects, processes, or other patterns. When patterns designate processes, they can be interpreted. Interpretation implies carrying out the designated processes.

This outlook provides a conceptual framework for studying intelligence (human or otherwise), which may be more precisely defined as the ability to process symbols. Thus, human beings and computers are two members of a larger class defined as information processors, a class that includes many other information-processing systems—economic, political, planetary—and, in its generality, a class that threatens to embrace the universe. Human beings and computers, however, are not only information processors but also intelligent agents: they are able to compute something besides their own processes.

How did Newell, Simon, and their colleagues arrive at these definitions of form and function in intelligence? They were in a position to do it because they had a physical machine called a computer to study; they could observe (and alter) the machine's behavior, tracing up through its architectural hierarchy the explicit connections from level to level—from semiconductor materials and metals up through the gross configuration level, each level explicitly connected to levels above and below it.

The working assumptions of the physical symbol system have led to two important but slightly different hypotheses about the nature of mind. One of them, which posits an intelligent agent working in a milieu called the knowledge level, is from Newell, and grows directly out of the physical symbol system hypothesis. It is generally hierarchical in design. The other, from Marvin Minsky at MIT, uses the same basic assumptions of the physical symbol system, but posits a "society" of agents (some intelligent, some not) working more heterarchically to produce the results we call a mind.

Mind, Allen Newell suggests, is an intelligent agent, a member of that special class of information processors that can compute something besides their own processes. Such intelligence as the mind exhibits is a result of the aggregate behavior of a hierarchy of functions, starting at the most primitive level and working up to the most complex.[6]

Newell can identify specific correspondences between the system levels of a human being as an intelligent agent and those of a computer system, each level of the systems with its own physical medium and rules of operation. The most basic is the device level, made up of semiconductor materials in computers and biochemicals in humans; then comes the circuit level, made up of resistors, inductors, and capacitors in computers, of cells in the human. The highest level has generally been thought to be the configuration level: in computers, the gross behavior of memories, tapes, disks, and input-output devices; in humans, the body that contains the brain.

But perhaps, Newell speculates, another level should be added above the configuration level, beyond the individual body that contains the brain. Newell calls it the knowledge level, and following his earlier taxonomy, the system at this level is the agent; the components are goals, actions, and bodies. The medium at the knowledge level is, of course, knowledge.

Thus an agent—a human or a computer system—has knowledge (encoded, however, at the symbol level, not the knowledge level), which it processes to determine actions to take. Knowledge requires both structures and processes: one kind of knowledge, structural, is impotent without the other kind, procedural. Behavior at the knowledge level is regulated by the principle of rationality; actions are selected to attain the agent's goals. Rationality, however, is not perfect, but limited.

In a recent book addressed to nonspecialists and called *The Society of Mind*, Marvin Minsky offers another view of what mind might be, ideas distilled from a professional lifetime devoted to AI research.[7] While he shares the AI assumption that intelligence grows out of matter (or nonintelligence), he takes a somewhat less hierarchical view of the whole process than Newell.

Minsky suggests that the entity called mind is the product of many agents working sometimes together, sometimes in conflict, each with greater or lesser short-term goals and shallow knowledge, but together producing all the phenomena we are used to talking about with regard to mind: the self, individuality, insight and introspection, memory, intelligence, learning, and so forth. In a delightful and powerful metaexample, the book itself is composed of many brief essays, often less than a page in length, the whole forming an instance of the larger point Minsky is making. (In a postscript, Minsky says he tried to write it differently, but it just didn't work. "A mind is too complex to fit the mold of narratives that start out *here* and end up *there;* a human intellect depends upon the connections in a tangled web—which simply wouldn't work at all if it were neatly straightened out."[8])

Within those brief essays Minsky deals with nearly every aspect of thought, which "is not based on any single and uniform kind of 'logic,' but upon myriads of varied kinds of processes, scripts, stereotypes, critics and censors, analogies and metaphors. Some of these are acquired through the operation of our genes, others are learned from our environments, and yet others we construct for ourselves. But even there inside our minds, nobody ever really learns alone, since every step employs so many things we've learned before, from language, family, friends—as well as from our former Selves [states of being]. Without each stage to teach the next, no person could construct anything so complex as a mind."[9]

Do people think logically? Not really. Do computers? Not those either. Instead, both use connections—processes that involve causes, similarities, and dependencies. The connections between agents are myriad, often indirect. Minsky doubts that the scientific laws of intelligence that will eventually emerge can ever be as simple as the laws of physics, because intelligence—symbol manipulation—is more complicated than matter.

THE SCIENCE OF ARTIFICIAL INTELLIGENCE

Since the beginning of modern computing it has been widely believed that if only people could communicate with computers in ordinary, natural language, many severe communication problems would be eased. (Indeed, this belief continues: a significant portion of effort in the Japanese fifth-generation project to develop large-scale intelligent computers is focused on natural-language processing.[10]) Early computational approaches to natural-language understanding relied on formal, virtually mathematical, models of language, and whatever their elegance, produced unsatisfactory results. The problem of automatic translation between natural languages, for example, one of the first nonmathematical problems tackled in postwar computation, created high hopes and then dashed them; it has had episodic waxing and waning ever since.

AI researchers in language have taken a number of approaches, and one of the most influential has been that of Roger Schank and his colleagues at Yale. Early in the 1970s Schank formulated a theory of *conceptual dependency,* which suggests that concepts, not words, are the proper primitives for linguists to deal with (concepts such as possession-changing-action standing for *give* or *take* or *buy* or *sell*). Schank proposes a universal representation system at the conceptual dependency level. At that level, when two sentences are identical in meaning, regardless of language, then there is only one representation. This work, in its attention to larger contexts, has little interest in focusing on simple sentence-by-sentence interpretations.[11] Schank reports that each implementation of his general theory has opened up new, unanticipated problems and has both refined and expanded the premises the theory is based on.

Nevertheless, AI research in language (and the Schankians represent only one approach) has come a long way. Thirty years ago scholars would scoff: How could a computer ever understand the difference between *the pen is in the box* and *the box is in the pen?* The answer is that an intelligent program can often resolve linguistic ambiguity, rephrase a simple narrative, infer answers to questions about it, and even tell simple stories.

As the computer proliferated after World War II, and its information-processing potential impressed a small number of researchers, some found the parallels between the on-off nature of the neuron and the electronic switch irresistible. In the early 1940s a brilliant University of Illinois neurophysiologist, Warren McCulloch, joined with a young mathematician, Walter Pitts, to try to define the mind mathematically as a net of interconnected neurons, on-off devices. The McCulloch-Pitts work, while influential for a decade or more, lost favor with the AI community. Many turned away from it, preferring a more information-processing view.

Thirty years later, with the availability of powerful new computers, the neural network idea has reemerged, dramatically revitalized and renamed connectionism. While connectionism, or neural net research, aims to build a model of natural intelligence using computer components, few are now led to compare the neuron with the on-off switches of the computer.

It bears repeating that all approaches in artificial intelligence share three assumptions: that intelligent behavior is explicable in scientific terms, that it can take place outside the human skull, and that the computer is the best laboratory instrument for exploring those propositions. Which particular approach will prove the best remains to be seen.

In the mid-1960s a small group of Stanford researchers, led by Edward Feigenbaum and Joshua Lederberg (now president of Rockefeller University), decided to transform their impatience with the toy problems that had preoccupied AI research efforts—chess, abstract game-playing, and the like—into an exploration of a real-world problem. Their stated aim was to try to simulate scientific induction: How do scientists, confronted with a problem, reason their way toward a solution? As a test they selected the difficult problem of spectrographic analysis, a complicated procedure for analyzing the composition of organic molecules, then the domain of Ph.D. chemists.

DENDRAL, the program that eventually emerged from this effort, was the first expert system, a method of capturing human expertise that has proved itself in various domains, causing considerable excitement in the marketplace as commercial ventures discovered the advantages of expert systems applications.

In principle, the expert system is simple. It consists of three connected subsystems:

1. A *knowledge base,* comprising facts, assumptions, beliefs, heuristics ("expertise"), and methods of dealing with the data base to achieve desired results, such as a diagnosis or an interpretation or a solution to a problem.

2. A *data base,* a collection of data about objects and events on which the knowledge base will work to achieve desired results.

3. An *inference engine,* which permits inferences to be drawn from the interactions between the knowledge and data bases.

The system is presented with a problem, evokes data from the questioner, and eventually offers advice toward the solution. It can be questioned in natural human language, which not only makes the expert system valuable to busy professionals but also makes it a fine instructional device for novices. From such relatively simple beginnings has developed a multimillion-dollar worldwide business that promises soon to be earning a great deal more.

Artificial intelligence, addressing as it does the central interests of human beings, their symbolic capacities, cannot fail to affect many other domains. Who can say which is likely to be the most important? The elucidation of human intelligence is obviously important; so, however, is its augmentation or amplification, with the help of mechanical intelligent assistants. But there are other, less obvious terrains where it may soon show its influence. Consider, for example, the present situation in the visual arts. Many of the fine arts long ago removed themselves from everyday access and understanding. Still, critics assure us that if we had discernment and training, we would all see why a hunk of iron from Richard Serra's studio is different from a hunk of iron ready to be hauled off to Joe's Scrap Metals, why Andy Warhol's pictures of Campbell's soup cans or Brillo boxes are more significant than the cans and boxes themselves, why it is worthy of our attention that the late Joseph Beuys deposited a lump of lard on the floor of the Guggenheim Museum and called it art.

The critics are correct. Still, we sometimes suspect a gigantic con game, and our suspicions are not much allayed by the monumental disputes among the credentialed experts themselves. It seems that discernment and training, while necessary, are clearly not sufficient. If outsiders are baffled, professional art discourse—so largely histori-codescriptive, so often frustratingly inexact—seems to verge on the arbitrary, and it is easy to suspect confidence games.

I return to AARON and its work, an apt conclusion for an essay on artificial intelligence. When Harold Cohen first began to work on AARON, he wished "to understand more about the nature of art-making processes than the making of art itself allows, for under normal circumstances the artist provides a near-perfect example of an obviously present, but virtually inaccessible body of knowledge."[12] AARON's drawings were not especially intended to be aesthetically pleasing, though the program was capable of generating such drawings. The objective was to allow the examination of certain properties of freehand drawing—what Cohen calls, in a deliberately general phrase, "standing-for-ness."

Specifically, Cohen wanted a more precise answer to certain important questions. What is an image? How do two-dimensional marks on a surface evoke in the human mind real objects in the world? Do certain universals exist within our cognitive structures that permit humans to infer meanings from two-dimensional images?

In brief, Cohen sought not only the grammar of two-dimensional images (closed figures standing for solid objects, occlusion standing for the third dimension of spatial relations) but also the beginnings of their semantics—the minimal conditions required for a set of marks to function as an image. AARON's first images were abstract, sharing with paleolithic art (and perhaps most human image-making) in the attempt to minimize the problem of dimension. Nothing was implied about depth by the spaces between pictorial elements. AARON then moved on to studies of edges and of implied depth.

Lately the program has surprised its longtime viewers by doing figurative drawing, which Harold Cohen the painter avoided, but which Harold Cohen the student of image- and art-making feels is necessary to explore. "The first time the program accumulated closed forms into something it knew to be an approximation of a figure, and I found an array of quasi-people staring eyelessly at me from my old 4014, I recoiled in fright. What was I getting myself into?"[13] Those quasi-people are distinctively AARON's: seen to frolic in recognizable though fantastical tropical gardens, on playing fields, or (perhaps in homage to Cézanne) on bathing beaches, they can be identified by gender.

To repeat, AARON cannot "see" human figures, trees, leaves, playing fields, or any other part of the material world. Instead, Cohen has provided his program with ideas about these things, indirect knowledge. In the manner of an artist who is required to conceptualize what a traveler tells him about a distant place he has never visited, or in the manner of an artist who illustrates a fairy tale, AARON has taken off. The human figures appear in many poses— AARON knows how joints move, how human figures keep their balance. He is able to summon up a nearly infinite repertoire of plausible human poses. When these figures are placed within a landscape, the general ideas AARON has about plant growth allow it to generate a great variety of individual plants and trees.

In AARON a central idea of artificial intelligence is exemplified: the program is able to generate the illusion of a complete and coherent set of images out of a comparatively simple and sparse lower representation. But if AARON can stand as a representation of present AI research, it also stands, in my view, as an example of the surprising influence AI can have on fields very distant from its origins in the mathematical sciences and engineering.

What Aaron does is clearly image-making, but is it art? Yes, Cohen answers serenely, standing aside from his creation, his protegé, as he calls it, which busies itself with its drawings. "Within Western culture," he goes on, "we have always afforded the highest level of responsibility—and praise or blame—to the individual who works on the highest conceptual level. We may hear a hundred different performances of a Beethoven quartet without ever doubting that we were listening to Beethoven. We remember the names of architects, not those of the builders who made their buildings. And, particularly, we value those whose work leaves art in a different state to the state in which they found it."[14]

The program AARON, he believes, stands in relation to its individual drawings the way a Platonic ideal stands in relation to its earthly instantiations. It is a paradigm. That Cohen has found a way to work his will upon and through the paradigm rather than upon a single instantiation simply means that his level of involvement is much higher, conceptually speaking, than has ever before been possible for the visual artist. It is similar to the way a composer writes a score instead of giving a performance, although in AARON the program is responsible for all the performances. It is as if a score could play itself (a desire of composers throughout this century).[15]

Art, Cohen argues, is humanity's most varied and subtle exercise in knowledge representation. The history of art is not simply a record of shifts in meaning or style, but of shifts in the relationship of meaning and style, all smaller by far within a specific culture than between cultures.

A UNIVERSAL SYMBOLIC CODE?

We have the capacity to understand times that are not our own, cultures that are not our own. Let us take all this much further, into the realm of speculation, and, borrowing Schank's continuum of language understanding, say that there are times when we encounter an artifact from a culture or a time not our own that makes sense, that allows us to achieve a more profound cognitive understanding, that makes for a deeper empathetic understanding.

Yet, with some modernism and with what has followed it, we are often bewildered; we need to depend on experts who do not agree among themselves. We lack an objective, precise, and coherent language for defining, measuring, and otherwise interpreting the process or the products of representation—in this case, visual images.

Cohen, for one, is dubious about the existence of such a code, dismissing the concept as the "telecommunications model of art."[16] He suggests the transaction between image-maker and image-reader takes place at a simple level of cognition; the sense of meaningfulness is generated by the structure of the image rather than by its content. Thus, the interpretations of the three drawings offered at the beginning of this essay rest on one individual's life of acculturation, nothing more. Cohen would allow me my acculturated interpretations, satisfied that AARON's pictorial generative power had drawn me into a transaction that is not an image of two people in an imagined paradise but rather the pictorial record of an act of will— AARON's, and finally, Harold Cohen's. And this accords with the belief of a number of prominent aestheticians and philosophers that this is all that can be confidently said about any work of art.[17]

Cohen may well be right to doubt the universality of higher representational forms (in the end Freud and Jung were unsuccessful in that search). At the same time he shows universality at a lower cognitive level, where certain motifs are ubiquitous in human expression—zigzags, crosses, squares, mandalas, combs, etc.—all built from even simpler elements.

Yet suppose that he is not right. Suppose that at some level, yet to be defined, a set of universal concepts underlies all human symbolic expression, the visual arts being only one aspect of this. Can that level be elucidated? If it can, will it clarify the human urge to express things symbolically? Will it suggest that we cannot really speak meaningfully to one another or pretend that we do so? Precise expression, after all, has introduced a certain kind of cross-disciplinary muteness to science even as it has also introduced a set of larger universals.

Artificial intelligence has properly set many ambitious goals for itself: a rigorous understanding of intelligence, wherever it manifests itself, including fuller evidence for the physical symbol system hypothesis; more precise concepts of mind, understanding, learning, knowledge representation, and the uses of natural language. If Harold Cohen's doubts are mistaken—if artificial intelligence can begin to illuminate a universal code, if such a thing indeed exists, a level of meaning underlying the most important symbolic expressions of human experience—then the questions already raised in studies of linguistic utterances and visual representations will become apparent also in other places. If such a question is to be moved beyond mere rhetoric (a phrase to chill any writer) and answered with empirical knowledge, artificial intelligence—of all things—is our best hope.

ENDNOTES

Figures 1–3 are reproduced courtesy of Harold Cohen.

[1]Except where noted, this and other material on the early history of artificial intelligence that follows, with its references, is presented in Pamela McCorduck, *Machines Who Think* (San Francisco: W. H. Freeman & Co., 1979).

[2]Joseph Needham, *Science in Traditional China* (Cambridge: Harvard University Press, and Hong Kong: Chinese University Press, 1981).

[3]Patrick Henry Winston, *Artificial Intelligence* (Reading, Mass.: Addison-Wesley, 1977).

[4]McCorduck, *Machines Who Think.*

[5]Allen Newell and Herbert Simon, "Computer Science as Empirical Inquiry: Symbols and Search," *Communications of the Association for Computing Machinery* (March 1976).

[6]Allen Newell, "The Knowledge Level," *Artificial Intelligence* 18.

[7]Marvin Minsky, *The Society of Mind* (New York: Simon and Schuster, 1986).

[8]Ibid.

[9]Ibid.

[10]Edward A. Feigenbaum and Pamela McCorduck, *The Fifth Generation: Japan's Computer Challenge to the World* (Reading, Mass.: Addison-Wesley, 1983; paperback edition, New York: Signet, 1984).

[11]Roger Schank, with Peter Childers, *The Cognitive Computer* (Reading, Mass.: Addison-Wesley, 1984).

[12]Harold Cohen, "What is an Image?" *Proceedings of the Sixth International Joint Conference on Artificial Intelligence—Tokyo* (1979).

[13]Private conversation with Harold Cohen.

[14]Pamela McCorduck, *The Universal Machine. Confessions of a Technological Optimist* (New York: McGraw-Hill, 1985; paperback edition, New York: Harcourt Brace Jovanovich, 1986).

[15]Ibid.

[16]Private correspondence with Harold Cohen.

[17]See, for example, Arthur Danto's *The Transfiguration of the Commonplace* (Cambridge: Harvard University Press, 1981).

Jack D. Cowan and David H. Sharp

Neural Nets and Artificial Intelligence

NEURAL NETS are aggregates of interconnected nerve cells, or neurons. The human brain, for example, is a neural net comprising about ten billion interconnected neurons. Somehow, such a net learns and remembers, thinks and feels. It is the substrate for behavior and the embodiment of mind. In the past half-century many attempts have been made to model the ways in which neural nets work, particularly those involved in seeing and moving. In this article, however, we shall concentrate on a somewhat more abstract, but fundamental, problem—the representation of external events inside neural nets. In our view this problem is central to any understanding of intelligent behavior in minds or machines. We will conclude by discussing neural nets in relation to contemporary studies of artificial intelligence.

INTRODUCTION

Neurons are living cells capable of receiving and transmitting electrochemical signals in highly specialized ways. Their complexities can be accurately simulated only by intricate computer chips, and nets comprising many such chips are needed to simulate even the simplest processes that are thought to occur in the brain. The modeling of neural nets, however, started long before such complexities were

Jack D. Cowan is a professor of applied mathematics and theoretical biology in the department of mathematics at the University of Chicago.

David H. Sharp is a theoretical physicist in the theory division of Los Alamos National Laboratory.

apparent. Perhaps the first major contribution was in a paper by Warren S. McCulloch and Walter H. Pitts published in 1943.[1] In this paper McCulloch and Pitts applied symbolic logic to the problem of describing what neural nets can do. In effect they proved that all processes that can be described with a finite number of symbolic expressions (e.g., simple arithmetic; classifying, storing and retrieving finite sets of data; and recursive application of logical rules) can be embodied in nets of what they called "formal" neurons. Fig. 1 shows several examples of McCulloch-Pitts neurons.

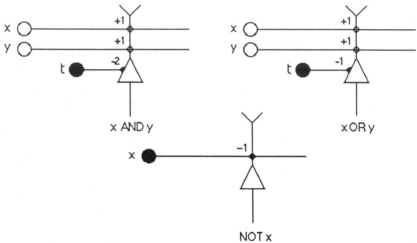

Fig. 1. McCulloch-Pitts formal neurons. Each unit is activated if and only if its total excitation reaches or exceeds zero. For example, the first unit is activated if and only if both the units x and y are activated, for only then does the total excitation, $(+1)x + (+1)y$, balance the threshold of -2 set by the threshold unit, t, whenever both x and y equal $+1$ (activated). The t-unit is always active. The numbers (± 1) and so on shown above are called weights. Positive weights denote excitatory synapses; negative weights, inhibitory synapses. Similarly, open circles denote excitatory neurons; filled circles, inhibitory ones.

McCulloch-Pitts Nets

Nets of formal neurons, or McCulloch-Pitts nets, as they are now called, are extremely simplified representations of the real thing. For example, they are synchronous: switching occurs only at regular, discrete intervals. Thus, formal neurons are just simple logical switches, quite unlike real neurons. Despite these simplifications, McCulloch-Pitts nets are important in that they can embody whatever operations and processes can be described in logical terms.

Donald M. Mackay has expressed this capacity as follows: if you assert that there is a certain process that a computer cannot go through, and if you can describe in words exactly what constitutes such a process, then at least one McCulloch-Pitts net that can embody and carry out the process exists.[2] McCulloch and Pitts thus proved that formal neural nets, if supplemented with indefinitely large memory stores, are equivalent to a class of computing machines that Alan M. Turing has shown to be computationally universal.[3]

Reliable Computing with Unreliable Neurons

McCulloch-Pitts nets were the first examples of model neural nets designed to perform specific logical tasks. But what happens if such nets malfunction from time to time or are damaged? This problem attracted one of the leading mathematicians of this century and a pioneer in the development of digital computers, John von Neumann. By introducing redundancy—using many neurons to do the job of one[4]—von Neumann solved the problem of making McCulloch-Pitts nets function reliably. In such nets one bit of information (the choice between one and zero) is signaled by the synchronous activation of many neurons rather than by the all-or-nothing activation of one formal neuron: one obtains whenever more than half are activated, zero otherwise. Von Neumann proved that redundant McCulloch-Pitts nets operating in such a fashion can be designed to carry out arithmetical calculations with high reliability. Subsequent work by Shmuel Winograd and Jack D. Cowan provided more efficient ways of constructing highly reliable redundant neural nets, at the cost of requiring more complicated microchiplike neurons, each with many contacts, to implement the needed logical functions.[5] The Winograd-Cowan construction was noteworthy in that it utilized a distributed representation of information: one bit of information was represented redundantly by many neurons, as in von Neumann's net, but in addition each neuron partially represented many bits.

These solutions to the reliability problem provided an insight into the way neural nets in the brain might function reliably despite damage. Ever since John Hughlings Jackson's neurological studies of brain-damaged patients[6] and Karl S. Lashley's demonstration of the spared cognitive abilities of brain-damaged rats,[7] it has become apparent that although different regions of the brain are specialized for differing functions, the scale of such a localization of function need not extend to single neurons. In terms of the von Neumann–Winograd-Cowan analysis, the representation of a bit of information need not be unary, but may be redundant or even distributed. There has been much debate on this point. Lashley, for example, proposed that the various brain regions are equipotent with respect to function[8] (any region can implement a given task)—the very antithesis of regional localization. Conversely, Horace B. Barlow asserted that the further one moves from peripheral to central regions of the brain, the more the level of redundancy in brain functioning is reduced.[9] Movement toward the central region culminates in a unary representation of information deep in the brain. In current terminology, we speak of "grandmother" neurons, supposedly activated only when a grandmother is perceived.

Cell Assemblies and Hebb Synapses

Lashley's notion of the equipotentiality of brain regions is reflected in the work of Donald O. Hebb.[10] In 1949 Hebb proposed that the connectivity of the brain is continually changing as an organism learns differing functional tasks and that cell assemblies are created by such changes. Hebb followed up an early suggestion of Santiago Ramon y Cajal and postulated that the repeated activation of one neuron by another through a particular contact, or synapse, increases its conductance, so that groups of weakly connected cells, if synchronously activated, tend to organize into more strongly connected assemblies. Here again, the representation of a bit of information is distributed. Hebb's proposal has proved to be very influential. Despite the lack of definitive evidence to support Hebb's ideas, the cell-assembly theory has triggered many investigations of learning in neural nets and of the way in which synchronized neural activity is generated and propagated.

PATTERN RECOGNITION, LEARNING, AND MEMORY

Hebb's proposal of synaptic modification during learning triggered much work on adaptive neural nets, which can learn to perform specified tasks. Early work on these nets was carried out in the 1950s by Albert M. Uttley, who demonstrated that neural nets with Hebb-like modifiable connections could indeed learn to classify simple sets of binary patterns (111010100, 101110101, etc.) into equivalence classes (e.g., all those beginning with 101).[11]

The problem of pattern classification, or pattern recognition, is central to any theory of intelligent behavior in either animals or machines. Pitts and McCulloch were among the first investigators to address this problem.[12] They noted that animals need to recognize many different versions of the same pattern, just as we need to be able to read many different versions of the same text—handwritten; printed in different sizes, fonts, colors; seen in different kinds of lighting. In effect, the need is to recognize not just one example of a pattern but all its examples. Pitts and McCulloch constructed two neural nets, each of which partly solves the problem. The first net attempts to find invariant properties of a given pattern (i.e., properties common to all possible variants of the pattern). The second net transforms any externally presented variant into a standard representation. Pitts and McCulloch then took a bold step: they proposed that the neural nets of the auditory and visual cortices embodied the first solution and that the neural net in the superior colliculus (involved in the control of eye movements) embodied the second solution. Both cortices were presumed to contain a mechanism that sampled or scanned all variants of a pattern at a frequency corresponding to the well-known alpha rhythm of the cortex,[13] approximately ten cycles per second. McCulloch and Mackay later carried out experiments that proved the scanning hypothesis to be false.[14]

Perceptrons

Some ten years after the publication of Pitts and McCulloch's paper, a major approach to the pattern-recognition problem was introduced by Frank Rosenblatt, who showed how McCulloch-Pitts nets with modifiable connections could be "trained" to classify certain sets of patterns as similar or distinct.[15] Rosenblatt called such nets *perceptrons,* and we shall use this term in what follows. Fig. 2 shows the architecture of a typical elementary perceptron. It consists of a set of "sensory" units connected, through a single layer of McCulloch-Pitts neurons (which we shall refer to as M-P units), to a set of "motor" units. Initially, the strengths or weights of all contacts or synapses in the net are set to arbitrary values so that stimulation will generate an arbitrary response. To obtain a desired response from the net requires that all these synaptic weights be adjusted. Rosenblatt found a way to

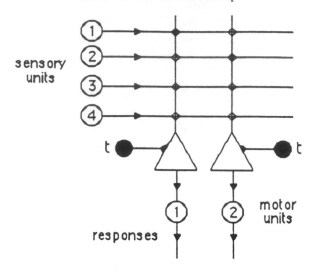

Fig. 2. An elementary perceptron, i.e., an adaptive McCulloch-Pitts neural net with modifiable synaptic weights that are changed if they generate incorrect responses.

obtain the desired response with the following training procedure: first, note an M-P unit's responses to a given stimulus. Some of its responses will be correct (i.e., will be the responses desired); others will be incorrect. Therefore, adjust the unit's weights as follows: make no adjustments if the unit's response is correct. If it is incorrect, however, increase the weights of all activated synapses if the unit should be activated but isn't; decrease the weights if the opposite obtains. Do the same for all possible desired stimulus-response patterns. It can be shown that after only a finite number of presentations of stimulus-response patterns, the weights converge to a set of values representing whatever computation or classification is embodied in these patterns.[16]

Adalines

Shortly after Rosenblatt's first publications there appeared a closely related variant of the perceptron invented by Bernard Widrow and M. E. Hoff. They called it the *adaline* (for adaptive linear neuron).[17] The only difference between perceptrons and adalines lies in the training procedure. In an adaline the excitation delivered to a given M-P unit is subtracted from its desired activity (taken to be +1 for activation and −1 for nonactivation, rather than 1 and 0). Call the result *d*. The weight of an activated synapse is increased if *d* is positive, decreased if *d* is negative. Conversely, the weight of an inactivated synapse is increased if *d* is negative, decreased if *d* is positive. This rule corresponds closely to the perceptron's, for if an M-P unit is not activated by a given sensory unit when it should be, the weight of the relevant synapse increases, or if the converse is true, decreases.

Limitations of Elementary Perceptrons and Adalines

There are limits to the performance of elementary perceptrons and adalines. Seymour A. Papert and Marvin L. Minsky proved that elementary perceptrons cannot distinguish between such simple patterns as *T* and *C*.[18] The difficulty lies in the nature of M-P units. As we said earlier, single units of this type can compute only such simple logical functions as *x* AND *y*, *x* OR *y*, NOT *x*, *x* AND NOT *y*, and so on. However, the function *x* OR ELSE *y* and its negation, NOT (*x* OR ELSE *y*), each require several M-P units. The reason is simply that *x* OR ELSE *y* is the same as (*x* AND NOT *y*) OR (*y* AND NOT *x*). This situation is unfortunate because the function NOT (*x* OR ELSE *y*) is computationally universal in Turing's sense: every other function can be expressed as a string of NOT (*x* OR ELSE *y*)'s. Fig. 3 shows the architecture of the simplest M-P net that implements

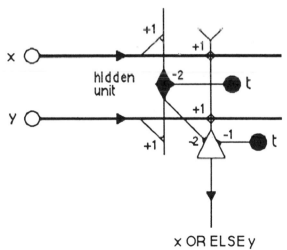

x OR ELSE y

Fig. 3. An M-P net that implements the logical function *x* OR ELSE *y*. The net comprises two M-P units, one of which is a hidden unit, and two threshold units. The weights of the hidden unit cannot be correctly modified with the procedures described earlier.

the function x OR ELSE y. It comprises two M-P units and two t-units. One of the M-P units lies entirely within the net; its output drives only the M-P unit, not the motor unit. In current terminology the interior unit is said to be "hidden," and what Papert and Minsky proved is that an elementary perceptron or adaline, which consists of only a single layer of M-P units, is not computationally universal, even with modifiable connections. In addition, they conjectured that hidden units in multilayer perceptrons cannot be trained—in other words, that the problem of assigning credit to hidden units is unsolvable.

It turns out that the limitations of simple perceptrons and adalines can be overcome. In fact, in 1961 Rosenblatt introduced a training procedure that almost solved the problem.[19] Despite this innovation, successful training procedures did not appear until 1985. We describe these in a later section.

Associative Memory

Another notable feature of the perceptron is that its memory of the learned task is distributed over all the connections modified during the training phase and is therefore less likely to be disrupted by damage. In these respects, it answers some of Lashley's concerns about human memory. However, there is an important aspect of human memory that perceptrons do not directly address—namely, that human memory seems to be associative as well as distributed. Whatever is common to two differing memories binds them together, so that one may elicit the other if the two have sufficient overlap.

Neural nets with associative memory have been extensively studied since the mid-1950s, beginning with the work of Wilfrid K. Taylor.[20] Fig. 4 shows the structure of Taylor's original net. It consists of a layer of associative units sandwiched between arrays of sensory and motor units. It is similar in structure to a three-layer perceptron, except that all contact weights in the net are modifiable, and the units are not M-P neurons but analog devices. (Consider the difference between a dimmer and a light switch. With a dimmer one can change the level of illumination in a smooth fashion, whereas with a switch it is all or nothing. Analog devices operate like dimmers rather than like switches). The training procedure, also different from the perceptron's, is simply Hebb's rule that activated synaptic weights increase if they activate their target units. Such changes have been

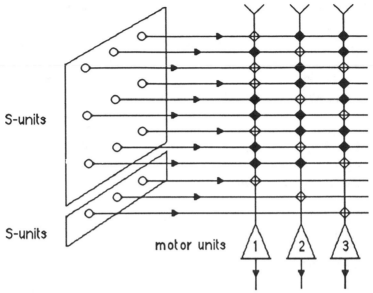

Fig. 4. A Taylor net. This net uses analog units with modifiable weights and can be trained to associate differing sets of stimulus patterns.

observed in brain tissue.[21] The net learns to associate differing sensory patterns through repeated presentation of pairs of patterns, one of which initially elicits a motor response. Eventually, the other pattern triggers the response. Thus, Taylor nets exhibit simple Pavlovian conditioning,[22] and the associated memory is stored in a distributed fashion in the pattern of weights.

In later work Taylor constructed a more elaborate net in which motor units reconnect with sensory units and with each other. Such a net is capable of forming associations with paired stimuli in a more reliable and controllable way than the earlier net and is also capable of pattern discrimination in the style of perceptrons and adalines. Taylor suggested that the association areas of the cerebral cortex and the thalamus contained such nets.[23]

Shortly after this, a very similar net was introduced by Karl Steinbuch—the "learning matrix."[24] It consists of an array of switches interposed between sensory and motor units. As in Taylor's scheme, the net learns to associate sensory patterns with motor patterns. The associated memory is stored in the pattern of open or closed switches. Learning matrices have a particularly simple mathematical structure, and their performance can be readily analyzed.

Following Steinbuch, but in most cases quite independently, many others devised similar nets—for example, James A. Anderson,[25] David J. Willshaw, O. Peter Buneman and H. Christopher Longuet-Higgins,[26] David Marr,[27] and Teuvo Kohonen,[28] all of whom discovered that associative nets are also content-addressable (i.e., stimulating such a net with some fragment of an associated memory will elicit the complete response). Thus, the net can be addressed with the partial content of a memory rather than just its location. Because of this property, associative nets are now generally referred to as associative content-addressable memories (ACAMs). Marr's work on this property is particularly interesting in that it is formulated as a theory of how the cerebellum enables animals to make delicate and precise voluntary movements and how memories may be temporarily stored in the hippocampus.

A Theory of the Cerebellum

The cerebellum ("little brain") is present in all vertebrates. It comprises roughly as many neurons as does the cerebrum (brain) and is thought to be the organ that controls voluntary movements. Compared with the cerebrum, the cerebellum has a strikingly regular and simple architecture. This architecture was revealed in the 1960s,[29] but its precise function and mode of operation remain to be discovered. Marr introduced the idea that the cerebellum is an ACAM that is trained by the cerebrum to control the execution of sequences of voluntary movements.[30] In Marr's theory (see Fig. 5), each of the five types of neuron comprising the cerebellar net is assigned a specific function. It is known that ACAMs work most efficiently when the stored patterns are uncorrelated with each other. Marr assigns to the granule cells the task of decorrelating activity patterns arriving along the mossy fibers. The resulting patterns are stored in the cerebellum via Hebb synapses, between granule and Purkinje cells and under the control of climbing fiber activation, exactly as patterns are stored in a learning matrix. It is easy to overload ACAMs with too many mossy fiber patterns. Golgi cells are supposed to prevent overload by raising the thresholds of granule cells. Since Golgi cells are themselves driven by mossy fiber activity, the more they are active, the more they inhibit and therefore raise the thresholds of granule cells. Thus, Golgi cells act like the automatic volume controls of radios and televisions. To retrieve patterns correctly from the store, the activation thresholds

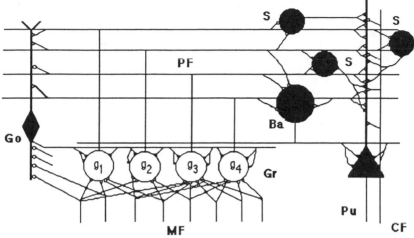

Fig. 5. Marr's theory of the cerebellum. Granule cells (g) are the only excitatory cells in the cerebellum; all others are inhibitory. Golgi cells (Go) control granule cell thresholds; basket (Ba) and stellate (S) cells control Purkinje cell (Pu) thresholds. The net is trained in the standard ACAM style to associate mossy fiber (MF) and climbing fiber (CF) patterns.

of Purkinje cells must be set high enough to suppress unwanted patterns. It is the task of basket and stellate cells, operating in a fashion similar to Golgi cells, to maintain these thresholds. The result of all this is that climbing fiber activation trains the cerebellar net to respond appropriately to mossy fiber activation patterns. This training is postulated to correspond to learning to execute complicated sequences of voluntary movements (e.g., driving, flying, playing the piano).[31]

Marr's theory is noteworthy in that for perhaps the first time, a specific function was assigned to each neuron in a part of the brain. This theory was slightly modified by James S. Albus, who noted that since Purkinje cells inhibit cells in the cerebellar nucleus, it is more likely that granule-Purkinje cell synapses are weakened rather than strengthened by coincident activation (i.e., training weakens the inhibition of cerebellar nucleus cells by Purkinje cells).[32] Since the publication of the Marr-Albus papers, a number of attempts have been made to test the theory.[33] It is fair to say that its validity or otherwise has not yet been definitively determined, although some recent experimental results appear to support Albus's version of the theory.

A Theory of the Hippocampus

Marr applied a very similar analysis to another part of the brain, the hippocampus,[34] so called because its shape resembles that of a sea horse. The hippocampus lies in the temporal lobe of the cerebrum and is thought to be a region where short-term, or working, memories are formed, particularly those related to the spatial aspects of an animal's environment.[35]

Like the cerebellum, the hippocampus has a particularly regular structure. Its principal region, the *cornu ammonis* (CA), comprises a single sheet of "output" neurons, the so-called pyramidal cells, together with ancillary "interneurons," mostly stellate neurons. In Marr's theory the pyramidal cells are analogous to cerebellar Purkinje cells, and the various interneurons are analogous to cerebellar granule, Golgi, basket, and stellate cells. Thus, the hippocampus, like the cerebellum, is modeled as an ACAM. However, there are important differences between the two structures. According to Marr, the hippocampus has to learn to form its own internal classifications of the many input patterns it has to store. It therefore needs granule cells with modifiable synapses as well as pyramidal cells. In fact, Marr showed that at least two sheets of modifiable granule cells are needed for reliable operation. In addition, the hippocampus, given only a small fraction of the relevant cues, has to be able to retrieve patterns. It can do so only if the CA's pyramidal cells are interconnected via modifiable excitatory Hebb synapses, so that the entire sheet of CA pyramids acts cooperatively.

A Theory of Cerebral Neocortex

Marr's theory of the hippocampus is actually a specialization of his more general theory of the function of the cerebral neocortex.[36] The neocortex, containing most of the neurons in the brain, is the major part of the cerebrum. Marr postulated that the primary function of neocortical nets is to form internal representations of classes and subclasses of objects, using perceptron-like procedures. In providing a role for climbing fibers to activate and guide the formation of new classificatory neurons, this theory differs from his theory of the hippocampus. To date, neither of these models has been definitively tested. However, considerable evidence has accumulated that many of the excitatory synapses on hippocampal pyramidal cells can be strengthened for long times (from seconds to minutes) by suitable presynaptic stimulation. This effect, called long-term potentiation (LTP),[37] is consistent with Marr's cortical theories.

CURRENT DEVELOPMENTS

Following Marr's work, there was a long hiatus in which little progress was made on how to train neural nets to represent information. Much work was done on how the brain develops[38] and on neurodynamics,[39] the generation and propagation of synchronized neural activity. It was not until the early 1980s, however, that real progress was made on the problems pioneered by Rosenblatt and Marr. These new investigations are generally classified under the term *connectionism*, which stands for the old notion that information is stored in the brain in the pattern of synaptic weights laid down during learning. This idea has been around almost since Ramon y Cajal first discovered neurons,[40] and as we have noted, was elaborated by Hebb in 1949. It forms the basis for most of the work on perceptrons and adalines since then. We shall therefore use the term *neoconnectionism* to refer to current work.

Hopfield Nets

As our first example of neoconnectionism we describe the work of John J. Hopfield,[41] who demonstrated the formal analogy between a net of neuronlike elements with symmetric connections,* now called a Hopfield net, and a material discovered in the past decade, called a spin glass.[42] The origins of this work are to be found in a very penetrating paper published in 1954 by the neuroanatomist Brian G. Cragg and the physicist Nevill V. Temperley.[43] Cragg and Temperley noted that just as neurons can be either activated or quiescent, so atoms in an assembly or a lattice can be in one of two states: they can be in spins pointing "up" or in spins pointing "down" (see Fig. 6). Furthermore, just as neurons either excite or inhibit one another, so atoms exert on their neighbors forces that tend to set their spins in either the same or the opposite direction. The properties of neurons in a densely connected net are probably somewhat similar to those of

---

*If x and y are two neurons, then their connections are symmetric if the weight of the x to y synapse equals the weight of the y to x synapse.

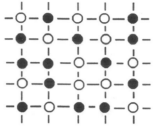

Fig. 6. Lattice spin system. "Up" and "down" spins are arranged in a square lattice. Each spin interacts with its nearest neighbors to take up a stable configuration.

atoms (or binary alloys) in a crystal lattice. Crystals, alloys, and other atomic assemblies can display differing types of order and disorder. These range from short-range order, in which, on the average, every "up" spin is surrounded only by "down" spins, to long-range order, in which, on the average, "up" spins persist at, say, every third lattice site in any given direction. Systems of spins showing various kinds or order provide good models of the properties of magnetic materials. For example, a ferromagnet, which consists of atoms tending to force each other to spin in the same direction, has long-range order; an antiferromagnet, which consists of atoms tending to force each other to spin in the opposite direction, also has long-range order; on the other hand, a paramagnet, which consists of atoms spinning both up and down in random patterns, is disordered. It is possible that neural nets exhibit analogous properties. Cragg and Temperley therefore suggested (a) that the domain patterns that are a ubiquitous feature of ferromagnets, comprising patches of up or down spins, should show up in neural nets as patches of excited or quiescent neurons and (b) that neural domain patterns, once triggered by external stimuli, would be stable against spontaneous random activity and could therefore constitute a memory of the stimulus.[44] It is interesting to note that twenty years later William A. Little, via the mathematical analysis of a lattice spin system, arrived at virtually the same conclusions concerning the existence of persistent neural states as Cragg and Temperley did.[45]

In 1975 David Sherrington and Scott Kirkpatrick discovered a new magnetic material consisting of a random mixture of both ferromagnetically and antiferromagnetically interacting spins and exhibiting no net magnetism.[46] They called this material a spin glass. Spin glasses have interesting properties, one of which is the capacity to store many different disordered spin patterns. Hopfield nets have similar properties, but they are not neural nets, since each element must both excite and inhibit its neighbors (see Fig. 7). Nevertheless, they are of interest as

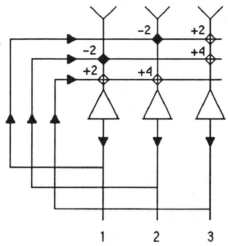

Fig. 7. A Hopfield net with symmetric connections. Units 1 and 2 excite one neighbor and inhibit another.

artificial neural nets, particularly for memory storage.

Hopfield recognized the formal analogy between a net of neuron-like elements with random symmetric connection weights and a spin glass and, using Hebb's postulated rule for synaptic weight modification, showed that the weights can be modified so as to stabilize net activity.* Given such weights, any initial configuration of active and inactive elements will evolve toward a stable configuration. Thus, the stable configurations can be used to store information in a reliable fashion. Hopfield nets, in fact, serve as reliable ACAMs and are similar in many respects to those constructed by Taylor, Steinbuch, Marr, and their associates.

Hopfield nets represent an important conceptual advance in the theory of neural nets. Although they are not very realistic as models for

---

*Hebb's rule can be stated as follows. Suppose neurons x and y are connected. Let $X = \pm 1$ be the state of the neuron x, and $Y = \pm 1$ the corresponding state of the neuron y. Then the synaptic weight of the x to y contact is proportional to the average value of the product XY. This is an example of a local rule. The weight is determined only by the correlated activities of the neurons x and y.

nerve nets, the principle they embody—storing information in dynamically stable configurations—is profound. Such a principle has its origins in the work of one of the early cyberneticians, W. Ross Ashby, who coined the term *ultrastability* to describe the way in which he thought brain activity patterns always tend toward dynamically stable configurations.[47] This principle is implicit in the work of many others.[48]

Computing with Hopfield Nets

Hopfield nets have proved to be of interest for solving computational optimization problems. A well-known application of these nets is the "traveling salesman problem," in which a salesman needs to visit each of a number of cities once on a schedule that minimizes the length of his journey. This is an example of what is called a constrained optimization problem.[49] S. Kirkpatrick, C. D. Gelatt, Jr., and M. P. Vecchi have shown that the equilibrium configurations taken up by a spin glass provide solutions to this problem.[50] John J. Hopfield and David W. Tank have demonstrated that certain Hopfield nets also find good solutions.[51] Fig. 8 shows a solution involving

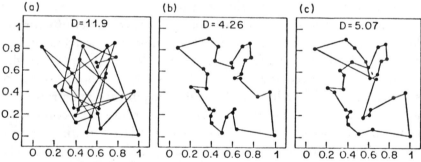

Fig. 8. Comparison of procedures for solving the traveling salesman problem: (a) a random tour, of total length D = 11.9; (b) a tour found by the Kernighan-Lin procedure, D = 4.26; (c) a tour found by the Hopfield-Tank procedure, D = 5.07. It will be seen that the Hopfield-Tank tour is nearly as short as the Kernighan-Lin tour. (Redrawn from J. J. Hopfield and D. W. Tank, " 'Neural' Computation and Constraint Satisfaction Problems and the Traveling Salesman," *Biological Cybernetics* 55 [1985]: 141].)

thirty cities. Although the Hopfield net does not find the shortest tour, it does find one that compares quite favorably with the solution found through the Kernighan-Lin procedure,[52] one of the better procedures for solving constrained optimization problems. Recently

Richard Durbin and David J. Willshaw have devised another neuronlike net that finds even shorter tours and works better on big problems.[53]

Boltzmann Machines

Hopfield nets suffer from one defect in their ability to find the best solution in constrained optimization problems. They can get trapped in metastable configurations. To find the true global minimum, the net must make random configurational changes from time to time, thereby gaining the ability to escape from metastable configurations. This is the essence of a well-known version of the Monte Carlo procedure, introduced at the Los Alamos National Laboratory in 1953 by N. Metropolis, A. Rosenbluth, M. Rosenbluth, M. Teller, and E. Teller to find stable states.[54] In this procedure the change produced by a random "flip" of one of the net spins is computed. If the new configuration is more stable, it is retained. Otherwise the configuration is rejected (i.e., the flip is cancelled). Such a procedure, although slow, will eventually find the most stable configurations. Geoffrey E. Hinton and Terrence J. Sejnowski accordingly used the Monte Carlo procedure to find stable configurations in Hopfield nets,[55] in effect repeating Kirkpatrick, Gelatt, and Vecchi's use of Monte Carlo methods in spin-glass problems. In doing so they discovered a process by which the resulting nets, which they called Boltzmann machines, can modify their connectivity in a way that solves the hidden-unit credit assignment problem.

The Boltzmann machine, an adaptive Hopfield net with hidden units, implements a Monte Carlo procedure for finding the stable configuration of active and inactive units; these units are not simple M-P neurons, which are all or nothing in their responses, but analog devices. Hinton and Sejnowski demonstrated that with these devices, stable configurations can be reached if contact weights change via the following rule: let p be the average probability of two units being simultaneously active when the S-units are activated by a stimulus pattern that clamps the motor units into some activation pattern, and let p' be the corresponding probability when the machine is freely running in the absence of stimulation. Let w be the weight of the contact between the two units. The rule by which w changes is very simple: if p is greater than p', increase w; if p is less than p', decrease it. (The reader should compare this rule with the perceptron and adaline training rules given on pages 90 and 91). With such a rule in place, Boltzmann machines are capable of solving a variety of constrained optimization problems.[56] Many such problems occur in computational approaches to vision.

Learning Representations

The Boltzmann machine also provides a solution to the credit assignment problem for hidden units, albeit in the special case of adaptive Hopfield nets. The rule given above solves the credit assignment problem for hidden units in terms of locally available information only (i.e., the change in weight of the contact between two units depends on their activation patterns alone). The Boltzmann machine learning process is autoassociative or unsupervised, depends only on correlations between pairs of units, and creates in the set of connection weights a distributed representation of the correlations that exist in and between members of the set of stimulus patterns. To put it another way, a Boltzmann machine can form a representation that eventually reproduces relations between classes of events in its environment.[57] It therefore provides a possible solution to Marr's problem of how to construct such representations *ab initio* in the granule cells of the hippocampus and the neocortex. More generally, it provides a way in which distributed representations of abstract symbols can be formed and therefore permits the investigation by means of adaptive neural nets of symbolic reasoning.[58]

Back-Propagation

The Boltzmann machine represents a considerable advance in unsupervised machine learning. However, because the machine uses a version of the Monte Carlo procedure to find stable configurations, the learning is very slow. In addition, the Boltzmann machine is a Hopfield net with only symmetric connections. These limitations have recently been overcome by David E. Rumelhart, Geoffrey Hinton, Robert J. Williams, and others in a successful implementation of the procedure originally suggested by Rosenblatt.[59] Fig. 9 shows the structure of the net. It is essentially a two-layer perceptron. It is also the basic architecture of Marr's model of the cerebellum, without inhibitory interneurons. The rules by which contacts are modified differ considerably from those of Marr's model, however,

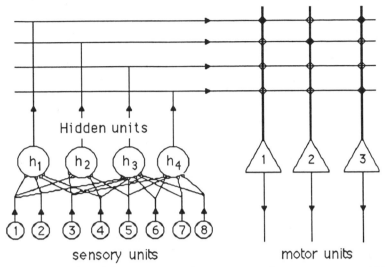

Fig. 9. Structure of a multilayer perceptron. In contrast to an elementary perceptron (cf. Fig. 2), there is a layer of hidden units, the synaptic weights of which are also modifiable. This structure is, in fact, a subset of Marr's model of the hippocampus, but the procedure for changing weights is different.

and derive from the adaline rules given earlier. Recall that in an adaline, weight changes are proportional to the differences between the desired activation pattern and the unit's total excitation. Rumelhart et al. have shown that for analog units a simple extension of the adaline rule solves the hidden-unit credit assignment problem.

The actual computations are effected in two stages. In the first, the forward stage, the net is stimulated and motor unit responses are noted. In the second, the backward stage, these responses are used to adjust the weights of the motor units themselves, and then hidden-unit weights are adjusted—hence the description of the procedure as back-propagation. It is here that the difference between the analog elements used by Rumelhart et al. and the simple M-P units used in elementary perceptrons and adalines proves decisive. The adaline procedure for modifying motor-unit synaptic weights can be extended to hidden-unit weights. Consider the weights in Fig. 10, which shows a section of the net depicted in Fig. 9. The requisite change in the hidden-unit weight W_{43} is related to the weights and weight changes of all units "downstream" of h_3. Thus, given the changes in w_{31} and so on, which are determined by a slight modification of the

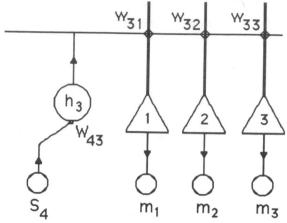

Fig. 10. How back-propagation works. The net is first stimulated, in this case via the unit S_4. The motor responses m_1, m_2, and m_3 are then obtained. The weights w_{31}, w_{32}, and w_{33} are then adjusted, and then the weight W_{43} is adjusted.

adaline procedure described earlier (adapted to analog units), the change in W_{43} can be computed.

The procedure of Rumelhart et al. provides a solution to the credit assignment problem and makes multilayered analog perceptrons and adalines into powerful tools for investigating supervised learning in adaptive neural nets. In what follows we describe a few applications of back-propagation.

The x OR ELSE y Problem

We have previously remarked on the failure of elementary perceptrons and adalines to compute the logical function x OR ELSE y. This function is true if and only if x is true and y is false or vice versa, and is false otherwise. The truth table corresponding to x OR ELSE y is shown on page 105. With back-propagation the net shown in Fig. 11 is obtained after training comprising 558 sweeps through the four patterns shown in the truth table. In this case both the hidden units and the motor unit have negative thresholds and are active unless sufficiently inhibited. The hidden unit h_1 is active if neither S-unit is active, and when h_1 is active it turns off the motor unit. The motor unit is also inactivated if both S-units are active. This net differs somewhat from that shown in Fig. 3, in which all threshold biases are positive; nevertheless, it also computes the logical function x OR ELSE y.

x y	x OR ELSE Y
+1 +1	−1
+1 −1	+1
−1 +1	+1
−1 −1	−1

Truth Table for *x* OR ELSE *y*. A + 1 denotes "true" and a − 1 "false." Thus *x* OR ELSE *y* is false when *x* and *y* are both true or both false. Otherwise *x* OR ELSE *y* is true.

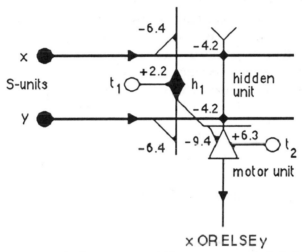

x OR ELSE y

Fig. 11. Net obtained via back-propagation, which computes correctly the logical function *x* OR ELSE *y*. The units t_1 and t_2 have zero threshold and are always active. (Redrawn from David F. Rumelhart, Geoffrey E. Hinton, and Robert J. Williams, "Learning Internal Representations by Error Propagation," in vol. 1 of *Parallel Distributed Processing: Explorations in the Microstructure of Cognition*, ed. David E. Rumelhart and James L. McClelland [Cambridge: MIT Press, 1986].)

The T/C Problem

Another problem solved by back-propagation is a geometric one—distinguishing between the letters *T* and *C* independently of translation and rotation. Fig. 12 shows the patterns, and Fig. 13 the architecture, of the net used by Rumelhart et al. to solve the problem.[60] This structure is more or less the same as that used by Rosenblatt and many others on similar problems. It is noteworthy in that the hidden units are connected only with small regions of the

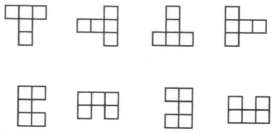

Fig. 12. *T* and *C* patterns to be distinguished by a three-layer back-propagating perceptron. (Redrawn from Rumelhart et al. [see Fig. 11].)

sheet of *S*-units (called receptive fields), whereas the motor unit is connected with many widely separated hidden units. This connection pattern mimics the architecture of the visual brain to some extent.[61]

After some 5,000 to 10,000 presentations of the *T* and *C* patterns, together with the appropriate responses, the net learns the appropriate task. In doing so, the hidden-unit receptive fields become adapted to the task in a number of ways, the effect of which is to facilitate distinguishing *T*'s from *C*'s via the final motor unit.

NETtalk

In an even more striking application, Terrence Sejnowski and Charles R. Rosenberg trained another similar net to read and speak English text.[62] The net comprises 203 *S*-units arranged in seven groups of 29;

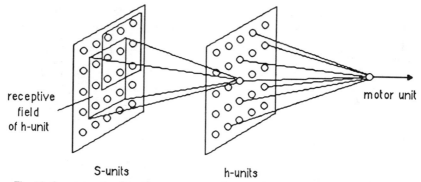

Fig. 13. Structure of a three-layer perceptron that can distinguish *T*'s from *C*'s. The input layer of *S*-units is a two-dimensional sheet, as is the layer of hidden units. The receptive field of each *h*-unit comprises a 3 × 3 square of *S*-units; that is, it is area-limited (cf. Minsky and Papert, *Perceptrons: An Introduction to Computational Geometry* [Cambridge: MIT Press, 1969]). Hidden-unit weights are adjusted via back-propagation during the course of about 10,000 presentations of *T* and *C* patterns and converge to a set that distinguishes *T* from *C* patterns. (Redrawn from Rumelhart et al. [see Fig. 11].)

80 *h*-units; and 26 motor units. In each group of *S*-units, 26 encode one letter of the English alphabet, and the remaining 3 units encode punctuation and word boundaries. A stimulus pattern is thus a string of seven characters. The motor units encode speech sounds, or phonemes, and also stress and syllable boundaries. The net was trained by using back-propagation on a number of texts. One experiment used phonetic transcriptions of the informal continuous speech of a child. Approximately 1,000 words from this corpus were used, and after some 50,000 presentations, the net was able to read and speak with an accuracy of about 95 percent. Fig. 14 shows the

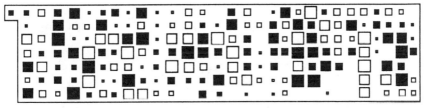

A B C D E F G H I J K L M N O P Q R S T U V W X Y Z

Fig. 14. Receptive field of a hidden unit in NETtalk. It comprises 203 *S*-units plus 1 *h*-unit to set its threshold. The *S*-units are arranged in seven groups of 29. Twenty-six of the 29 *S*-units encode letters of the alphabet, and 3 of them encode punctuation and spaces. Thus, each hidden unit responds to a string of seven characters in a specific fashion defined by its weights. The area of each square is proportional to the weight: open squares correspond to positive weights, filled squares to negative ones. (Redrawn from T. J. Sejnowski and C. R. Rosenberg, *NETtalk, A Parallel Network that Learns to Read Aloud,* Technical Report JHU/EECS—86/01 [Baltimore, Md.: Johns Hopkins University, Electrical Engineering and Computer Science, 1986].)

receptive field of one of the hidden units. It is evident that this unit has a distributed representation of many attributes of input strings.

The net was then presented with a 439-word continuation of text from the same child (containing many novel words), which it read and spoke with an accuracy of 78 percent. This is an example of generalization. The Sejnowski-Rosenberg net, called NETtalk, generalizes very well. In fact, multilayer perceptrons and adalines generalize quite well over a variety of tasks, just as Rosenblatt claimed many years ago.[63] Another property exhibited by NETtalk is resistance to damage. A substantially damaged NETtalk can still read and speak with an accuracy of some 40 percent, and it recovers quickly with retraining. Such properties are to be expected in all nets with distributed representations, as suggested in the Winograd-Cowan theory. Overall, NETtalk works surprisingly well, but it is limited in its ability to deal with syntactic and semantic ambiguities. More elaborately structured versions of NETtalk may be expected to perform better in this respect.

Family Trees

We describe as a final example of back-propagation a net that is trained to store abstract relationships[64] (see the information in the two family trees shown in Fig. 15). The net comprises 24 *S*-units,

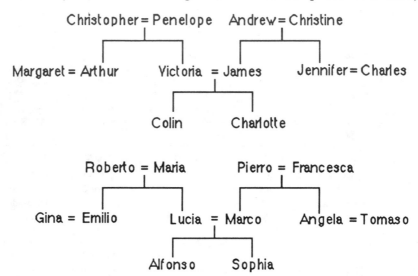

Fig. 15. Two isomorphic family trees. The information can be expressed as a set of triples of the form ⟨person 1⟩ ⟨relationship⟩ ⟨person 2⟩, where the possible relationships are {father, mother, husband, wife, son, daughter, etc.}. A layered net can be said to "know" these triples if it can produce the third term of each triple when given the first two. (Redrawn from David E. Rumelhart, Geoffrey E. Hinton, and Robert J. Williams, "Learning Representations by Back-Propagating Errors," *Nature* 323 [1986]:533.)

each representing a person; a further 12 *S*-units, each representing a relationship; 30 hidden units arranged in three layers; and 24 motor units, each representing a person. Fig. 16 shows the activity levels in such a net after it has been trained. The net learns both of the family trees, essentially by generalizing from one tree to the other, after about 1,500 presentations of the various triples. Once again, hidden-unit receptive fields adapt to the task. Fig. 17 shows the fields of two units in the first hidden layer. Unit 5 encodes the distinction between English and Italian, whereas unit 6 encodes which branch of the

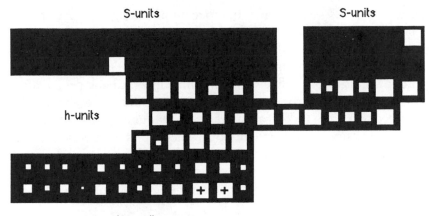

Fig. 16. Activity levels in a five-layer net after it has been trained. The top layer has 24 S-units on the left to represent ⟨person 1⟩ and 12 S-units on the right to represent ⟨relationships⟩. The white squares show activity levels of the various units. The S-units activated correspond to ⟨Colin⟩ ⟨has aunt⟩. Each of the two input groups is totally connected to its own group of 6 *h*-units in the second layer. These groups learn to encode people and relationships as distributed activity patterns. The second layer is totally connected to the central layer of 12 *h*-units, and these are connected to the next layer of 6 *h*-units. Activity in this layer must activate the correct motor units, each of which represents a particular ⟨person 2⟩. In this case, there are two correct answers (marked with +) because Colin has two aunts. (Redrawn from Rumelhart et al. [see Fig. 15].)

Fig. 17. Receptive fields of two hidden units encoding family tree information. (Redrawn from Rumelhart et al. [see Fig. 15].)

family 1 comes from. With such hidden-unit receptive fields, the net is able to generalize correctly when presented with novel triples.

Receptive Fields and Neurobiology

The examples described above show clearly that hidden units learn about the stimulus patterns that are presented to them, subject to feedback driven by the intended response of the net to such patterns. In learning about stimulus patterns, hidden units develop specialized receptive fields (determined by their input weights) in a highly cooperative fashion (each field is affected by all the others in the net) and form a distributed representation of the stimulus class. This result has important implications for experimental neurobiology, for although it is highly unlikely that anything like the back-propagation procedure is employed in the brain, the end product—receptive fields adapted to a given task—can supply clues about how real neural nets performing similar tasks might work. These clues have very practical consequences, since one of the few ways neurobiologists can directly observe brain operation is by determining which stimulus patterns activate the neuron nearest to a microelectrode implanted in the brain.

A first application of back-propagation along these lines has recently been reported by Richard Andersen and David Zipser in connection with the receptive fields of neurons in the monkey's posterior parietal cortex.[65] In such neurons, information about eye position in relation to the head and to the position of the image on the retina is combined to locate objects with respect to the position of the head in space. Neurons in this area have very large overlapping receptive fields, and their responses are tuned so that they fire at rates proportional to the difference between preferred and actual eye position. Andersen and Zipser modeled this situation with a three-layer back-propagating perceptron trained to learn spatial positions. After less than 1,000 trials, motor-unit responses accurately encoded object locations in head-centered coordinates, given eye and retinal image coordinates. The net learned to associate eye and retinal image positions, and of course the hidden-unit receptive fields reflected this. What is more important, these receptive fields resemble those in the monkey's parietal cortex. It is evident that multilayer perceptrons can be used in many similar situations to predict receptive field properties.

Extension of the Back-Propagation Procedure

The back-propagation procedure described above represents a major advance in the theory of perceptrons and adalines, and more generally in the theory and practice of supervised learning. There are, however, a few problems with the procedure. First, although it is much faster than the Monte Carlo procedure used in the Boltzmann machine, back-propagation is still rather slow. Much work is now being devoted to finding faster and more efficient procedures.[66] Another problem concerns performance on very large problems. It does not always follow that procedures that work well on small problems also work well on larger versions of the same problem. This is known as the scaling problem. Two approaches to this problem have recently appeared.

In the first of these, Dana H. Ballard notes that sometimes multilayer perceptrons using back-propagation become "trapped" in a pattern of activity that does not solve the given task, particularly in nets with more than one layer of hidden units.[67] Ballard's solution to this situation is twofold. First, construct autoassociative learning modules in which the outputs of hidden units feed back to influence S-units. Learning in such a net is unsupervised, and the hidden units form a representation of correlations existing in and between S-unit patterns, just as in the Boltzmann machine. Second, use such autoassociative nets as modules in a hierarchically organized net. These modules can be coupled in ways that permit the solving of larger and larger problems, so that the scaling problem is solved. In a related piece of work, Hinton and his colleagues have devised a similar procedure, called recirculation, that minimizes the rate of change of activity in the net and is claimed to be more neurobiologically plausible than back-propagation.[68]

Eric Mjolsness and David H. Sharp have recently introduced another procedure that has been shown to scale well on certain problems and is based on the fact that the connectivity of a large class of nets can be specified recursively, that is, by the repeated application of a few simple rules.[69] Such nets can be modified through rule changes rather than weight changes. Moreover, the procedure is designed to penalize nets with a large number of contacts and thus to increase the likelihood that such nets will generalize to larger input sets. This approach is closely related to what are called genetic algorithms, in which rules for generating adaptive nets are themselves subject to adaptation.[70] The point is that genetic nets scale better than nets specified directly by weights.

Master-Slave Nets

Many other variants of Hopfield nets, Boltzmann machines, and multilayer perceptrons now exist.[71] A particularly interesting example is the "master-slave" net recently introduced by Alan S. Lapedes and Robert M. Farber.[72] As we have previously noted, Hopfield nets (and Boltzmann machines) are not realistic as models of neural nets, since all their connections are symmetric. Nevertheless, the ability of these nets to find globally stable configurations is valuable. Conversely, multilayer perceptrons need not be symmetrically connected, but their operation is synchronous: they have no intrinsic dynamics other than what an external clock provides. The master-slave net introduced by Lapedes and Farber has the best of both worlds. The slave is an asynchronous, asymmetric net of neurons, the weights of which are controlled and modified by a master Hopfield net. The different stable states of the master net can be used to control the weights of the slave net in such a way as to encode any desired dynamical behavior. Master-slave nets are, in fact, dynamical generalizations of multilayer perceptrons and can be used to encode representations, not just those of static S-unit patterns and correlations but also those of S-unit patterns that change in time.

Neural Nets for Prediction and Simulation

But if neural nets can learn to represent time-varying correlations, they can be used as predictors and as simulators of a variety of dynamical processes. Lapedes and Farber have recently extended their investigation of generalized back-propagation in this direction and have demonstrated the efficacy of neural nets for such purposes.[73] With this development, the theory of perceptrons and adalines has renewed contact with cybernetics, the branch of engineering that deals with predicting, filtering, and simulating dynamical processes.[74]

In this respect, it is of considerable interest to compare the structure of a multilayer perceptron with that of the learning filter invented in 1954 by Dennis Gabor,[75] one of the early pioneers of communication theory and cybernetics and the inventor of holography. This filter operates in the following fashion. A long sample of a noisy message is stored on magnetic tape and sent periodically through the filter. The filter output and an advanced or a retarded copy of the message are fed into a comparator, which generates the difference between the two signals. This difference is then used to adjust the filter so as to minimize the difference. Thus the filter output ends up looking like the message sample. Gabor showed that such a machine could be trained to predict and filter messages of various kinds and also to recognize patterns. The adjustable filter is clearly analogous to a net of S, h, and motor units. (It seems evident that

Gabor solved the equivalent of the credit assignment problem in 1954!) Lapedes and Farber recognized the analogy and have shown that generalized back-propagating multilayer perceptrons are much more powerful and flexible simulators than the Gabor learning filter.

NEURAL NETS AND ARTIFICIAL INTELLIGENCE STUDIES

In this section, drawing on the material presented earlier in the paper, we discuss the relationship between neural nets and research on artificial intelligence.

We take AI to be the attempt to embody in computing machinery a repertoire of intelligent behavior comparable with human behavior in similar contexts. Until recently this attempt has taken place almost entirely within the framework of the standard AI paradigm: first specify the context, next describe the logic of the desired behavior, and then try to achieve it by using various heuristics (i.e., search methods based on a background of prior knowledge supplied by the designer).[76] It is evident that such a system will succeed only if the designer has analyzed the class of problems to be solved and is able to represent this class and the problem-solving heuristics in a suitable programming language. It is not clear if this approach can succeed in situations that have to be reanalyzed because the context has changed. Part of the problem lies in the need for context-sensitive logical descriptions. This is where neural nets (more specifically, multilayer perceptrons) become relevant. The designer of a multilayer perceptron needs no precise logical description, only an informal understanding of the complexities of the desired behavior sufficient to construct the overall architecture of an appropriate neural net. Back-propagation takes care of the rest of the details. Thus, given some overall hard-wiring, local connection weights can be soft-wired into the net by training. The resulting neural net embodies an implicit description of the desired behavior rather than the explicit declarative logical statements that control an AI system. In this respect, it is interesting to recall a remark of John von Neumann's concerning the question of whether every behavior can be expressed completely and unambiguously in words and therefore in logical symbols. Von Neumann foresaw the problem of vision as immensely complicated:

It is not at all certain that ... [a visual object] might not constitute the simplest description of itself. ... [Further,] it is ... not at all unlikely that it is futile to look for a precise logical concept, that is, for a precise verbal description [say] of "visual analogy." It is possible that the connection pattern of the visual brain itself is the simplest logical expression or definition of this principle.[77]

Of course, multilayer perceptrons have not yet been used for problem solving in the way AI systems have, and it may be that as more difficult problems are tackled, the complexities of the required hard-wiring will prove to be too formidable. In this respect, the attempts by Ballard, Hinton, Mjolsness, and Sharp to build hierarchically organized soft-wireable nets may prove useful. In any event, it seems reasonable to expect improved multilayer perceptrons to be capable of embodying implicit descriptions of very complicated behavior, provided some prior understanding of the logical structure of this behavior is encoded in the overall architecture.

Memory

There is also the problem of memory. One of the factors limiting the development of AI systems is the cost of large, fast memories.[78] ACAMs in the form of Taylor-Steinbuch nets, or in their modern form as Marr nets,[79] or more likely in the form of improved Hopfield nets, are likely to play a key role in providing such memories, particularly in light of the development of very large-scale integrated (VLSI) circuitry, which can be soft-wired for a variety of tasks.[80] Such memory stores, in combination with the trainable nets described above, may well provide a suitable substrate for the embodiment of truly intelligent behavior in machines.

Future Prospects

Can we therefore expect to see autonomous intelligent robots with silicon brains, built from hierarchically organized improved multilayered perceptrons and ACAMs, in the not too distant future? It is our belief, based on the investigations we have described in this paper, that there is still a very long way to go before any kind of truly intelligent robot can be produced. It is clear that all progress to date in the soft-wiring of nets to perform intelligent tasks rests on prior analysis by a designer of the context-dependent tasks to be performed. The intention and the meaning are supplied by the designer.

AI rests on the idea expressed very succinctly by Kenneth J. W. Craik in 1943, that "thought parallels reality through symbolism."[81] But we have noted that explicit symbolic descriptions may not exist for many important thought processes, so can trainable neural nets "describe" such processes? The answer seems to be yes, but the trainer needs to know a lot about the structure of these processes.

What about Hopfield nets and Boltzmann machines, which learn without trainers? Because of the restriction to symmetric weights, these seem more promising as models of how real brains work; several investigators have devised Hopfield nets with modifiable synaptic weights for this purpose. Christoph von der Malsburg, for example, has used such nets to model associative thinking, in which novel combinations of representations are produced by means of very rapid synaptic modifications.[82] Such synapses have recently been referred to as Malsburg synapses.[83] It is not clear, however, that Malsburg nets solve the credit assignment problem. Boltzmann machines certainly do, but only if there is a hidden external net that signals to hidden units that the net is being stimulated. (As we have said, the Boltzmann machine learning procedure requires that hidden units know the difference between stimulated and freely running activity.) This is a primitive attention mechanism. That such a mechanism is needed to control learning and thinking is not, of course, novel. In thinking about the brain, Francis Crick has suggested that such a mechanism exists not in the cerebral neocortex but in the thalamus, the part of the brain that lies between the neocortex and the brain stem and that contains all the nets that control bodily functions. The need for such a mechanism in Hopfield nets has already been appreciated by Mjolsness as a way to serialize the search process that finds stable configurations.[84] Can such nets replace back-propagating multilayer perceptrons? In our view, the answer is likely to be yes, but once again, only if a great deal of hard-wiring already exists in the net.

It is hard-wiring that embodies prior knowledge and, in a sense, the intent of the designer. In the human brain the hard-wiring is the end product of a billion years of evolutionary adaptations to changing environments expressed through the action of gene products during the course of brain development. In a sense, evolution has acted not as a trainer to soft-wire neural nets but as a critic to hard-wire them: if it works, it survives, so that further soft-wiring is effective. Should we expect to be able to telescope one billion years of evolution acting on protoplasm into a few decades of neural-net and AI research on VLSI silicon chips? Until we understand how ideas and intentions are embodied in the human brain, rapid progress seems unlikely. On the other hand, the developments we have described in the theory and practice of multilayer perceptrons permit the experimental investigation of hard-wiring itself. We predict that the top-down approach of conventional AI and the bottom-up approach of neoconnectionism will eventually join to produce real progress in what McCulloch once called experimental epistemology, the study of how knowledge is embodied in brains and may be embodied in machines.[85]

ENDNOTES

Jack Cowan acknowledges with thanks the hospitality of the Centre for Mathematical Biology, Mathematics Institute, University of Oxford; the Institute for Theoretical Physics, the University of California at Santa Barbara; and the Mathematics Department, University of Southern California; as well as the financial support provided in part by the Los Alamos National Laboratory, the Science and Engineering Research Council of Great Britain (Grant No. GR/D/13573), the National Science Foundation (Grant No. PHY82–17853, supplemented by funds from the National Aeronautics and Space Administration), the System Development Foundation (Grant No. SDF 55), and the Program in Neural, Informational, and Behavioral Science (NIBS) of the University of Southern California. David Sharp thanks the University of Chicago and the Institute for Theoretical Physics, the University of California at Santa Barbara, for their hospitality, and the U.S. Department of Energy for its financial support.

[1] Warren S. McCulloch and Walter H. Pitts, "A Logical Calculus of the Ideas Immanent in Nervous Activity," *Bulletin of Mathematical Biophysics* 5 (1943):115.

[2] Donald M. Mackay, "On Comparing the Brain with Machines," *American Scientist* 42 (1954):2.

[3] Alan M. Turing, "On Computable Numbers with an Application to the Entscheidungsproblem," in *Proceedings of the London Mathematical Society* 42 (1936):230; 43 (1937):544.

[4] John von Neumann, "Probabilistic Logics and the Synthesis of Reliable Organisms from Unreliable Components," in *Automata Studies,* ed. C. E. Shannon and John McCarthy (Princeton, N.J.: Princeton University Press, 1956).

[5] Shmuel Winograd and Jack D. Cowan, *Reliable Computation in the Presence of Noise* (Cambridge: MIT Press, 1963).

[6] J. Taylor, *Selected Writings of John Hughlings Jackson* (London: Hodder and Stoughton, 1932).

[7] Karl S. Lashley, "Persistent Problems in the Evolution of Mind," *Quarterly Review of Biology* 24 (1) (1942):28.

[8]Karl S. Lashley, "In Search of the Engram," *Symposium of the Society for Experimental Biology* 4 (1950):454.

[9]Horace B. Barlow, "Single Units and Sensation: A Neuron Doctrine for Perceptual Psychology?" *Perception* 1 (1972):371.

[10]Donald O. Hebb, *The Organization of Behavior* (New York: John Wiley, 1949).

[11]Albert M. Uttley, "The Classification of Signals in the Nervous System," *EEG Clinical Neurophysiology* 6 (1954):479.

[12]Walter H. Pitts and Warren S. McCulloch, "How We Know Universals: The Perception of Auditory and Visual Forms," *Bulletin of Mathematical Biophysics* 9 (1947):127.

[13]O. Lippold, *The Origin of the Alpha Rhythm* (Edinburgh and London: Churchill Livingstone, 1953).

[14]Donald M. Mackay, "Some Experiments on the Perception of Patterns Modulated at the Alpha Frequency," *EEG Clinical Neurophysiology* 5 (1953):559.

[15]Frank Rosenblatt, "The Perceptron, a Probabilistic Model for Information Storage and Organization in the Brain," *Psychological Review* 62 (1958):386.

[16]A. Novikoff, "On Convergence Proofs for Perceptrons," in *Symposium on the Mathematical Theory of Automata,* ed. J. Fox (New York: Polytechnic Press, 1963): 615.

[17]Bernard Widrow and M. E. Hoff, "Adaptive Switching Circuits," *WESCON Convention Record* 4 (1960):96.

[18]Marvin Minsky and Seymour Papert, *Perceptrons: An Introduction to Computational Geometry* (Cambridge: MIT Press, 1969).

[19]Rosenblatt, "The Perceptron."

[20]Wilfrid K. Taylor, "Electrical Simulation of Some Nervous System Functional Activities," in *Information Theory,* ed. E. C. Cherry (London: Butterworths, 1956), 3.

[21]G. S. Brindley, "The Classification of Modifiable Synapses and Their Use in Models for Conditioning," in *Proceedings of the Royal Society of London* B (1967).168, 361.

[22]R. A. Rescorla and A. R Wagner, "A Theory of Pavlovian Conditioning: Variations in the Effectiveness of Reinforcement and Nonreinforcement," vol. 2 of *Classical Conditioning,* ed. A. H. Black and W. F. Prokasy (New York: Appleton-Century-Crofts, 1972).

[23]Wilfrid K. Taylor, "Cortico-Thalamic Organization and Memory," in *Proceedings of the Royal Society of London* B (1964):159, 466.

[24]Karl Steinbuch, "Die Lernmatrix," *Kybernetik* 1 (1) (1961):36.

[25]James A. Anderson, "A Memory Storage Model Utilizing Spatial Correlation Functions," *Kybernetik* 5 (1968):113.

[26]David J. Willshaw, O. Peter Buneman, and H. Christopher Longuet-Higgins, "Non-holographic Associative Memory," *Nature* 222 (1969):960.

[27]David Marr, "A Theory of Cerebellar Cortex," *Journal of Physiology of London* 202 (1969):437; Marr, "Simple Memory: A Theory for Archicortex," *Philosophical Transactions of the Royal Society of London* B 262 (841) (1971):23.

[28]Teuvo Kohonen, *Associative Memory: A System-Theoretical Approach* (Berlin: Springer-Verlag, 1977).

[29]J. C. Eccles, M. Ito, and J. Szentágothai, *The Cerebellum as a Neuronal Machine* (New York: Springer-Verlag, 1967); R. Llinás, ed., *Neurobiology of Cerebellar Evolution and Development* (Chicago: American Medical Association, 1969).

[30] Marr, "A Theory of Cerebellar Cortex."

118   Jack D. Cowan and David H. Sharp

[31]S. Blomfield and David Marr, "How the Cerebellum May Be Used," *Nature* 227 (1970):1224.

[32]James S. Albus, "A Theory of Cerebellar Function," *Mathematical Bioscience* 10 (1971):25.

[33]M. Ito, *The Cerebellum and Neural Control* (New York: Raven, 1984); P. L. Strick, *Science* 229 (1985):547.

[34]Marr, "Simple Memory: A Theory for Archicortex."

[35]J. O'Keefe and L. Nadel, *The Hippocampus as a Cognitive Map* (Oxford: Clarendon Press, 1978).

[36]David Marr, "A Theory for Cerebral Neocortex," *Proceedings of the Royal Society of London* B (176) (1970):161.

[37]T. V. P. Bliss and T. Lomo, "Long-Lasting Potentiation of Synaptic Transmission in the Dentate Area of the Unaesthetized Rabbit Following Stimulation of the Perforant Path," *Journal of Physiology of London* 232 (1973):357.

[38]David J. Willshaw and Christoph von der Malsburg, "How Patterned Neural Connections Can Be Set Up by Self-Organization," in *Proceedings of the Royal Society of London* B (194) (1976):431; D. J. Willshaw and Ch. von dan Malsburg, "A Marker Induction Mechanism for the Establishment of Ordered Neural Mappings: Its Application to the Retinotectal Problem," *Philosophical Transactions of the Royal Society of London* B (287) (1979):203; S. E. Fraser and R. K. Hunt, "Retinotectal Specificity: Models and Experiments in Search of a Mapping Function," *Annual Review of Neuroscience* 3 (1980):319; V. A. Whitelaw and Jack D. Cowan, "Specificity and Plasticity of Retinotectal Connections: A Computational Model," *Journal of Neuroscience* 1 (12) (1981):1369.

[39]E. M. Harth et al., "Brain Functions and Neural Dynamics," *Journal of Theoretical Biology* 26 (1970):93; H. R. Wilson and Jack D. Cowan, "Excitatory and Inhibitory Interactions in Localized Populations of Model Neurons," *Biophysics Journal* 12 (1972):1; H. R. Wilson and Jack D. Cowan, "A Mathematical Theory of the Functional Dynamics of Cortical and Thalamic Nervous Tissue," *Kybernetik* 13 (1973):55; S. Grossberg, "Contour Enhancement, Short-term Memory, and Constancies in Reverberating Neural Networks," *Studies in Applied Mathematics* 52 (3) (1973):213; G. B. Ermentrout and Jack D. Cowan, "Temporal Oscillations in Neural Networks," *Journal of Mathematical Biology* 7 (1979):265; "A Mathematical Theory of Visual Hallucination Patterns," *Biological Cybernetics* 34 (1979):137.

[40]Santiago Ramon y Cajal, *Histology du Système Nerveux* (reprinted, Madrid: Consejo Superior de Investigaciones Cientificas, 1972).

[41]John J. Hopfield, "Neural Networks and Physical Systems with Emergent Collective Computational Abilities," *Proceedings of the National Academy of Sciences* 79 (1982):2554; Hopfield, "Neurons with Graded Response Have Collective Computational Properties Like Those of Two-State Neurons," *PNAS* 81 (1984):3088.

[42]David Sherrington and Scott Kirkpatrick, "Spin Glasses," *Physics Review Letters* 35 (1975):1972; S. F. Edwards and P. W. Anderson, "Theory of Spin-Glasses: I," *Journal of Physics F: Metal Physics* 5 (5) (1975):965; Edwards and Anderson, "Theory of Spin-Glasses: II," *Journal of Physics F: Metal Physics* 6 (10) (1976):1927.

[43]Brian G. Cragg and H. Nevill V. Temperley, "The Organisation of Neurones: A Cooperative Analogy," *EEG Clinical Neurophysiology* 6 (85) (1954):37.

[44]Brian G. Cragg and H. Nevill V. Temperley, "Memory: The Analogy with Ferromagnetic Hysteresis," *Brain* 78 (2) (1955):304.

[45]William A. Little, "The Existence of Persistent States in the Brain," *Mathematical Bioscience* 19 (1974):101.

[46]Sherrington and Kirkpatrick, "Spin Glasses."

[47]W. Ross Ashby, "The Stability of a Randomly Assembled Nerve-Network," *EEG Clinical Neurophysiology* 2 (1950):471.

[48]S-I. Amari, "Characteristics of Random Nets of Analog Neuron-like Elements," *Institute of Electronic and Electrical Engineers Transactions on Systems, Man, and Cybernetics*, SMC–2 (5) (1972):643; R. L. Beurle, "Properties of a Mass of Cells Capable of Regenerating Pulses," *Philosophical Transactions of the Royal Society of London* B (240) (669)(1956):55; Jack D. Cowan, "The Problem of Organismic Reliability," *Progressive Brain Research* 17 (1965):9; B. G. Cragg and H. N. V. Temperley, "The Organisation of Neurones"; S. Grossberg, "Contour Enhancement, Short-term Memory, and Constancies in Reverberating Neural Networks," *Studies in Applied Mathematics* 52 (3) (1973):213; W. A. Little and G. L. Shaw, "A Statistical Theory of Short and Long-Term Memory," *Behavioral Biology* 14 (1975):115; H. R. Wilson and Jack D. Cowan, "Excitatory and Inhibitory Interactions in Localized Populations of Model Neurons," *Biophysics Journal* 12 (1972):1; H. R. Wilson and Jack D. Cowan, "A Mathematical Theory of the Functional Dynamics of Cortical and Thalamic Nervous Tissue," *Kybernetik* 13 (1973):55.

[49]E. L. Lawler et al., eds., *The Traveling Salesman Problem* (New York: John Wiley, 1985).

[50]S. Kirkpatrick, C. D. Gelatt, Jr., and M. P. Vecchi, "Optimization by Simulated Annealing," *Science* 229 (4598) (1983):671.

[51]John J. Hopfield and David W. Tank, " 'Neural' Computation and Constraint Satisfaction Problems and the Traveling Salesman," *Biological Cybernetics* 55 (1985):141.

[52]S. Lin and B. W. Kernighan, "An Algorithm for the TSP Problem," *Operations Research* 21 (1973):498.

[53]Richard Durbin and David J. Willshaw, "An Analogue Approach to the Travelling Salesman Problem Using an Elastic Net Method," *Nature* 326 (1987):689.

[54]Nicholas Metropolis et al., "Equations of State Calculations by Fast Computing Machines," *Journal of Chemical Physics* 21 (1953):1087.

[55]Geoffrey E. Hinton and Terrence J. Sejnowski, "Optimal Perceptual Inference," in *Proceedings of the Institute of Electronic and Electrical Engineers Computer Society on the Conference on Computer Vision and Pattern Recognition* (Washington, D.C.: IEEE, 1983); D. H. Ackley, G. E. Hinton and T. J. Sejnowski, "A Learning Algorithm for Boltzmann Machines," *Cognitive Science* 9 (1985):147.

[56]Dana H. Ballard, Geoffrey E. Hinton and Terrence J. Sejnowski, "Parallel Visual Computation," *Nature* 306 (5938) (1983):21.

[57]F. A. Hayek, *The Sensory Order* (Chicago: University of Chicago Press, 1952).

[58]Geoffrey E. Hinton, *Distributed Representations*, Technical Report CMU–CS–84–157 (Pittsburgh: Carnegie-Mellon University, Computer Science, 1984).

[59]David E. Rumelhart, Geoffrey E. Hinton, and Robert J. Williams, "Learning Internal Representations by Error Propagation," *Parallel Distributed Processing: Explorations in the Microstructure of Cognition*, vol. 1, *Foundations*, ed. David E. Rumelhart and James L. McClelland (Cambridge: MIT Press, 1986); Y. Le Cun, "A Learning Scheme for Asymmetric Threshold Networks," in *Proceedings*

Cognitiva 85 (1985):599; D. B. Parker, "A Comparison of Algorithms for Neuron-Like Cells," in *Proceedings of the AIP Conference* 151, *Neural Networks for Computing*, ed., J. S. Denker, AIP.

[60] L. Uhr, ed., *Pattern Recognition* (New York: John Wiley, 1966).

[61] D. H. Ballard, "Cortical Connections and Parallel Processing," *Behavioral and Brain Sciences* 9 (1) (1986):67.

[62] Terrence J. Sejnowski and Charles R. Rosenberg, *NETtalk: A Parallel Network that Learns to Read Aloud*, Technical Report JHU/EECS–86/01 (Baltimore, Md.: Johns Hopkins University, Electrical Engineering and Computer Science, 1986).

[63] Rosenblatt, "The Perceptron."

[64] David E. Rumelhart, Geoffrey E. Hinton, and Robert J. Williams, "Learning Representations by Back-Propagating Errors," *Nature* (323) (1986):533.

[65] Richard Andersen and David Zipser, "A Neural Net Model of Posterior Parietal Cortex," in *Neurobiology of Neocortex* (Berlin: Dahlem Conferenz, 1987), 50; J. Altman, "A Quiet Revolution in Thinking," *Nature* 328 (1987):572.

[66] W. S. Stornetta and B. A. Huberman, "An Improved Three-Layer Back-Propagation Algorithm," a preprint from Xerox Corporation, Palo Alto, 1987.

[67] Dana H. Ballard, "Modular Learning in Neural Networks," a preprint from the University of Rochester Department of Computer Science.

[68] G. North (1987), "A Celebration of Connectionism," *Nature* 328 (1987):107.

[69] Eric Mjolsness and David H. Sharp, "A Preliminary Analysis of Recursively Generated Networks," in *Proceedings of the AIP Conference on Neural Networks for Computing*, ed. J. S. Denker (1986): 151; E. Mjolsness, David H. Sharp, and B. K. Alpert, "Recursively Generated Networks," YALEU/DCS/RR–549, a preprint from Yale University, 1987.

[70] J. H. Holland, *Adaptation in Natural and Artificial Systems* (Ann Arbor: University of Michigan Press, 1975).

[71] R. P. Lippmann, "An Introduction to Computing with Neural Nets," *IEEE ASSP Magazine* 4 (2) (1987):4.

[72] Alan Lapedes and Robert Farber, "A Self-Optimizing, Nonsymmetrical Neural Net for Content Addressable Memory and Pattern Recognition," *Physica D* 22 (1986):247.

[73] Alan Lapedes and Robert Farber, "Nonlinear Signal Processing Using Neural Networks: Prediction and System Modeling," LA–UR–87–2662, a preprint from Los Alamos National Laboratory.

[74] Norbert Wiener, *Cybernetics, or Control and Communication in the Animal and the Machine* (New York: John Wiley, 1948).

[75] Dennis Gabor, "Communication Theory and Cybernetics," in *IRE Transactions* CT–1 (4) (1954):19.

[76] David L. Waltz, "The Prospects for Building Truly Intelligent Machines," *Dædalus* (Winter 1988):191–212.

[77] John von Neumann, "The General and Logical Theory of Automata," in *Cerebral Mechanisms in Behavior, the Hixon Symposium*, ed. L. A. Jeffress (New York: John Wiley, 1951).

[78] Waltz, "The Prospects for Building Truly Intelligent Machines."

[79] P. Kanerva, *Self-Propagating Search: A Unified Theory of Memory* (Cambridge: MIT Press, in press).

[80] J. S. Denker, ed., *Proceedings of the AIP Conference on Neural Networks for Computing* (1986): 151.

[81]Kenneth J. W. Craik, *The Nature of Explanation* (Cambridge: Cambridge University Press, 1943).

[82]Christoph von der Malsburg, "Nervous Structures with Dynamical Links," *Berichte Bunsenges Physikalische Chemie* 89 (1975):703.

[83]Francis Crick, "Function of the Thalamic Reticular Complex: The Searchlight Hypothesis," *PNAS* 81 (1984):4586.

[84]Eric Mjolsness, "Control of Attention in Neural Networks," YALEU/DCS/RR–545, a preprint from Yale University.

[85]Warren S. McCulloch, "A Historical Introduction to the Postulational Foundations of Experimental Epistemology," in F. S. C. Northrop and H. H. Livingston, eds., *Cross-Cultural Understanding: Epistemology in Anthropology* (New York: Harper and Row, 1964).

Jacob T. Schwartz

The New Connectionism: Developing Relationships Between Neuroscience and Artificial Intelligence

P ART OF THE CONFIDENCE with which artificial intelligence researchers view the prospects of their field stems from the materialist assumptions they make. One is that "mind" is simply a name for the information-processing activity of the brain. Another is that the brain is a physical entity that acts according to the laws of biochemistry and is not influenced by any irreducible "soul" or other unitary, purely mental entity that is incapable of analysis as a causal sequence of elementary biochemical events. This broadly accepted view, together with the rapidly mounting mass of information concerning nervous system physiology, microanatomy, and signaling behavior and with the current technology-based push to construct analogous computing systems involving thousands of elements acting in parallel, has encouraged a shift in emphasis among AI researchers that has come to be identified as "the new connectionism." The emphases that characterize this school of thought are as follows:

1. The brain operates not as a serial computer of conventional type but in enormously parallel fashion. The parallel functioning of hundreds of thousands or millions of neurons in the brain's subtle information-extraction processes attains speed. Coherent percepts

Jacob T. Schwartz is a professor at the Courant Institute of Mathematical Sciences at New York University.

are formed in times that exceed the elementary reaction times of single neurons by little more than a factor of ten. Especially for basic perceptual processes like sight, this observation rules out iterative forms of information processing that would have to scan incoming data serially or pass it through many intermediate processing stages. Since extensive serial symbolic search operations of this type do not seem to characterize the functioning of the senses, the assumption (typical for much of the AI-inspired cognitive science speculation of the 1960–80 period) that serial search underlies various higher cognitive functions becomes suspect.

2. Within the brain, knowledge is stored not in any form resembling a conventional computer program but structurally, as distributed patterns of excitatory and inhibitory synaptic strengths whose relative sizes determine the flow of neural responses that constitutes perception and thought.

AI researchers developing these views have been drawn to involvement in neuroscience by the hope of being able to contribute theoretical insights that could give meaning to the rapidly growing, but still bewildering, mass of empirical data being gathered by experimental neuroscientists (many of whom regard theoretical speculation with more than a little disdain). These AI researchers hope to combine clues drawn from experiment with the computer scientists' practiced ability to analyze complex external functions into patterns of elementary actions. By assuming some general form for the computational activities characteristic of these actions, they hope to guess something illuminating about the way in which the perceptual and cognitive workings of the brain arise. That is to say, computer scientists hope to relate to experimental neuroscience much as theoretical physicists relate to experimental physics—by contributing unifying theoretical insights and theoretically based conjectures that can guide experimentation along fruitful paths.

The awesome complexity of the brain poses major obstacles to easy realization of this aim. The magnitude of the problems that need to be unraveled is indicated by a few intimidating estimates and a brief review of some basic facts of neuroscience. The human brain consists of approximately 100 billion neurons, possibly even ten times as many. Neurons usually communicate by transmitting discrete electrical spikes (action potentials) to a population of follower neurons. As far as is known, the precise amplitude and shape of such a spike, and the precise time of its arrival within an interval of two milliseconds or so, are physical details that the nervous system is not able to exploit. Hence, one can model each spike as a single information-carrying "bit" in a neuron's output stream and say that a neuron outputs information at a rate of approximately 100 bits per second. This way of thinking leads to an estimate of 10 trillion bits per second, give or take a factor of 100, for the internal "bandwidth" of the brain.

The computational activity of each neuron involves a great variety of mechanisms, still most imperfectly understood. Nevertheless, a considerable mass of experimental evidence supports the following general picture. A neuron transmits information to its follower neurons at interneuron junctions called synapses. A single neuron can have as many as 10 thousand synaptic inputs, though in some cases many fewer inputs, and in other cases as many as 100 thousand inputs, converge on single neurons. The total number of synapses in the brain can be estimated as 1,000 trillion, though this estimate, like all those offered in the next few paragraphs, is uncertain by a factor of roughly 100. Input signals transmitted to a neuron (generally chemically) across a synapse trigger a wide variety of reactions. One is modulation of the ionic conductivity of the affected neuron's membrane, which either raises the voltage of a portion of its interior (excites the neuron) or lowers this voltage (inhibits the neuron). After attenuation in space and time in a manner determined by the chemistry and geometry of the affected neuron and its synapses, the neuron then combines the voltage changes generated by such synaptic effects. If the resulting combined (summed, for example) voltage exceeds a reaction threshold, the neuron generates an output spike or other electrical signal. This is then transmitted to all its output synapses. Though many other mechanisms play a role, this kind of effect seems basic to many of the fastest computations performed by the brain.

Other forms of synaptic input are known to have slower but longer-lasting biochemical effects than these ionic effects, which probably support the bulk of the brain's information-transmuting activity. Stimulation of certain synapses can, for example, trigger enzymatic activities within a neuron that modify its biosynthetic activities—for instance, by increasing or decreasing its susceptibility to excitatory or inhibitory stimuli that are acting ionically. Depending on the chemical effects involved, such synaptic modification of fast ionic responses may last for as little as fifty milliseconds or for as long as several seconds, minutes, or days; it may even become permanent. Other synaptically triggered enzymatic reactions can initiate sequenced biochemical changes. For example, a neuron's electrical response may be enhanced for several tens of milliseconds but then inhibited for a longer period, leading to complex patterns of alternation between excitation and inhibition. The variety of single-neuron behaviors that the wide spectrum of enzymatic actions can engender has been explored in simple animals such as *Aplysia,* some of whose neurons are known to have highly individualized patterns of continuing, periodic, or burst activity.

Though it is not easy to summarize the wide range of synaptic response patterns with a few numbers representing the information-processing power and storage capacity of a single neuron, the following estimates do not seem unfair. One byte (eight bits, about one printed character) may well suffice for representing the long-term strength of each synapse. Four additional bytes can then be taken to give a sufficiently complete representation of the short-term biochemical state of both sides of a synapse and of the state of the corresponding synaptic gap, as determined by its stimulation history up to a given moment. Such exceedingly rough quantitative guesses lead us to estimate that the long-term memory available to the brain is about 10,000 trillion bytes and that the amount of shorter-term data needed to characterize the state of each of its synapses is roughly the same. The logical activity of each neuron can then be regarded as a process that combines approximately 10 thousand input bytes with roughly 40 thousand synapse status bytes at a rate of 100 times each second. The amount of analog arithmetic required for this estimate is (again very roughly) 10 million elementary operations per neuron per second, suggesting that the computing rate needed to emulate the entire brain on a neuron-by-neuron basis may be as high as 1,000,000 trillion arithmetic operations per second. (Of course, computation rates many orders of magnitude lower might suffice to represent the logical content of the brain's activity if it could be discovered what this is.)

It is interesting to compare these exceedingly coarse estimates with corresponding figures for the largest supercomputer systems likely to be developed over the next decade. These will probably not attain speeds in excess of 1 trillion arithmetic operations per second, which is about one one-millionth of the computation rate that we have estimated for the brain. Today's large magnetic storage disks hold around 1 billion bytes of digital information each, which is roughly one ten-millionth of the storage capacity that we have ascribed to the brain. Even if we assume continuing rapid advances in storage technology and systems equipped with hundreds of storage disks, supercomputers seem unlikely to achieve more than 1 percent of the brain's storage capacity over the next decade. Clearly, the neuroscientist confronts a system whose workings are difficult to approach physically and whose operations are of awesome complexity.

CLUES TO BRAIN FUNCTION

One of the most salient clues from which the "connectionist" theorists hope to work is the observation that mental (especially sensory) processes seem to be of very restricted "depth," in the sense that not many successive elementary neural reactions are required to form the higher-level reactions that the brain generates. There is simply not time for very many successive reactions to be involved.

This is only a weak clue, however. Since neurons are vastly more complex than the elementary switches used to construct computers, a single stage of neural processing may compare to ten or more stages of electronic processing by elementary switchlike elements. Hence, outputs that the brain can generate in one-tenth of a second may compare in complexity with outputs requiring a hundred or more stages of processing by electronic switches. Moreover, so little is understood concerning the logical significance of the interconnections in the nervous system (even in cases where we know a great deal about the microanatomical structures involved) that it is hard to rule out any one of hundreds of conjectures about the way in which electronic devices should be connected so as to imitate the workings of the brain. A computer scientist, given a vast, almost totally unknown computer like the brain, with trillions of active elements connected in unfathomed ways, and asked to guess its mode of functioning with no other clue than the statement that it generates its outputs using highly parallel computations involving only a few hundred serially successive stages of processing, could feel only the most minimal confidence in whatever guess he or she ventured. The problem is not that we cannot imagine how known properties of neurons could serve to support intelligent function; it is that too many lines of speculation lie open for definitive choice between them to be feasible without additional evidence. The theorist's task is therefore to cultivate a sensitivity to the clues that are available in the enormous and growing, but confusing, mass of data that laboratory neuroscience already furnishes. In the paragraphs that follow I review a few of the most helpful clues.

Direct recording of the activity of single neurons has been possible for several decades, and by correlating controlled sensory inputs with single-neuron recordings one can get a crude picture of the workings of the brain's sensory systems, at least for the initial stages of neural processing. These stages seem to prepare incoming data for the first (still entirely mysterious) acts of recognition. Studies of this type suggest that certain general structures are common to several sensory modalities. In many cases, neurons that handle information generated by primary sensory systems having a natural one- or two-dimensional layout seem to be arranged in successive two-dimensional sheets (either within the cerebral cortex or in various smaller brain structures underneath the cortical lobes). The arrangement of cells in these sheets often seems to reflect the natural geometry, or at any rate some informationally significant dimension, of the sensory data itself. For example, the cells that accomplish the very first stages of image processing in the visual cortex are arranged *retinotopically,* which is to say in relatively precise one-to-one continuous correspondence with the retina of the eye (or, equivalently, with the geometry of images falling onto the retina). Cells devoted to the analysis of tactile sensations detected in the skin are arranged in much coarser, *somatotopic* correspondence with regions of the skin, while cells in the first stages of the auditory system are arranged *tonotopically*—that is, according to the auditory frequencies to which they react. Cells reacting to subtler properties of incoming stimuli are also arranged in regular geometries. For example, the angle of maximum response for orientation-sensitive cells of the visual cortex rotates systematically as one moves through small regions of the cortex; cells with corresponding retinal fields in the right and left eye reside in thin vertical strips of cortical tissue (ocular dominance columns) adjacent to, but sharply distinguished from, each other. Presumably these cell arrangements facilitate the interchange of information needed to detect significant features in incoming sensory streams, by highlighting sharp intensity and/or color changes, edge orientations, or sharp corners, for example. The picture suggested by the available evidence is one of the successive transformation of imagelike (because one- or two-dimensional) data structures to produce secondary imagelike structures in which stimulus features that are potentially useful for the formation of higher-level responses have been made explicit—a form of processing that is unsurprising in computer science terms. Even in the sensory realm, we do not know more than a few of the specific transformations that incoming data flows undergo, but we do know enough to think of this data and its processing in geometrically extended, imagelike terms. Beyond these early, relatively well-understood processing stages, one enters terra incognita, in which it has thus far proved impossible to correlate observed neural activity with any specific property of external stimuli.

Additional insight, consistent with the evidence just reviewed, comes from neuroembryology—from consideration of the pattern in which the cells of the brain knit themselves together. Neurons, like the cells constituting all other tissues, are initially motile—that is, capable of migrating from their original positions, usually via a form of slow "walking" that is guided by the selective adhesiveness of a migrating cell to the tissues over which it pulls itself. This biochemically regulated cell motility plays a fundamental role in shaping the tissues and organs of the body during embryonic development: the sheets of cells that come to constitute these tissues are in many cases erected by the collective migration of their constituent cells, somewhat in the manner that a large circus tent can be erected by the collective motion of many people walking along under it and pulling on its expanding edges.

In neurons, however, similar patterns of motility act in a significantly different way. After the earliest phases of embryonic development, instead of the cell body itself migrating, a neuron throws out projections (its axons and dendrites to be), the ends of which carry small motile units known as growth cones. Each of these cones has twenty or so "feet" (pseudopodia) about one one-thousandth of a millimeter in diameter and thirty times as long, which allow the cone to move over the surface of any tissue with which it comes in contact. The pseudopodia extend themselves in an apparently random manner from the growth cone in which they originate till they make contact with some nearby tissue surface. They then adhere to it with a force that is determined by the sugar- or starchlike side chains attached to modified protein molecules (glycoproteins), which are present in the cell membranes of the two contacting cells. Once contact is made, the pseudopodia contract, pulling the growth cone and the growing axon that develops behind this cone, apparently in the direction of the greatest adhesivity, just as a fly is forced to walk in the direction of maximal stickiness along flypaper on which it is trapped. Though other direction-determining forces are undoubtedly involved, these adhesive effects, much elucidated through the brilliant work of Gerald Edelman and his collaborators at Rockefeller University, now appear basic not only to definition of interconnection patterns in the nervous system but also to embryological development in general.

Neurons' growth cones continue their walk, each apparently until it contacts any destination cell that is marked with some chemical substance to which the pseudopodia are sensitive, at which point some unknown enzymatic reaction destroys the capacity of the pseudopodia to continue moving. The growth cone then metamorphoses into a synapselike structure that subsequently develops into a mature synapse.

This picture of the nervous system's development does not suggest that the pattern of connections formed in complex mammalian brains can be entirely specific in the sense of creating perfectly determinate connections between specifically identified neurons, as if the neurons were transistors on an artificially engineered silicon chip, and the connections between them were formed by laying down metal in very precise fashion. Rather, this picture suggests a system, perhaps containing hundreds, thousands, even tens of thousands of neuron subspecies, possibly distinguishable biochemically and perhaps differing significantly in their detailed reaction to external stimuli but probably interconnected with relatively coarse specificity. The rules of growth that apply may, for example, only specify that a neuron of a particular type originating at a certain point in a particular brain layer will connect via an axon and a synapse to any neuron of some second type that is close to some other position in another brain region. Known growth mechanisms are sufficient to yield structures having this degree of specificity, but that they can produce the vastly more specific structures that characterize computer circuitry and that often enter into the neural system models of speculative thinkers coming from computer backgrounds seems doubtful.

It is worth noting, in this connection, that we presently lack not only detailed knowledge of the interconnection pattern of the brain but also comprehensive understanding of the more fundamental and rudimentary question of how many biochemically distinct species of neurons inhabit the brain. Partly for this reason, theorists who propose abstract brain models often begin by assuming that all neurons are functionally identical and accordingly model neurons as simple threshold elements that emit signals whenever the sum of their incoming excitatory stimuli, minus the sum of their incoming inhibitory stimuli, exceeds some fixed or adjustable threshold value. It is as if an investigator faced with the problem of analyzing an immense computing system of wholly unknown internal architecture began by assuming that all its integrated circuit chips were identical simply because at first glance they looked roughly the same and because any hypothesis closer to the truth was too dispiriting. Cursory microscopic examination of the brain's population of neurons, however, shows them to differ from one another as much as garden shrubs differ from giant redwoods. Moreover, even cells of apparently identical external morphology may differ biochemically in ways that cause their reactions to similar patterns of incoming stimuli to be widely different. Over the next decade or two, systematic use of the increasingly powerful battery of monoclonal antibodies available as ultrasensitive biochemical reagents will probably dispel much of our present ignorance about the varieties of neurons.

Nevertheless, while ignorance persists, the utility of even standard neuroanatomical information is compromised, since what is wanted is knowledge of the manner in which informationally significant (and, presumably, biochemically distinguishable) cell *populations* interconnect. In contrast, the information available concerns only the manner in which brain *regions* interconnect.

The massive cell death that occurs immediately after birth confirms the impression that the brain is designed to function correctly even if the neurons constituting it link up in a manner that is only approximately correct. It is well known that in newborn mammals some 15 percent of the neurons present in the neonate die out in early infancy. Evidence suggests that many of those neurons represent either overgrowth or neurons that for some reason have formed improper connections and are therefore failing to receive the electrical or chemical stimuli needed to keep them viable. Still further evidence suggesting that the interconnections in the brain are not entirely specific comes from experiments in which the synaptic connections made by a population of neurons are destroyed by cutting the axons connecting these synapses to their originating cell bodies. Such cutting usually causes the sprouting of nearby neurons and subsequently the formation of abnormal synaptic connections among neurons that would not ordinarily form connections in the affected brain region. This evidence suggests that a mechanism of competitive growth is involved in the development of interconnections among neurons and that neurons invade unoccupied synaptic space in much the same way that growing grasses tend to invade an initially empty field—not a situation that favors computerlike wiring precision.

These considerations suggest that the brain may be incapable of using the patterns of information processing that are most effective for artificial computers, even very large parallel computers. Artificial computing systems can often generate desired results most effectively (sometimes with remarkable efficiency) by using carefully designed and coordinated sequences of elementary processing steps. In such processing, the arrays of data being processed move through a sort of closely coordinated, massively parallel square dance, during which each data item interacts with all the items it encounters in such a way as to leave the desired output in place at the end of the procedure. Any failure in synchronization or in a local operation combining two operands when they meet generates a wave of error and leaves a meaningless result at the end. Such delicately balanced parallel processes only generate their intended results, or for that matter any useful result, if each motion of every one of the thousands of data items being processed takes place precisely at the moment specified for it and if every one of the millions of arithmetic or logical operations involved works perfectly. The evidence I have cited suggests that biological systems are not wired precisely enough to support this extremely delicate style of information processing. In particular, we have no evidence that the nervous system operates in other than perfect asynchrony, so that no form of information processing that requires close synchronization or that becomes substantially less expensive in its absence is an attractive candidate for use in neural systems.

Evolutionary considerations also suggest that the brain makes no use of delicately balanced processing patterns of the kind that are so common and effective in computer practice. Indeed, evolution proceeds by the accumulation of tiny random changes, each typically affecting but one detail of one of the thousands or tens of thousands of protein molecules whose interaction determines cell biology and function. For evolutionary pressures to carry change very far, each successive evolutionary step must provide change-carrying organisms with enough of an advantage to favor their survival, at least marginally. This observation seems to rule out major qualitative jumps from an established pattern of activity to some other radically different and delicately balanced programlike pattern, no part of which is useful until an entire structure is put in place. Clever information-processing algorithms require exactly such complex interlocking logical constructions—another reason their use in a biological setting is inappropriate.

Our still insufficiently developed knowledge of neuroanatomy and the biochemistry of neurons does not provide the information that would enable us to model the activity of the nervous system at all specifically. Partly for this reason, theorists have remained attracted to homogeneous neural models and to highly conjectural (even if appealing) theories that the brain or important parts of it progress— from an informationally blank initial condition to a state in which much usable information is encoded—via a process of learning that acts at the synaptic level. The commonest theory of this type is one that Hebb initially proposed in the 1940s. According to Hebb, synapses receiving excitatory stimuli during periods in which the neuron to which they attach is active grow more sensitive and hence act more strongly on subsequent occasions to stimulate the firing of the same neuron. The efficacy of synapses not involved in a pattern of synaptic stimuli that repeatedly cause a cell to fire may then diminish in relative, perhaps also in absolute, terms; eventually, such synapses become partly or wholly incapable of stimulating their cell.

Hebb's proposed mechanism allows initially undifferentiated cells to become selectively conditioned to a variety of patterns that can originate directly in sensory systems or indirectly in the earlier stages of neural processing. His hypothesis has appealed to theoretically minded neural modelers, since it does not conflict with any available evidence yet suggests a way in which learning can mold neural structures about which little needs to be assumed. Moreover, it is easy to imagine biochemical mechanisms, compatible with Hebb's hypothesis, that might allow very powerful information-processing capabilities, such as general forms of associative memory, to develop.

In spite of this appeal, only recently have we begun to have hard experimental evidence to support Hebb's conjecture, and this only for a very few regions of the brain, most notably the cerebellum. Recent research on this important brain structure shows that it functions, at least in small part, as a mechanism for storage of simple conditioned reflexes. This function has been demonstrated by showing that suitably patterned and intense simultaneous stimulation of appropriate neurons (specifically, the cerebellar "climbing" fibers and the parallel fibers originating in the granule cells of the cerebellum) causes long-lasting changes in the sensitivity of the large cerebellar Purkinje cells. These are the same cells as are presumably involved in the formation of simple Pavlovian conditioned reflexes. It is possible in this way to establish a conditioned reflex (for example, conditioning to a preceding auditory stimulus of the primitive eye-blink reflex triggered by a corneal air puff), even if one or both of the experimental factors (air puff or auditory stimulus) normally entering its formation is replaced by direct electrical stimulation of corresponding cerebellar input. The modifications that occur during the formation of such electrically induced artificial conditionings can be localized to a single class of synapse, namely the synapses between parallel fibers and the multiple Purkinje cell layers these fibers traverse. This experimental work brilliantly verifies the theoretical conjectures concerning the role of the cerebellum that David Marr and James Albus put forth years earlier. These conjectures were inspired by the striking abstract resemblance between cerebellar microanatomy and the physical layout of certain types of computer memory.

Beyond these profoundly intriguing, but still limited, insights, learning-based theories of the origin of neural function remain subject to the objection that we know hardly anything yet about the actual locus or mechanism of other memory storage within the brain and even less about the way memories are modified to accomplish abstract learning. Though it is widely believed that synapses represent the elementary loci of memory storage and that memory storage is somehow accomplished by modifying synaptic reactivity, we have not yet been able to develop much clear biochemical evidence to support this belief. Most of the evidence relating to mammalian brains is still very indistinct. For example, certain often-cited studies indicate simply that experimental rats raised in stimulating environments apparently develop larger numbers of synapses than rats imprisoned in stimulus-free environments. Moreover, the process of synaptic modification revealed in studies of simpler nervous systems (Eric Kandel's famous work on *Aplysia,* for example) is not specifically Hebbian. The governing synaptic changes seen in these investigations seem to occur in the transmitting (presynaptic) rather than in the receiving (postsynaptic) side of synapses and hence are not in agreement with the mechanism Hebb assumed. Thus, theorists who take some hypothesis about learning as their starting point are choosing to begin in a particularly dark area of neuroscience.

To function effectively, theorists with research backgrounds in computer science and artificial intelligence need to extract an appropriate notion of neurocompatibility from the diffuse mass of evidence coming from wet-lab neuroscience. This notion must both reflect any detailed knowledge of nervous system function that is likely to cast light on the information-processing activities of the nervous system and define constraints on the modes of neural processing that can best guide the theorist's attempts to guess what is going on. Thus far, the following clues seem most useful:

1. The nervous system must make use of highly parallel algorithms involving only very limited numbers of successive stages of transformation of incoming data streams.

2. The best-known stages of early sensory processing seem to involve successive transformations of imagelike data structures to highlight data features that are probably important to subsequent formation of higher-level responses. The layout of this data in the neural sheets that process it is often in correspondence with continuous, varying parameters inherent in the data being processed (retinal position or edge orientation in the case of the eye, for example, and pitch in the case of the auditory system).

3. Neurons differing in the information they extract from a common incoming data stream are observed in the sensory system. Their existence may point to the existence of morphologically similar,

but biochemically distinct, neuron subspecies within local areas of tissue, which might serve to carry separate dimensions of an incoming information flow. The number of these informationally significant subspecies is unknown and may possibly be large. The manner in which such subspecies make connection with each other and the geometry of the dendrite and axon arborizations they form may be significant for the data transformations that are then realized.

4. The crude picture of neurons as devices that sum incoming excitatory and inhibitory signals and that pass along as much of this sum as exceeds an inherent threshold may need to be sophisticated to allow for complex time lags and nonlinear effects, easily allowed by the very complex internal biocycle of all cells, neurons included.

5. The level of wiring accuracy in the nervous system seems to be low, and it seems to make no use of processing steps that involve tight synchronization of data motion or highly artificial interconnection patterns. Forms of processing that would arise naturally in neuron populations, possibly consisting of multiple subspecies that are interconnected in ways determined by simple growth rules, are most appealing as conjectures.

NEURAL NET MACHINES

Besides reflecting a desire to give theoretical assistance to experimental neuroscientists in their search for the way the living brain functions, the rapidly growing involvement of computer scientists with neuroscience has a second motive. This is to use knowledge of the brain to guide the design of new, very highly parallel computers— the so-called neural net machines. Though by no means likely to yield results quickly or easily, the contributions of computer science to neuroscience will come to attain full scientific legitimacy. Whether today's neuroscience will guide computer design in the near term seems far more doubtful. A substantial list of arguments supports this judgment:

1. Even in regard to the best-understood sensory systems, little is yet known about the detailed workings of the brain. Of brain function outside the sensory systems, we know essentially nothing.

Hence, any claim that a specific computer architecture imitates a neural system is pure conjecture.

2. The living nervous system and the patterned silicon networks constituting computers differ much as technologies. The nervous system is three-dimensional and unsynchronized; it must probably tolerate very high degrees of miswiring but can form tens or hundreds of thousands of connections to each of its active computational elements, the neurons. At least for the moment, electronic circuit patterns are largely restricted to the two-dimensional surfaces of silicon chips and also (except where special, very regular patterns are used) to a few tens of connections per active element and a few hundred per chip; these circuits can, however, be wired with nearly perfect precision so that they operate in close synchrony.

3. Computers can exploit any artificial pattern of hardware interconnection or software processing that the intellectual work of machine and algorithm designers brings to light. We have argued that only an unknown minuscule fraction of these processing patterns is available for the evolution-constrained activity of the living brain. It is revealing to note that all the current major projects to design and build large parallel machines make use of highly artificial structures for communication and processing. This remark applies equally well to the Thinking Machines Corporation's Connection Machine (hypercube and rectangular grid communication), to NASA's Massively Parallel Processor, to ICL's Digital Array Processor (rectangular grid), to Intel Corporation's Hypercube (hypercube communication), to IBM's RP3, and to New York University's Ultracomputer (omeganet communication). Moreover, computations on these machines regularly use highly artificial and efficient parallel algorithms, not procedures suggestive of the constraints likely to affect information processing in natural neural structures.

Thus, enthusiastic discussion envisaging vast potential for some obscurely characterized form of neural net machine (and especially proposals to build such devices) seems suspect. At any rate, no serious argument justifying such claims has as yet appeared. The difficulties encountered in past research certainly afford little encouragement.

However, one exception must be made to this reservation about the prospect for neural analogies in electronic device design, in favor of the striking work on integrated electronic sensors of Carver Mead at the California Institute of Technology. Mead's idea can be put as follows. Although as used in digital circuitry, a single transistor accomplishes only the most elementary operations of Boolean logic (so that, for example, several dozen transistors are required to implement operations as simple as the addition of two decimal digits), much more is possible if the same transistor is used in analog rather than digital fashion. The analog use of circuitry treats circuit voltages as representations of numerical values, accurate to one or more decimal digits; digital use gives thresholds to these voltages by classifying them as high or low. The digital approach has become overwhelmingly popular because it decisively improves the logical stability of electronic computations and somewhat simplifies circuit fabrication, but the loss of information and of potential processing speed is substantial. If used in analog fashion, a few transistors can do arithmetic operations as complex as multiplication or extraction of logarithms, at least approximately; done digitally, the same operations require hundreds of transistors.

Though this potential advantage of analog computation has been well understood for decades, analog systems have steadily lost ground to their digital competitors. In the first place, the precision of digital systems can readily be extended to any desired level simply by adding as many digits as one likes to the representation of a numerical quantity. Only standard components of fixed cost are required. In contrast, the precision of analog systems is inherently limited by the accuracy with which their component devices can be fabricated and isolated from outside physical disturbances such as temperature changes. A consequence is that the cost of analog devices escalates very rapidly with each additional digit of precision required and soon reaches a limit of absolute infeasibility.

A second advantage of digital systems is that they can retain information with perfect accuracy for indefinitely long periods by storing it in devices of essentially perfect stability—in the now commonplace computer "memories." Since analog information (voltage values, for example) inevitably degrades and drifts with time, nothing directly corresponding is available in the analog sphere. Purely analog computers cannot, therefore, store their programs in the same sense that digital systems can. Hence, the control information for analog systems that are at all complex, plus any extensive tables of constants or auxiliary functions that may be necessary, must be stored digitally and converted to analog form when needed for analog computation. Still worse, all intermediate data must be reconverted to digital form if it is to be stored for any length of time. The clumsiness and inherent limitations of this situation have restricted analog computation to a steadily narrowing sphere until, at present, large-scale computation of this sort is almost nonexistent.

Mead's insight is that there is an important area in which the disadvantages of analog computation are irrelevant, namely, in the processing of streams of sensory information like audio information or moving images. Here the precision of digital systems is of little advantage, since conversion from some raw analog sensory form is required in any case, implying that the incoming data fed to an analysis system, whether digital or analog, will necessarily be of limited precision. Moreover, many of the common procedures in the initial processing of this data, and especially those standing in any conjectural relationship to initial sensory processing in the nervous system, make little or no use of prestored information, so the absence of memory in analog systems is not an objection. Consequently, there is reason to hope that analog networks can process sensory data in a manner that will profit from their great simplicity and compactness in relation to comparably functional digital systems. Mead has constructed two interesting systems that do so: a sound-spectrum analyzer modeled after the cochlear membrane of the inner ear, and an optical motion detector whose structure is similar to the retinal neuroanatomy of the eye. His work may suggest many other applications that allow combination of the performance advantage of analog computation with the extremely sophisticated, ultra–high-density packaging that current very large-scale integration (VLSI) technology supports. It may inspire much imitation and open a new direction in electronic design.

Nevertheless, in my opinion, Mead's work is interesting as analog VLSI rather than silicon neuroscience; in particular, his sound-spectrum analyzer models the mechanical structure of the inner ear rather than the neural structures that receive its outputs.

PERSPECTIVE

Stunning new discoveries can be expected from experimental neuroscience during the coming decade. The astonishing successes of molecular biology constitute one major ground for this optimistic assessment. Once the presence of some biochemically important, even if initially quite unknown, protein is suspected in a tissue of interest, molecular techniques can be used to produce substantial quantities of antibody to this protein. Once available ("raised," in the jargon of the molecular biologist), such an antibody (which is simply a protein containing a portion complementary to some molecular detail of the protein) detects the presence of its target protein with exquisite sensitivity. Moreover, the antibody can readily be marked radioactively, magnetically, or optically and can be used to make the particular cells containing the target protein, or even particular microanatomical features of these cells, visible under the electron microscope. In addition, the walls of glass tubes can be coated with the antibody, and these columns can then be used to concentrate the protein by factors of a million or more. Such concentration opens a path to the chemical and structural analysis of the protein and from this to the identification of biochemical antagonists to its normal activity. Then, by dosing living brain tissue with these antagonists, one can paralyze the portion of normal function that is mediated by the protein and thereby pinpoint its specific physiological role and relevance for the information-processing activity of the brain.

As investigations of this sort are pursued more and more comprehensively for the entire battery of proteins significant as surface receptors in neurons, cell populations will become identifiable by the collections and concentrations of receptor molecules that their surfaces carry. Moreover, we will come to know the manner and speed with which neurons respond to the activation of particular surface receptors. These responses may be fast and electrically mediated or slow and activated through long chains of intermediate biochemical effects triggered by initial receptor molecules.

As noted earlier, biochemical identification of the subpopulations of neurons resident in the brain will give new focus to the work of neuroanatomists, increasing the relevance of their painstaking tracing of the brain's internal connections to our understanding of the brain's information processing. Embryological studies of the specialization and migration of biochemically identified cell populations within the developing brain will reveal the mechanisms that guide the formation of these connection patterns and improve our sense of what information-processing schemes the brain's substructures use and how complex they are. New chemically and optically mediated techniques are already beginning to improve our ability to observe the brain's electrical activity directly. Now, for instance, we can record the electrical activity of up to several hundred interconnected cells simultaneously. At some point we will also gain insight into the specific biochemical mechanism (or perhaps the many mechanisms) underlying memory, and that will enable us to formulate far more specific models of the memory processes, be these Hebb-like or not.

Though these massive experimental efforts will involve thousands of biochemists and neuroscientists for many years, we can expect investigations like these as well as ingenious, entirely new techniques eventually to uncover a very revealing mass of detail concerning brain function. As this information surfaces, the present aspiration of computer scientists to integrate their knowledge with that of neuroscientists will grow in relevance. Those in the computer science community who have paid their dues to experimental neuroscience by digesting and tracking its mounting mass of information may then be able to play an important part in extracting broad systematizing principles from an initial forest of experimental detail. These will surely be insights standing at the very pinnacle of science.

George N. Reeke, Jr., and Gerald M. Edelman

Real Brains and Artificial Intelligence

A RTIFICIAL INTELLIGENCE is a science that finds itself in somewhat the same epistemological position as Aristotelian dentistry. Aristotle stated that women have fewer teeth than men[1] and attributed this characteristic to women's supposed lesser need, men being stronger and more choleric,[2] but he never bothered to look in Mrs. Aristotle's mouth to verify his theory. Similarly, AI has developed as an almost entirely *synthetic* enterprise, quite isolated from the complementary, *analytic* study of the biology of natural intelligence represented by psychology and the neurosciences. To a biologist, the AI approach to the study of intelligence seems like a strange way of trying to understand the brain, which is, after all, at the basis of human intelligence. Nonetheless, biologists and computer scientists for the most part share the monistic view that mental events, including the manifestations of intelligence, necessarily reflect the activity of neurons in the brain.

It is important, then, to ask whether the goals of AI are really so different from those of neurobiology as to require entirely different methods of investigation and demonstration. For if they are not, there is much to be gained by joining experiment with theory and synthetic modeling to make a whole science of the brain.

We shall argue that the ultimate goals of AI and neuroscience are quite similar but that they have become obscured by erroneous

George N. Reeke, Jr., is associate professor of developmental and molecular biology at The Rockefeller University.

Gerald M. Edelman is Vincent Astor Professor at The Rockefeller University and director of The Neurosciences Institute.

epistemological assumptions drawn on the one hand from the arguments of Alan Turing and Alonzo Church about the universal problem-solving capabilities of computers (suggesting that the brain may be understood as a computer) and on the other hand from the reductionism of molecular biology (suggesting that the brain may be understood as a collection of units that exchange chemical signals). These confining assumptions, along with enormous practical and experimental difficulties, have kept the practitioners of both approaches very busy, while placing the goals always well out of their reach. In fact, consideration of the magnitude of the problem with due modesty suggests that perception alone is hard enough to understand, without attempting to jump directly from perception to learning, through learning to social transmission and language, and from there to all the richness of ethology. At present, it is still a large challenge to understand how an animal can even move, and it would be well for AI to look first to such fundamental issues.

As biologists (that is, as evolutionists) seeking to understand what we perceive as the nearly dogmatic neglect of our science—at least in recent years—by those attempting to create AI, we shall begin by asking just what it is that AI seeks to accomplish, and what are the basic assumptions about the nature of the solution that engender the standard paradigms of AI. We shall discuss some problems that have arisen in the application of these paradigms and some recent attempts to overcome them by what we call "looking sideways to biology," or "the physicist's approach to neural networks."

These new approaches, the misleading label "neural network computing" notwithstanding, draw their inspiration from statistical physics and engineering, not from biology. They are immensely appealing to the AI community for several reasons. They provide a practical recipe for parceling out AI computations among large numbers of simple processors, with a potentially enormous increase in computing speed. Parallelism has proven difficult to apply to AI, although it has already emerged in numerical computing as the only indefinitely extensible way to overcome the "von Neumann bottleneck" (the fundamental limits imposed on the speed of single processors by the laws of physics, for example, because signals cannot travel from one part of a computer to another faster than the speed of light). By virtue of their imitation of statistical systems, the new approaches also provide statistical approximations to optimization problems that have proven recalcitrant to all attempts at exact computation.

Nonetheless, these statistical approaches share with mainstream AI the implicit notion that objects and events, categories and logic are given and that the nature of the task for the brain is to process information about the world with algorithms to arrive at conclusions leading to behavior. This information-processing paradigm fundamentally fails to come to grips with certain basic problems concerning the nature of information and the ways that systems capable of analyzing information-bearing signals can come to exist. The assumption that categories and signals encoding information about them are the basic stuff around which computations are organized constitutionally biases AI to equate perceptual and intellectual performance with algorithms. This "category problem" leads directly to the inability of AI systems to cope with the complexity and unpredictability of the real world.

Our goal in this essay is to point out the fundamental nature of this problem. By characterizing observable forms of intelligence in the biological world (among others, human intelligence), we will introduce an approach based on the most basic of biological principles, namely, Darwin's theory of natural selection. We will present a theory that suggests how selection can provide the solution to the category problem and how it might occur in the nervous system.[3] We will describe several automata that carry out tasks involving perceptual categorization by selective mechanisms. Finally, we will discuss some ways that this purely biological principle might contribute to further progress in AI.

THE NATURE OF THE AI ENTERPRISE

Artificial intelligence is one of those terms with such an apparently self-evident meaning that it is rarely defined carefully. As a result, it has come to have an overly broad interpretation that adds confusion to the debate about its merits and prospects. Some have gone so far as to define AI as "whatever people in AI are working on." However, we will require a more meaningful, nonrecursive definition. To help us see the fundamental issues most clearly, we will exclude endeavors that have purely engineering goals, that is, projects aimed at devising effective computer solutions for problems that are already well understood in principle. (We include in this category essentially all work on so-called expert systems and logical programming.)

In his influential textbook *Artificial Intelligence,* Patrick Winston defines AI as "the study of ideas that enable computers to be intelligent." As for the goals of this study, he states (in this order) that "one central goal of Artificial Intelligence is to make computers more useful. Another central goal is to understand the principles that make intelligence possible."[4] Neurobiologists would find the mention of these two goals in the same discourse rather lacking in balance. They would acknowledge the great practical importance of the first but consider it to have very little fundamental interest. They would agree, on the other hand, that the second goal captures much of the essential nature of their own enterprise, although they would consider its formulation rather abstract. In contrast, neurobiologists would almost certainly refer to their own interest in discovering and validating such principles by observing existing intelligent systems. For the time being, such systems remain confined to the world of biological organisms.

Thus, as already suggested, the major goals of AI and neuroscience are indeed similar. AI, however, starts off with a more formal approach to these goals that directs it away from the study of "messy" biological systems. What are the subjects of inquiry that AI considers appropriate to a pursuit of its goals, and what are the research paradigms these subjects engender? In 1961 Marvin Minsky presented a list that most workers in AI would probably still accept today: to find effective procedures for search, pattern recognition, learning, planning, and induction.[5] Perhaps language understanding would now be added as a separate category; in agreement with Minsky, "search" would include a variety of optimization and reasoning problems as well as retrieval of coded information from memory, and "pattern recognition" clearly would have to encompass the decomposition of sensory data into component objects as well as the categorization of these objects and events after (or while) they were being recognized.

This choice of subject matter reflects the epistemological assumptions alluded to earlier. In the standard AI paradigm, as presented by Winston, the key to finding powerful procedures that can solve these problems is to discover appropriate representations of the relevant information. Once a representation is given that "make[s] the right things explicit and expose[s] natural constraints,"[6] it is a much simpler matter to devise purely computational procedures to manipulate the information, still in its encoded representation, so as to obtain the desired solutions. Winston is right. Once an appropriate representation is available, many problems do become amenable to automatic solution. In our view, however, the problem requiring intelligence is the original one of *finding* a representation. To place this problem in the domain of the system designer rather than in that of the designed system is to beg the question and reduce intelligence to symbol manipulation.

The line of reasoning that leads to this oversimplified and mechanical view of intelligence has distinguished origins. It can be traced back at least to Pascal and Leibniz, and it took on its present form in the earliest days of modern computers. The most important underpinning of the theory of digital computers, Turing's universality principle, was developed before any workable machines existed; perhaps this is why people were encouraged to think in very general, abstract terms about computers and their capabilities. The very real limitations of actual computers and computer programs only became clear later, after the initial excitement was over and the basic paradigm was well established. The limitations then came to be viewed as purely practical and eventually surmountable; after all, those who believed otherwise did not remain in the field to invest their creative energies in building what they saw as a house of cards. Thus, only now is it becoming more widely suspected, as it always was by some,[7] that AI may have fundamental difficulties as opposed to merely practical ones. This situation is quite unlike the case with such inventions as the steam engine, where practice preceded theory and guided it into the most fruitful channels.

The basic justification for AI, which we shall criticize in detail later, goes essentially like this:

1. Objects and events exist in the world. Information about them may be gathered by appropriate sensors. It is the goal of intelligent systems to process or transform this information so as to provide the basis for the "planning" and "induction" of which Minsky speaks.

2. Given a representation of information as strings of symbols, its manipulation can be carried out by purely formal rules that need

make no reference to the meanings of the symbols. These rules may be expressed as algorithms.

3. An algorithm may be executed by any universal Turing machine.[8] The very existence of these machines implies that the particular mechanism of operation of any one of them is unimportant. The important thing for understanding intelligence is the algorithms, not the hardware on which they are executed. In particular, what the brain does may be described by algorithms.

4. Church's thesis further suggests that if any consistent, terminating method exists to solve a given problem, then a method exists that can run on a Turing machine and give exactly the same results.[9] Therefore, at least for problems that can be solved consistently in a specified, finite amount of time, a Turing machine is as powerful as any other entity that can solve the problem, including the brain.

5. Since inconsistency makes science impossible and infinite time requires immortality, it only makes sense to discuss problems of the kind that can be solved by Turing machines.

6. Once the informational requirements for such a problem have been identified and an algorithm presented, the problem is in some sense understood. Other algorithms may be found that are more elegant or more efficient in some implementation, but all algorithms, including those used by the brain, are subject to the same informational requirements and may be understood in the same way.

7. Therefore, the brain is equivalent to a computer, or at least the computer is an adequate model for the interesting things the brain does.

The standard, entirely synthetic, paradigm for carrying out AI research immediately follows from this line of argument: Choose a significant problem that everyone would agree requires the exercise of intelligence for solution; identify the items of information needed to reach a solution to the problem; determine how this information might best be represented in a computer; find an algorithm that can manipulate the information to solve the problem; write a computer code implementing this algorithm; and test it with sample (usually also simple) instances of the problem.

This approach has led to a number of impressive demonstrations. For reasons that are no accident, the most successful of these have come in areas that most obviously meet the conditions for applying Church's thesis: logical problem solving and theorem proving (GPS, MACSYMA, and the Prolog language, for example), identification of objects in images (ACRONYM, CONSIGHT), playing chess and other games (CHESS, KAISSA, BELLE, PARADISE), understanding human language in limited domains (SHRDLU, BORIS), and expert systems, which combine rule-based inference and natural-language interface techniques with domain-specific data bases (MYCIN, DENDRAL, PROSPECTOR, XCON). However, all of these programs share a common quality that John McCarthy[10] and others have repeatedly pointed out: they are "brittle" in the sense that, if pressed around the edges, they tend to "crack." In other words, the programs lack commonsense knowledge and reasoning—they do not "know" their own limitations. They are insensitive to context and are likely to give quite incorrect responses to queries that are slightly outside the domains for which they were programmed. These responses are perfectly logical consequences of the rules built into each system, but to the observer equipped with normal human reasoning faculties, they can appear arbitrary and even mysterious.

A general solution to this problem of brittleness is not easy to find. While it may appear to be just another instance of the general difficulty of setting up and maintaining reliable large software systems, there seems to be a qualitative difference stemming from the open-endedness of natural language and the need for experience in the real world to acquire a competent repertoire of common sense. In the next section, we will look at some of the solutions to this problem attempted from within the standard AI paradigm. Then we will explain why we believe the problem lies with the paradigm itself and how the solution may be found by looking to real nervous systems and the ways they deal with complexity and novelty in the world.

LOOKING SIDEWAYS TO BIOLOGY

When one experiences difficulties in any large endeavor, the first impulse is to do more of the same or to do the same thing better. In the case of AI, this impulse has taken two directions—to improve the hardware and to improve the software. Each of these directions has given impetus to the development of new methods involving the representation of information by the states of simple processors and the connections between them (the so-called connectionist, or neural net, models).

First, improved hardware has made it possible to evaluate more conditionals (programmed logical tests) per second, to store larger data bases, and to examine images in more detail than before. This faster computation has certainly led to the improved performance of traditional AI systems. Chess automata, for example, can now "look deeper" (more moves ahead) into board positions.[11] Ultimately, however, hardware speeds can be improved only to a point. Eventually, parallel processing must be introduced to bring about further progress—but effective use of parallel processing requires new software techniques. Among the most intriguing of the new techniques being developed to replace traditional AI software are network models, which are ideally suited for implementation on multiprocessor systems whose physical arrangement matches or can be made to imitate the network structure of the models.

Second, new software techniques have been widely heralded as ways to approach the brittleness problem. Nonprocedural computer languages promise to relieve the programmer of the responsibility for specifying the sequence of steps needed to solve a particular problem (in reality, they substitute standard sequencing methods that are built into a compiler and that, on account of their generality, are rarely optimal for particular problems). These languages allow programmers to introduce large numbers of domain-specific rules into expert systems before the complexity becomes totally unmanageable. Some form of "nonmonotonic" reasoning[12] must then be introduced to mitigate the problems that arise when such rules are applied without precise consistency checks before the program is used. However, even these techniques require a vast software engineering effort for each problem that is attacked. The possibility of solving some of these problems with network-oriented methods that reduce the amount of explicit programming still further has provided the second major impetus for the development of simulated network methods within AI. Curiously, however, these developments have taken place in relative isolation from prior and contemporaneous work by biologists that was aimed at making models that incorporate some of the rich functional diversity of real nervous systems. (Some examples from our own work appear later in this article.)

We shall trace only the major currents in the development of these nonbiological networks; more details may be found in the works listed in the endnotes. While much of the activity has been recent, the notion that networks might be employed to carry out computations actually antedates the introduction of the programmable digital computer. The most influential of these early discussions was probably the 1943 paper of Warren McCulloch and Walter Pitts,[13] in which activity in neuronal* networks was identified with the operations of the propositional calculus. Actual simulations of recognition automata based on networks were carried out by Frank Rosenblatt before 1958,[14] but the theoretical limitations of his "perceptrons" were soon pointed out by Marvin Minsky and Seymour Papert,[15] and interest in network models waned until the recent introduction of more complicated nonlinear models that do not share these limitations. Other lines of development that have influenced many of the current models include networks that are specially crafted for specific purposes, such as the system of David Marr and Tomaso Poggio for computing stereo disparity,[16] and networks in which nodes are identified with cognitive "units" and interconnections with relationships between concepts, as in John R. Anderson's ACT model for retrieving information from memory.[17]

Thus the stage was set for the "physicist's approach to neural networks" as many scientists perceived a need to design networks for which convergence and learning properties could be predicted by mathematical theorems rather than by lengthy computer runs. Linear systems provided a relatively tractable starting point,[18] but nonlinearity is essential if categories are to be distinguished without overlap. A convenient physical analogy was the spin-glass, for which an extensive theory was already available. Never mind if the analogy had to be a highly strained one. The possibility of analysis was more important to these workers than whether what their systems did was related to the basic problem of intelligence. All one had to do was identify network nodes with spins and connections with spin interactions, and one could then speak of an "energy" that increased with the number of incompatibly connected spin pairs. From any starting state, the system would "relax" toward a state of minimum energy,

---

*We use the term *neuronal* when a close identification with the properties of actual neurons is implied. We use the term *neural* when only a general similarity to actual neurons is involved.

and these states could be identified with "memories" encoded in the connectivity coefficients of the network. Each memory would have a "zone of attraction" in the surrounding "state space." This description neatly tied in the neural networks with recent advances in the dynamics of nonlinear systems and the theory of chaos. The best-known models of this class are those of John Hopfield and his coworkers, who have been concerned primarily with the construction of ready-made networks for various tasks rather than with learning algorithms for such networks.[19] The latter element has been added in "Boltzmann machine" models, which take their name from their use of the concept of energy from statistical mechanics associated with the late nineteenth-century physicist Ludwig Boltzmann.[20] The representation of concepts from cognitive psychology in such networks has been zealously explored, and illustrative applications presented.[21]

Even with parallel computation and new learning algorithms, however, the possibility of training a network in a sufficient number of circumstances to confer *common sense* on it appears to recede forever into the distance as one contemplates the exceptions to the exceptions that are present in real-life situations. This unending compounding of exceptions comes close to revealing the true nature of the brittleness problem, which is that no amount of anticipation, planning, and programming can ever enumerate, a priori, all the variants of even a routine situation that may occur in daily life. It would seem, in what is perhaps an analogy to the classic "halting problem" in the analysis of algorithms (the problem of determining whether a given algorithm will run forever or eventually halt), that the only way to determine all the responses a system needs to have to deal with the vagaries of the real world is to expose it to the world and let it "run." Thus, each system will be different and fundamentally unprogrammable.

We say that connectionist models "look sideways to biology" because they take their inspiration and much of their terminology from the neural networks in living organisms, but they are not model neural networks (nor are they intended to be). Physicists, in their search for simplicity, are not prepared to deal with systems whose fundamental aspect lies in variability rather than regularity. In the attempt to find regularity in biological systems, many features have been introduced into their simulation in connectionist systems that are quite unbiological. These include the notion of memory as a replica or a transformation of "information" given in the world (human memories are highly context- and affect-sensitive and to some extent nonveridical); the conception of memory retrieval as the relaxation of a network to a stable state (a brain is continually exposed to changing input patterns and has no opportunity to freeze them while waiting for the approach to equilibrium); the idea of energy minimization through simulated annealing (a brain decides actions more quickly than known annealing procedures could attain in model networks operating at the speeds of real neurons); the notion of bidirectional and symmetric single connections (synaptic connections in the brain are monodirectional); and the idea that learning can proceed by clamping the output of the system to a desired value while synaptic weights are adjusted according to some rule (the motor output of a brain can in general not be imposed externally). Yet each of these elements is present in one or another of the connectionist models.

These unrealistic features should be a warning sign that something is seriously amiss in the basic assumptions behind the AI paradigm, even as modified by the introduction of parallel processing in neural-network–inspired systems. The *ad hoc* quality of these assumptions suggests that the true problem lies deeper than the details of the network simulations; it must have to do with the concept of information and the way it comes to be represented and transformed in the intelligent systems that have evolved in nature.

Standing at the start of the chain of deductions enumerated on pages 147–48, which for AI justify the notion of the brain as a computer, is the assumption that information exists in the world— that it is just there to be manipulated. There is also the idea that the organism is a *receiver* rather than a *creator* of criteria leading to information. Once the prior existence of such external information is conceded, it is entirely natural to proceed without further ado to the business of programming the rules to deal with it. At this point, the damage is already done. All efforts to program such rules run quickly into five vicious problems that have in common the transfer to the programmer of functions that belong properly to the putatively intelligent system:

1. *The coding problem.* The programmer must find a suitable representation of the information to put it in the proper form for

symbolic manipulation. It will usually not be clear in advance just what symbolic manipulations may be required and what the antecedent requirements on the representation may be.

2. *The category problem.* The programmer must specify a sufficient set of rules to define all the categories with which the program must deal. It is difficult to see in advance what these categories must be in a real world, much less how to define them.

3. *The procedure problem.* The programmer must specify in advance the actions to be taken by the system for all combinations of inputs that may occur. The number of such combinations is enormous and becomes even larger when the relevant aspects of context are taken into account. The behavior of biological organisms with real nervous systems becomes quite unpredictable in such circumstances.

4. *The homunculus problem.* Separate mechanisms are required to interpret the strings of symbols produced as output by any formal information-processing system. The strings can have no meaning within the formal system itself. But then, the necessary properties of intelligence are embodied in the observer, not the system. To avoid an infinite regress, the programmer is obliged to specify all the procedures the observer must follow.

5. *The developmental problem.* Can a programmed system come to exist without a programmer? Intelligent biological systems exist, yet they evolved and were not programmed, either as species or as individuals. Thus, the AI argument that brains carry out computations as computers do leads to a contradiction: brains must have programs, yet at the same time must not be programmed.

We hold that the solution to these conundrums may be found by examining existing natural intelligences and other biological systems in an attempt to understand how they come to exist and how they operate without prior programs. In the remainder of this essay, we shall argue that a form of selection, akin to Darwinian selection but operating among collections of neurons in the brain of a single organism during its lifetime, provides the only tenable basis for a theory of categorization and intelligence.[22] Evolution, by extending selection in this way to the individual brain, was able to remove the need for the programmer.

LOOKING DIRECTLY TO BIOLOGY

From the preceding analysis, it is clear that the notion of information preexisting in the world must be rejected. The essential requirement for learning, logic, and the other mental functions that are the usual subjects of AI research is the prior ability to categorize objects and events based on sensory signals reaching the brain. The variety of sensory experiences is both vast and unique for each individual. The categories themselves are not present in the environment but must be constructed by each individual according to what is adaptive for its species and its own particular circumstances. The a priori specification of rules for categorization, applicable to all individuals and all contexts, is precluded by the complexity, variability, and unpredictability of the macroscopic world. To make matters worse, the categories constructed by an organism cannot be fixed but must constantly change in response to new experiences and new realities in its part of the environment. The only way categories constructed in this individualistic manner can be validated is by constant coupling back to the world through behavior. However, once this adaptive categorization process has been established, the rest of the task—the construction of higher categories, memories, and associations—is enormously simplified.

Our first task, then, is to build a satisfactory theory that goes beyond the formal processing of information to a consideration of how that information comes to exist in an unlabeled world, what relationship exists between signals in the brain and the categories it has constructed, and how the interactions of those signals yield behavior without the benefit of prearranged codes to give them meaning or of prearranged algorithms to process them. The problems encompass memory as well as transient signals: How can memory function in the absence of a replicative store like that found in a computer, and how can memory be combined with current sensory signals to produce behaviors that enhance the survival of the organism? To make such a theory, we must consider the entire biological system, its evolutionary origins, and its development as an individual from embryo to functioning adult.

It would be well to begin by considering some basic facts of neurobiology. First, nervous systems are organized as networks with distinct areas having different patterns of connectivity, apparently specialized for different functions. Often these networks are connected to one another in a sequence of maps. We characterize this anatomy as a "heterarchy" (an arrangement in which the subnetworks are cross-connected in ways that do not follow a strict hierarchy). In such an arrangement, subnetworks with different functions interact to yield more complex functions that they do not possess alone. Successive regions appear to have been added gradually during the course of evolution, each contributing a new function but working in conjunction with older regions to confer a high degree of functional redundancy on the brain. There is no apparent analog to the functions of the clock and the instruction decoder in a computer. Instead, there is apparently a high degree of parallelism in the operations of the functional regions as well as in the responses of individual neurons. Extensive overlaps of dendritic and axonal arborizations suggest a functional degeneracy in which there are many alternative paths between any two points in the network, even within a single map. That no single neuron appears to be indispensable for any function suggests that only patterns of response over many neurons can have functional significance. Inasmuch as neurons have limited speed and dynamic range, they probably do not carry out computational algorithms in anything like the way a computer does.

The final, and most telling, observation is the enormous diversity of neuronal populations. This diversity is seen at all phylogenetic levels but, if anything, is greater in higher forms. Diversity extends to the number and arrangement of neurons in genetically identical animals and even to the detailed structure of individual neurons of known function in those animals in which such structures can be identified. It can easily be calculated that there is not enough information in the DNA to specify uniquely the locations of all these neurons and their connections. Thus, indeterminate, dynamic, epigenetic mechanisms (mechanisms reflecting the influence of the local environment on the unfolding genetic programs of individual cells) must operate during development to determine the fine structure of the nervous system. This is not what one would expect if nervous systems were optimized by design to carry out specific cognitive functions. Furthermore, the variability appears to be not just an unavoidable consequence of essential developmental processes but an evolutionarily selected trait. While such variation in wiring would lead to total failure in a computer, it seems to serve a functional role in the brain. The nature of this role will become clear when we consider how selective processes can act to give the kind of flexible, adaptive categorization that we have argued is necessary to enable an animal to deal with the world without benefit of a preordained program.

The biological facts we have pointed out, particularly the structural variation at all levels in the nervous system, together suggest that selection has a role not only in the development of nervous systems but also in their functioning at maturity. In selective systems the functional units are not specifically constructed to carry out their functions in an optimal way but instead are selected from much larger sets called "repertoires." The component units in a repertoire are constructed with a wide structural variety that is sufficient to cover, with overlap, the range of possible functions needed in any particular instantiation of the system. Selection occurs during experience without further alteration of the functional properties of units already constructed. Rather, the selected units are multiplied or amplified in such a manner as to make a larger contribution to the future responses of the system than the unselected units. Selective processes of this kind, with different amplification modes appropriate to each system, provide the basic mechanisms of the immune system and, of course, of evolution itself.

Consideration of the need for nervous systems to provide organisms with the behavioral adaptability to survive in a hostile environment without prior knowledge or programming, consideration of the structural variability found in all nervous systems, and other considerations have prompted the idea embodied in the neuronal group selection (NGS) theory[23] that the brain is in fact a selective system operating in somatic time (that is, during the lifetime of an individual organism). Population thinking, the fundamental theoretical mode of biology in which the properties of populations as well as those of individuals are taken into account, is thereby introduced into considerations of how individual brains work.

THE NEURONAL GROUP SELECTION THEORY

According to the NGS theory, two kinds of selection events play critical roles in shaping the development of the nervous system.

During the formation of the brain in the embryo, selection among competing neuronal cells and their processes determines the anatomical form and the pattern of synaptic connectivity of the nervous system. This selection for connectivity is elaborated through the developmental mechanisms of cell adhesion and movement, differential growth, cell division, and cell death. Because of their dynamic properties, these selective mechanisms introduce individual variance into the neuronal networks. Later, during postnatal experience, selection among diverse preexisting groups of cells, accomplished by differential modification of synaptic strengths or efficacies *without change in the connectivity pattern,* shapes the behavioral repertoire of the organism according to what is of adaptive value to it in its econiche.

A system must have three features if it is to be selective: (1) it must have an a priori repertoire of variant entities capable of responding to relevant environmental states; (2) the individual members of this repertoire must have extensive opportunities to encounter the rich diversity of the environment, providing opportunities for selection, and (3) the system must have a mechanism for differentially amplifying the relative contributions of those members of the repertoire that are in some sense favored or selected in their interactions with the environment. According to the NGS theory, the repertoires in the nervous system comprise groups of perhaps 50 to 10,000 neurons, capable, as a result of their interconnections, of responding to particular patterns of activity that arrive at their synapses. These interconnections are formed during development, prior to experience. The inputs to which the groups respond originate ultimately at the sense organs (encounter with the environment) but frequently are relayed first through other neuronal groups. Selective modification in the strengths of synaptic connections (differential amplification) leads to the compartition and stabilization of functioning circuits out of fixed networks. In higher forms, responses of neuronal populations are significantly influenced by similarities between present and past constellations of sensory signals. This reevocation of previous responses constitutes the basis of what we call memory. Memory is a consequence of selective amplification, which leads to increased speed or strength of selected responses when similar patterns of stimulation are repeated.

To be able to respond adequately to a wide range of novel inputs, a selective system must have a sufficient number of units in its repertoires. A relationship can be derived between the sizes of the repertoires and the specificities of the individual groups.[24] If recognition is too specific, the system will fail because there will be no way to place enough groups in a finite repertoire to recognize all possible stimuli; similarly, if specificity is too broad, the system will fail because stimuli with significant differences may be confused. The specificities must therefore be intermediate, allowing several groups to respond more or less well to any given stimulus. This phenomenon, which we call "degeneracy," is critical to an understanding of selective recognition systems. Degeneracy ensures that any perceptual problem has multiple potential solutions. Context determines exactly which combination of groups responds in a given situation and therefore which solution is selected. Degeneracy also ensures that the entire "space" of possible stimuli is covered and that the system has the functional redundancy needed to make it fail-safe against the loss of individual groups.

One additional concept that is critical to the NGS theory is that of "reentry," or the exchange of output signals, usually in a mapped arrangement, from one repertoire to another at the same or an earlier stage of neuronal processing. Reentry provides a mechanism for correlating responses at corresponding positions in related maps so as to ensure consistency across the entire system with respect to the current state and spatiotemporal continuity of the environment. Reentry ensures that subrepertoires at all levels in the nervous system are constantly mapped to each other and to the outside world, obviating any need for the context switching, time stamps, or other bookkeeping apparatus used in computers. It encompasses feedback but is more general. For example, two different repertoires in independent parallel pathways, each disjunctively sampling different aspects of signals, can classify stimuli according to different criteria and can be cross-connected at higher levels. Such interacting repertoires form "classification couples," which, by their mutual interaction, can perform classifications more complex than either repertoire could accomplish alone. Another form of reentry involves the total system of creature plus environment. In this "global" form of reentry, the motor output of the organism influences sensory systems by changing the relative arrangement of objects or the organism's position in space. Mappings at all levels of the nervous system thus become joined in a global loop. Iteration of activity in this loop can alter reentry in local maps and lead to modified behaviors that are more adaptive for the organism.

The NGS theory is consistent with the biological facts we have summarized. It takes advantage of the unavoidable variance in connectivity introduced by epigenetic events during the construction of neuronal networks to provide a plausible mechanism for categorization without programmed descriptions, homunculi, or reinforced learning. The theory is based on principles of selection similar to those that govern the evolution of species; the mechanisms, of course, are different. Such an approach is not all-inclusive, but it does give one a way to confront the fundamental problem of categories before taking on social psychology and all the intervening problems between perception and language.

Like any scientific theory, NGS must be tested by experiment. Data from several lines of study already provide significant support for it. Studies of development in the nervous system show that the dynamic regulation of a small number of cell-adhesion molecules is responsible for the growth patterns of neuronal processes,[25] and there is no evidence for the kind of extensive system of chemical markers that would be required if all connectivity were somehow genetically specified. Indeed, there is evidence for extensive variance of connectivity, even in genetically identical animals. In adult animals, data now show that neuronal mappings, such as those in the somatosensory cortex (a brain area that responds to touch receptors in the skin), are not nearly as rigid and unvarying as had previously been thought. [26] Rather, competition occurs to determine map boundaries. The evidence shows that certain connections that are anatomically present but not used in the normal functioning of these cortical regions can become active by selection when normal patterns of activation are disrupted. These inactive connections correspond to the ones not selected in normal functioning; their existence would make no sense in a nonselective system. A complete discussion[27] of this evidence[28] is beyond the scope of this article. Instead, we shall briefly describe a series of automata that we have constructed in computer simulations to test the self-consistency of NGS as well as to demonstrate the ability of selective recognition systems to carry out interesting recognition and categorization tasks. Such models can be invaluable in helping to focus experimental questions for the biologist. Ultimately, we hope also to learn from them how to construct machines capable of carrying out context-sensitive classification tasks far better than any computers that are now available.

SELECTIVE RECOGNITION AUTOMATA

We have been exploring the properties of selective recognition systems by constructing and testing a series of automata. These automata address some of the problems of the standard AI paradigm by avoiding preestablished categories and programming altogether. Instead, they are constructed as networks of simulated neuronlike units that, by a process of selection, can carry out simple categorization and association tasks in variant worlds full of novelty. Programming is used to instruct the computer how to simulate the neuronal units, but the function of these units is not itself programmed. The first automaton, called Darwin I, dealt with the process of recognition itself by using strings of binary digits as both recognizands and recognizers.[29] The second, Darwin II, was used for the recognition and classification of two-dimensional patterns presented on a retina-like array.[30] A third system, Darwin III, combines the recognition and categorization networks of Darwin II with motor circuits and effectors that act upon the environment to form a complete automaton capable of autonomous behavior. Unlike the previous two automata, Darwin III can be observed behaving without our looking into its "nervous system."

The arrangement of networks in Darwin III may be varied at will to suit various experimental protocols. A simplified functional schematic of one such arrangement, which we will describe in detail shortly, is shown in the diagram on page 162.

Networks may be constructed from multiple repertoires, corresponding to functional regions in the brain. Each repertoire may contain several layers of cells, just as the cerebral cortex does. Each layer may have its own rules for connectivity and synaptic modification. Once established, the connectivity is fixed, but the connection strengths vary in accordance with rules for synaptic modification that provide the mechanism of NGS. Stimuli are presented on a retinalike input array. An environmental module permits these stimuli to be generated and moved about in various ways in order to test the

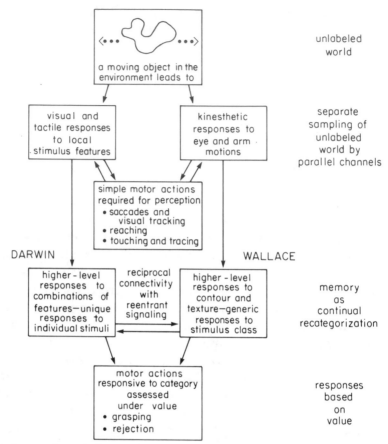

This diagram shows the functional relationships in one arrangement of Darwin III. The box at the top represents the environment, in which an unnamed object is moving about. The remaining boxes represent functions, each of which is subserved by several repertoires of neuronal groups with appropriate interconnections. The arrows suggest causal relationships, which generally reflect the existence of anatomical connections among the various regions. The two separate sampling systems of the automaton, Darwin and Wallace, are at the left and the right, respectively.

The result of the automaton's neuronal activity is externally apparent as motor activity responsive to its categorization of objects. This categorization proceeds according to internal criteria that emerge because the automaton has biases or values. For example, the value "seeing is better than not seeing" is expressed in terms of changes in connection strengths in oculomotor repertoires when visual units become more active following eye movements. Note that value does not prespecify categories, but when categories do emerge, it biases the selection of behaviors consequent upon them. Note also that the automaton reflects its experience in more or less stable alterations of connection strengths but does not have coded representations for memory. Instead, memory is exhibited as an enhanced ability to recognize and categorize objects in classes seen before.

responses of the automaton. Two devices are provided for motor output from Darwin III: a multijointed arm and a movable head with one or two eyes. Motions of the arm can actually displace objects in the environment, while motions of the head affect only their perceived positions. Specialized networks may be incorporated that respond by simple innate criteria to the relative adaptive value to the automaton of its various motor actions. Selective amplification may be made to depend on adaptive value as registered by these internal structures. External criteria for amplification (such as might be provided by a programmer) are not permitted.

An important rule, one that distinguishes the Darwin automata from AI systems with similar goals, is that no specific information about the stimulus objects to be presented is built into the system when it is constructed. General information about the kinds of stimuli that will be significant to the system (for example, the fact that they will be line drawings) is, however, implicit in the choice of feature-detecting elements that are used. This choice is akin to the specializations built into the receptor organs of each species during the course of evolution.

A part of Darwin III is specialized, like Darwin II, to deal with categorization. Psychological studies suggest that humans use several different methods to make classifications.[31] Accordingly, both automata incorporate two separate categorization functions. The first is to recognize aspects of individual objects according to their unique characteristics; the second is to recognize similarities among things in the same class and differences among things in different classes and thus to define objects. To accomplish these tasks, two sets of repertoires are used that operate in parallel. They both incorporate series of maps, but the maps are constructed differently and they make classifications according to quite different principles. These complementary subsystems interact via reentrant reciprocal connections to give associative functions not possessed by either set alone.

The two subsystems are arbitrarily named Darwin and Wallace (see the diagram). Darwin is the one designed to respond uniquely to individual stimulus patterns. Its responses loosely correspond to an approach to categorization known in the psychological literature as "matching to exemplars." In this approach, objects are compared to stored exemplars, and categories are assigned according to the maximum degree of match obtained with features; Darwin, however, does not store feature patterns but rather produces patterns of response corresponding to each unique input that it recognizes. In itself, Darwin cannot define an object, because it is insensitive to the continuities of features. Wallace, on the other hand, is designed to respond in the same way to different objects in a class by correlating a variety of features; this process loosely corresponds to a probabilistic matching approach to categorization and cannot in itself distinguish individuals. Of course, the particular response specificities of Darwin and Wallace (mainly to contour in a two-dimensional world) are intended to be merely exemplary, and other stimulus properties such as color and texture would also be represented in real nervous systems.

The Darwin and Wallace networks both have hierarchical structures. Each has a level that is connected directly to sensory input and that deals with features of the stimulus; connected to that is an abstracting or combining level that receives its main input from the first level and responds to combinations of the elementary responses that are relevant to categorization. The initial layer of the Darwin subsystem comprises groups of cells that respond to local features on the input array, such as line segments oriented in certain directions or with certain bends. These are connected in various combinations to higher-level abstracting groups that give the desired unique responses to each stimulus pattern. These responses include elements contributed by the surrounding context.

On the other hand, Wallace deals with object and class properties. In Darwin III, the Wallace subsystem makes use of the automaton's arm to trace over the contours of stimulus objects, much as a blind person reading braille text might do. The first-level repertoire of Wallace receives input from the arm's kinesthetic sensory neurons. It responds to correlations of trace activities that distinguish objects as entities from the background by their spatial continuity. Cells in this repertoire are in turn connected to an abstracting network similar to the one in Darwin. Because the trace responds to the presence or changes of direction of lines in the environment with little regard for their lengths and orientations, Wallace is insensitive to both rigid and nonrigid transformations of stimulus objects and tends to respond to class characteristics of whole families of related objects.

The networks in the two abstracting repertoires are connected to each other at higher levels to form a classification couple. It is important that in such a couple the earlier levels not be connected, for if they were, the separate modes of sampling for later classification would be confounded and their distinct characteristics lost. In other words, the sampling of the world by parallel channels must be disjunctive for rich, context-sensitive classification to occur.

The responses of the neuronal groups in Darwin III are determined by their present inputs and past histories in a manner that incorporates the most important features of the far more complicated responses of real neurons. Input connections are specified by lists that are constructed when the model is set up. These lists are constructed differently for each repertoire according to its function. Each input contributes to the output of the group according to the current strength of its connection. In addition, the groups are subject to random fluctuations in their activity analogous to those found in real neuronal networks. The recognition specificity of each group depends on its connection list and connection strengths; the best response is obtained when the most active inputs are connected via synapses with high connection strengths. For other inputs, a group will respond more or less well, overlapping in specificity with other groups and conferring degeneracy on the system as a whole.

The connection strengths among cells, both within and between groups, are modified during selective amplification. The amplification rule depends only on quantities that could reasonably have an influence on the efficacies of real synapses in real neuronal networks and is purely local in nature. In the scheme we have used most often, a connection is strengthened if the activities of both pre- and postsynaptic cells exceed specified thresholds. In other words, a connection from an active input to an active cell is strengthened and leads to a stronger response the next time a similar input is encountered. In certain other circumstances, connection strengths are weakened, preventing the system from eventually reaching a state in which all synapses have maximum efficacy. If this were to happen, any input would drive the network as a whole to a state of maximal activity corresponding to a kind of "epileptic seizure."

With appropriate stimulation sequences, Darwin II and Darwin III are capable of producing responses corresponding to behaviors such as categorization, recognition, generalization, and association. A detailed treatment of some typical experiments has been presented elsewhere.[32] *Categorization* is most evident in the Wallace responses.

It does not involve *naming*, which requires a linguistic convention, but only similarity of response to items in the same category. As we have already seen, such similarity is characteristic of the operation of Wallace. (The particular categories arrived at for various kinds of stimuli are dependent on the particular choice of kinesthetic trace correlations that Wallace groups respond to, and might or might not agree with the categories *we* define for the stimuli. The existence of discrepancies is consistent with the idea that categories are not inherent in the environment, but depend on the evolutionarily dictated predispositions of organisms to attend to categories that are relevant to their adaptive needs. The construction of information depends on these internal adaptive criteria.)

The effect of synaptic modification on the responses of groups in these networks is to alter cells that respond above a certain level (the amplification threshold) so that they will give a stronger response when later they experience a similar input pattern; groups with weaker responses generally are changed so as not to respond at all after amplification. Groups that are not involved in the response to a particular stimulus remain unchanged and available for response to novel stimuli not yet encountered. These selective changes demonstrate *recognition*, or the enhancement of meaningful response to a stimulus after it has been experienced before. In addition, amplification can be shown to improve the ability of the system to categorize.

Generalization occurs when responses to novel shapes are more like the responses to previously encountered shapes in the same class than would have been the case without prior experience. In Wallace, generalization is already present without amplification as a consequence of the feature-correlating property of that network, but in Darwin, generalization is not built in and can occur only with the help of Wallace. Reentrant connections between Darwin and Wallace make it possible for common patterns of response in Wallace to bias the units amplified in Darwin in accord with the class membership of the various stimuli. After a number of repetitions of this process, with shapes from several different classes, the Darwin responses become more alike within each class. To the extent that novel stimuli in the same class elicit responses in the feature-detecting layer of Darwin that have elements in common with the responses to the stimuli used during amplification, responses to these new stimuli will also become more similar, consistent with generalization in Darwin.

Reentrant connections in both directions between Darwin and Wallace are also essential for the process of *association*. Association is achieved when individual responses in Darwin are linked to different stimuli in the same class via Wallace in such a way that presentation of one of the individual stimuli evokes elements of the response in Darwin proper to another. Such associative properties among individuals could not be displayed by Wallace alone.

These capabilities of categorization, recognition, generalization, and association all underline the point that these critical aspects of perception can, and indeed must, occur before conventional learning. They also show how systems based on more than one principle of categorization can be joined in classification couples to give modes of classification not available to any single system.

Darwin III is also being used to study problems involving motion, perceptual invariance, figure-ground discrimination, and memory, among other phenomena. The NGS theory suggests that object motion is a critical factor in the selective process, particularly in early visual learning, where it provides to the perceptual system a major clue that the world in fact can be parsed adaptively into separate objects. This view is consistent with experiments suggesting that human infants have a conception of objects as spatially connected, coherent, continuously movable entities.[33] For this reason, the first experiments using the motor systems in Darwin III have been aimed at gaining a better understanding of this parsing process, beginning with the simple ability to track a moving object on a plain background.

In these experiments, connections are provided from retinotopically mapped visual layers (corresponding to the superior colliculus or optic tectum in various biological species) to motor layers connecting ultimately to the muscles that control the position of the eye. These connections are made indiscriminately to motor cells corresponding to all directions of eye movement. Thus, there is no a priori specificity with regard to input in any particular part of the visual field and there are no prearranged motor skills; performance can develop and improve only by selection from spontaneous movements generated by pairs of mutually inhibitory motor pattern-generating layers. Amplification of connections from sensory to motor regions is modulated by value schemes based respectively on the appearance of activity in a circumfoveal region and in the fovea itself. (The fovea is the region of greatest visual acuity near the center of the retina.) Thus, connections from a particular point on a visual layer to a particular motor area will tend to be strengthened when the appearance of an object at that point is correlated with activity in the motor area that leads to foveation of the stimulus. These same connections will tend to be weakened when the motor activity does not lead to foveation.

After a suitable period of experience with various moving stimuli, Darwin III in fact begins to make the appropriate saccades and fine tracking movements with no further specification of its task than that implicit in the value scheme. The automaton finally displays a system of behavior in which the eye scans at random when no stimulus is visible, makes a rapid saccade to any stimulus that appears within the outer limits of its widest visual field, and finely tracks any stimulus that has successfully been foveated. During fine tracking, the Darwin and Wallace networks are able to respond to the now-centered object, permitting position-independent categorization to occur. Habituation eventually sets in, permitting occasional saccades to other parts of the visual field. After such a saccade, a new stimulus object can take over as tracking target.

In a similar fashion, the multijointed arm of Darwin III can be trained to reach for and touch objects that are first detected and tracked by the visual system. This performance, which entails the coordination of gestural motions involving the various joints to different extents, requires the participation of a whole series of repertoires that perform functions similar to those thought to be carried out by the cerebellum in real nervous systems.

Of course, these selective systems make mistakes. For example, in the oculomotor system, amplification errors may occur when a stimulus crosses the edge of a visual field diagonally, and very large stimuli may confuse the tracking mechanism. By the use of standard engineering techniques, a better tracking system could surely be designed, one in which the correct motions for a spot of light at any location on the visual field would all be calculated in advance and incorporated in the logic of the design. The selective system needs experience to develop its functional capabilities. But this very lack of built-in function is its biggest advantage; the machinery in a selective system "doesn't know what it is for," permitting the same networks to accomplish various tasks depending on what we, acting as external agents of "evolution," decide they should find "adaptive." This flexibility is possible precisely because the functional organization of the system arises only *after* interaction with the environment. Equally simple training regimes should work for a wide variety of tasks, such as finding a desirable object in a background of distracting objects and picking it out with the arm. The modular combination of subsystems capable of carrying out recognition tasks provides an attractive approach to the construction of automata with increasingly complex perceptual capabilities and should have eventual significance for efforts at machine vision. As for output, the corollary for motor control is the ability to generate complex behavioral sequences by selection from simple and innate motion patterns. This has obvious significance for developments in robotics and the control of complex systems, particularly in connection with "attentional tasks."[34] Such context-sensitive tasks present an apparently insuperable barrier to traditional AI approaches.

From a purely economical point of view, it might be argued that artificial selective systems would be impractical because they must always contain some units that do not respond to any of the inputs actually encountered, and thus are never used at all. The fraction of such units does not increase with system size, however, and the extra units provide redundancy that may well yield overall cost savings because of reduced repairs and downtime. Speed of execution is also no barrier to the usefulness of selective systems implemented on parallel processors; responses require only a few times the response latency of the individual units because relaxation is not required as it is in systems based on the statistical-mechanical concept of lattice (network) energy minimization. It is therefore reasonable to expect that practical systems based on selection could be constructed with hardware that is presently available or forseeable in the near future. Such systems will have more components but a simpler overall design than possible systems based on information-processing network models. Obviously, such systems, if proven feasible, will have a great influence on the design of computer hardware.

SUMMARY AND CONCLUSIONS

The automata we have described are intended to illustrate certain aspects of the NGS theory without attempting to emulate real nervous systems in a detailed way. The experimental data and the computer resources to do that are not yet at hand. Thus, the models do not provide evidence for the applicability of the theory to real nervous systems; such evidence can come only from experiment. Nonetheless, NGS provides satisfying explanations for a whole panoply of perceptual processes involving categorization, and as inanimate examples of selective systems, the models can help to demonstrate the consistency of the theory as an abstract description of these processes. Such demonstrations are important for understanding complicated biological systems and at the same time can provide real insight into the computer-science problem of designing artificial systems with brainlike capabilities.

In particular, it is quite clear that nervous systems do not work in anything like the way that has been assumed in the standard AI paradigm, yet the performance of at least some nervous systems is definitive of the term *intelligence* as used in the phrase "artificial intelligence." It is therefore very curious that AI, even in its new connectionist guise, has for the most part neglected the fundamental biology of the nervous system, from which the very definition of intelligence is derived. We suggest that in order to make progress in overcoming the obstacles we have discussed, AI must recognize these origins and incorporate what can be learned from a study of nervous systems. It must stop reasoning by analogy with well-studied, but irrelevant, physical systems such as spin glasses, and must instead reason by analysis of relevant facts about biological systems that actually have intelligence. This change will require AI to abandon the notion of intelligence as a purely abstract information-processing activity.

A confrontation of the number of interactive levels in a real organism capable of intelligent behavior reveals a staggering complexity of nonlinear interactions. If social transmission through language is added, the complexity increases even more. It appears to be the height of arrogance, in the face of this complexity, to think that all problems intelligent creatures confront can be understood by just pondering them in the abstract. One must instead begin by analyzing such systems in terms of their basic necessary structures and functions and their modes of origin—developmental as well as evolutionary. The separation of hardware from software implicit in the traditional AI approach needs to be abandoned, even though it served well as a guiding principle in the development of von Neumann–type computers, which may be logic engines and—to some extent, culture engines—but are not biological engines. We believe that AI will eventually be achieved only in non–von Neumann systems in which specialized variants of hardware, based on a common theme of selection and population thinking, will work without programs to adapt to the particular environments in which they find themselves, just as biological organisms do. Programs and intelligence based on communication can come later.

ENDNOTES

We thank the International Business Machines Corporation and the Cornell National Supercomputer Facility for their support of part of this work.

[1] Aristotle, *Historia Animalium,* trans. D'Arcy Wentworth Thompson (Oxford: Clarendon Press, 1910), bk. 2, sec. 3, 501^b 20.

[2] Aristotle, *De Partibus Animalium,* trans. William Ogle (Oxford: Clarendon Press, 1912), bk. 3, sec. 1, 661^b 33.

[3] Gerald M. Edelman, *Neural Darwinism: The Theory of Neuronal Group Selection* (New York: Basic Books, 1987).

[4] Patrick Henry Winston, *Artificial Intelligence,* 2d ed. (Reading, Mass.: Addison-Wesley, 1984), 1–2.

[5] Marvin Minsky, "Steps Toward Artificial Intelligence," in *Proceedings of the Institute of Radio Engineers,* 49 (1961):8–30.

[6] Winston, *Artificial Intelligence,* 42.

[7] Hubert L. Dreyfus, *What Computers Can't Do* (New York: Harper and Row, 1972).

[8] Alan M. Turing, "On Computable Numbers, with an Application to the Entscheidungsproblem," in *Proceedings of the London Mathematical Society* 42 (1937):230–65. Turing defined a certain class of automaton, now known as the Turing machine, and showed that any member of this class could compute any of a large class of functions. All but a few special-purpose digital computers are Turing machines.

[9] Douglas R. Hofstadter, *Gödel, Escher, Bach: An Eternal Golden Braid* (New York: Basic Books, 1979), 561. Hofstadter points out that "like tea, the Church-Turing Thesis can be given in a variety of different strengths," and he presents several of these with a discussion of their implications for AI.

[10] John McCarthy, "Programs with Common Sense," in *Proceedings of the Teddington Conference on the Mechanization of Thought Processes* (London: Her Majesty's Stationery Office, 1960); John McCarthy, "Some Expert Systems Need Common Sense," *Annals of the New York Academy of Sciences* 426 (1984):129–35.

[11] Peter W. Frey, ed., *Chess Skill in Man and Machine,* 2d ed. (New York: Springer-Verlag, 1984).

[12] Raymond Reiter, "Nonmonotonic Reasoning," *Annual Reviews of Computer Science* (Palo Alto: Annual Reviews Inc., forthcoming).

[13] Warren S. McCulloch and Walter H. Pitts, "A Logical Calculus of the Ideas Immanent in Nervous Activity," *Bulletin of Mathematical Biophysics* 5 (1943):115–33.

[14] Frank Rosenblatt, *The Perceptron: A Theory of Statistical Separability in Cognitive Systems* (Ithaca: Cornell Aeronautical Laboratory Inc., Report No. VG-1196-G-1, 1958).

[15] Marvin Minsky and Seymour Papert, *Perceptrons: An Introduction to Computational Geometry* (Cambridge: MIT Press, 1969).

[16] David Marr and Tomaso Poggio, "Cooperative Computation of Stereo Disparity," *Science* 194 (15 Oct. 1976):283–87.

[17] John R. Anderson, "A Spreading Activation Theory of Memory," *Journal of Verbal Learning and Verbal Behavior* 22 (1983):261–95.

[18] Leon N. Cooper, "A Possible Organization of Animal Memory and Learning," in *Nobel Symposium*, no. 24 (1973), 252–64; Teuvo Kohonen, *Associative Memory: A System Theoretical Approach* (New York: Springer-Verlag, 1977).

[19] Reviewed in John J. Hopfield and David W. Tank, "Computing with Neural Circuits: A Model," *Science* 233 (8 August 1986):625–33.

[20] David H. Ackley, Geoffrey E. Hinton, and Terrence J. Sejnowski, "A Learning Algorithm for Boltzmann Machines," *Cognitive Science* 9 (January-March 1985):147–69.

[21] David E. Rumelhart, James L. McClelland, and the PDP Research Group, eds., *Parallel Distributed Processing: Explorations in the Microstructure of Cognition*, vols. 1,2 (Cambridge: MIT Press, 1986).

[22] Edelman, *Neural Darwinism*.

[23] Ibid.; and Gerald M. Edelman, "Group Selection and Phasic Reentrant Signalling: A Theory of Higher Brain Function," in *The Mindful Brain*, Gerald M. Edelman and Vernon B. Mountcastle, eds. (Cambridge: MIT Press, 1978), 51–100.

[24] Edelman, *Neural Darwinism*.

[25] Gerald M. Edelman, "Cell-Adhesion Molecules: A Molecular Basis for Animal Form," *Scientific American* 250 (April 1984): 118–29; Gerald M. Edelman, "Cell Adhesion Molecules in the Regulation of Animal Form and Tissue Pattern," *Annual Review of Cell Biology* 2 (1986):81–116.

[26] John H. Kaas, Michael M. Merzenich, and Herbert P. Killackey, "The Reorganization of Somatosensory Cortex Following Peripheral-Nerve Damage in Adult and Developing Mammals," *Annual Review of Neuroscience* 6 (1983):325–56; Michael M. Merzenich et al., "Topographic Reorganization of Somatosensory Cortical Areas 3b and 1 in Adult Monkeys Following Restricted Deafferentation," *Neuroscience* 8 (January 1983):33–55. Numerous other examples have been reported.

[27] Edelman, *Neural Darwinism*.

[28] Gerald M. Edelman and Leif H. Finkel, "Neuronal Group Selection in the Cerebral Cortex," in *Dynamical Aspects of Neocortical Function*, Gerald M. Edelman, W. Einar Gall, and W. Maxwell Cowan, eds. (New York: John Wiley, 1984), 653–95.

[29] Gerald M. Edelman, "Group Selection as the Basis for Higher Brain Function," in *Organization of the Cerebral Cortex*, Francis O. Schmitt et al., eds. (Cambridge: MIT Press, 1981), 51–100.

[30]Gerald M. Edelman and George N. Reeke, Jr., "Selective Networks Capable of Representative Transformations, Limited Generalizations, and Associative Memory," in *Proceedings of the National Academy of Sciences USA* 79 (1982):2091–95.

[31]Edward E. Smith and Douglas L. Medin, *Categories and Concepts* (Cambridge: Harvard University Press, 1981).

[32]George N. Reeke, Jr., and Gerald M. Edelman, "Selective Networks and Recognition Automata," *Annals of the New York Academy of Sciences* 426 (1984):181–201.

[33]Philip J. Kellman and Elizabeth S. Spelke, "Perception of Partly Occluded Objects in Infancy," *Cognitive Psychology* 15 (4) (October 1983):483–524.

[34]Anya Hurlbert and Tomaso Poggio, "Do Computers Need Attention?" *Nature* 321 (12 June 1986): 651–52.

W. Daniel Hillis

Intelligence as an Emergent Behavior; or, The Songs of Eden

SOMETIMES a system with many simple components will exhibit a behavior of the whole that seems more organized than the behavior of the individual parts. Consider the intricate structure of a snowflake. Symmetric shapes within the crystals of ice repeat in threes and sixes, with patterns recurring from place to place and within themselves at different scales. The shapes formed by the ice are consequences of the local rules of interaction that govern the molecules of water, although the connection between the shapes and the rules is far from obvious. After all, these are the same rules of interaction that cause water to suddenly turn to steam at its boiling point and cause whirlpools to form in a stream. The rules that govern the forces between water molecules seem much simpler than crystals or whirlpools or boiling points, yet all of these complex phenomena are somehow consequences of those rules. Such phenomena are called *emergent behaviors* of the system.

It would be very convenient if intelligence were an emergent behavior of randomly connected neurons in the same sense that snowflakes and whirlpools are emergent behaviors of water molecules. It might then be possible to build a thinking machine by simply hooking together a sufficiently large network of artificial neurons. The notion of emergence would suggest that such a network, once it reached some critical mass, would spontaneously begin to think.

W. Daniel Hillis is the designer of the Connection Machine, a parallel computer that was the subject of his Ph.D. thesis at the Massachusetts Institute of Technology.

This is a seductive idea because it allows for the possibility of constructing intelligence without first understanding it. Understanding intelligence is difficult and probably a long way off, so the possibility that it might spontaneously emerge from the interactions of a large collection of simple parts has considerable appeal to the would-be builder of thinking machines. Unfortunately, that idea does not suggest a practical approach to construction. The concept of emergence in itself offers neither guidance on how to construct such a system nor insight into why it would work.

Ironically, the apparent inscrutability of the idea of intelligence as an emergent behavior accounts for much of its continuing popularity. Emergence offers a way to believe in physical causality while simultaneously maintaining the impossibility of a reductionist explanation of thought. For those who fear mechanistic explanations of the human mind, our ignorance of how local interactions produce emergent behavior offers a reassuring fog in which to hide the soul.

There has been a recent renewal of interest in emergent behavior in the form of simulated neural networks and connectionist models, spin glasses and cellular automata, and evolutionary models. Each of these is a model of some real system. For neural networks and connectionist models, the system being modeled is a collection of biological neurons, such as the brain; for spin glasses it is molecular crystals. Cellular automata and evolutionary models are based on the ontogenesis and phylogenesis of living organisms. In all of these cases, both the model and the system being modeled produce dramatic examples of emergent behavior.

Most of these models are not new, but interest in them is being stirred because of a combination of new insights and new tools. The insight/s come primarily from a branch of physics called dynamical systems theory. The tools come from the development of new types of computing devices. Just as we thought of intelligence in terms of servomechanism in the 1950s, and in terms of sequential computers in the sixties and seventies, we are now beginning to think in terms of parallel computers, in which tens of thousands of processors work together. This is not a deep philosophical shift, but it is of great practical importance, since it is now possible to study large emergent systems experimentally.

Inevitably, antireductionists interpret such progress as a schism between symbolic rationalists, who oppose them, and gestaltists, who support them. I have often been asked which "side" I am on. Not being a philosopher, my inclination is to focus on the practical aspects of this question: How would we go about constructing an emergent intelligence? What information would we need to know in order to succeed? How can this information be determined by experiment?

The emergent system that I can most easily imagine would be an implementation of symbolic thought rather than a refutation of it. Symbolic thought would be an emergent property of the system. The point of view is best explained by the following parable about the origin of human intelligence. As far as I know, this parable of human evolution is consistent with the available evidence (as are many others), but because it is chosen to illustrate a point, it should be read as a story, not as a theory. It is different from most accepted theories of human development in that it presents features that are measurable in the archeological records—such as increased brain size, food sharing, and neoteny—as consequences rather than causes of intelligence.

Once upon a time, about two and a half million years ago, there lived a race of apes that walked upright. In terms of intellect and habit they were similar to modern chimpanzees. The young apes, like young apes today, had a tendency to mimic the actions of others. In particular, they had a tendency to imitate sounds. If one ape shrieked "ooh, eeh, eeh," another would repeat "ooh, eeh, eeh." Some sequences of sounds, or "songs," were more likely to be mimicked than others.

Let us ignore the evolution of the apes for the moment and consider the evolution of the songs. Since the songs were replicated by the apes, and since they sometimes died away and were occasionally combined with others, we may consider them (very loosely) a form of life. They survived, bred, competed with one another, and evolved according to their own criterion of fitness. If a song contained a particularly catchy phrase that caused it to be repeated often, then that phrase was likely to be incorporated into other songs. Only songs that had a strong tendency to be repeated survived.

The survival of a song was only indirectly related to the survival of the apes; it was more directly affected by the survival of other songs. Since the apes were a limited resource, the songs had to compete with one another for a chance to be sung. One successful competition strategy was for a song to specialize; that is, for it to find a particular niche in which it was apt to be repeated. Songs that fit particularly well with specific moods or activities of apes had a special survival value for this reason. (I do not know why some songs fit well with particular moods, but since it is true for me, I do not find it hard to believe that it was true for my ancestors.)

Before songs began to specialize they were of no particular value to the apes. In a biological sense the songs were parasites, taking advantage of the apes' tendency to imitate. As songs became specialized, however, it became advantageous for apes to pay attention to the songs of others and to differentiate between them. By listening to songs, a clever ape could gain useful information. For example, an ape could infer that another ape had found food or that it was likely to attack. Once the apes began to take advantage of the songs, a symbiotic relationship developed: songs enhanced their own survival by conveying useful information to apes; apes enhanced their own survival by improving their capacity to remember, replicate, and understand songs. Thus the blind forces of evolution created a partnership between the songs and the apes that thrived on the basis of mutual self-interest. Eventually this partnership evolved into one of the world's most successful symbionts: the human race.

Unfortunately songs do not leave fossils, so unless some natural process has left a phonographic trace, we may never know if the preceding story describes what really happened. But if the story is true, the apes and the songs became the two components of human intelligence. The songs evolved into the knowledge, mores, and mechanisms of thought that together are the symbolic portion of human intelligence. The apes became apes with bigger brains, perhaps optimized for late maturity so that they could learn more songs. *Homo sapiens* is a cooperative combination of the two.

It is not unusual in nature for two species to live together so interdependently that they appear to be a single organism. Lichens are symbionts of a fungus and an alga that live so closely intertwined that they can only be separated under a microscope. Bean plants need living bacteria in their roots to fix the nitrogen they extract from the soil, and in return the bacteria need nutrients from the bean plants. Even the single-celled *Paramecium bursarra* uses green algae living inside itself to synthesize food.

Another example of two entirely different forms of "life" that form a symbiosis may be even closer to the example of the songs and the apes. In *The Origins of Life,* Freeman Dyson suggests that biological life is a symbiotic combination of two different self-reproducing entities with very different forms of replication.[1] Dyson suggests that life originated in two stages. While most theories of the origin of life start with nucleotides replicating in some "primeval soup," Dyson's theory starts with metabolizing drops of oil.

In the beginning these hypothetical replicating oil drops had no genetic material, but were self-perpetuating chemical systems that absorbed raw materials from their surroundings. When a drop reached a certain size it would split; about half of its constituents would go to each part. Such drops evolved efficient metabolic systems even though their rules of replication were very different from the Mendelian rules of modern life. Once the oil drops became good at metabolizing, they were infected by another form of replicators that, like the songs, had no metabolism of their own. These were parasitic molecules of DNA; like modern viruses, they took advantage of the existing machinery of the host cells to reproduce. The metabolizers and the DNA eventually coevolved into the mutually beneficial symbiosis that we know today as life.

This two-part theory of life is not conceptually far from the two-part story of intelligence. Both suggest that a preexisting homeostatic mechanism was infected by an opportunistic parasite. The two parts reproduced according to different sets of rules, but were able to coevolve so successfully that the resulting symbiont appears to be a single entity. Viewed in this light, choosing between emergence and symbolic computation in the study of intelligence is like choosing between metabolism and genetic replication in the study of life. Just as the metabolic system provides a substrate in which the genetic system can work, so an emergent system may provide a substrate in which the symbolic system can operate.

Currently the metabolic system of life is far too complex for us to fully understand or reproduce it. By comparison the Mendelian rules of genetic replication are almost trivial, and it is possible to study them as a system unto themselves without worrying about the details of the metabolism that supports them. In the same sense, it seems likely that symbolic thought can be fruitfully studied and perhaps even recreated without worrying about the details of the emergent system that supports it. So far this has been the dominant approach in artificial intelligence and the approach that has yielded the most progress.

The other approach is to build a model of the emergent substrate of intelligence. This artificial substrate for thought would not need to mimic in detail the mechanisms of the biological system, but it would need to exhibit those emergent properties that are necessary to support the operations of thought.

What is the minimum that we would need to understand in order to construct such a system? For one thing, we would need to know how big a system to build. Information theory suggests that the appropriate unit of measure is the number of binary digits, or bits, required to store the information. How many bits are required to store the acquired portion of human knowledge of a typical human? We need to know an approximate answer in order to construct an emergent intelligence with humanlike performance. Currently the amount of acquired information stored by an average human brain is not known to within even two orders of magnitude, but it can in principle be determined by experiment. There are at least three ways to estimate the storage requirements for emergent intelligence.

One way would be through an understanding of the physical mechanisms of memory in the human brain. If information is stored primarily by modifications of synapses, then it would be possible to measure the information-storage capacity of the brain by counting the number of synapses. Elsewhere in this issue of *Dædalus*, Jacob T. Schwartz estimates that the brain contains roughly 10^{15} synapses. Each synapse could store several bits. But even knowing the exact amount of physical storage in the brain would not completely answer the question of storage requirement, since much potential storage capacity might be unused or used inefficiently. But at least this method can help establish an upper bound on the requirements.

A second method for estimating the storage requirements for emergent intelligence is to measure the information in symbolic knowledge by some form of statistical sampling. For instance, it is possible to estimate the size of an individual's vocabulary by testing him or her on words randomly sampled from a dictionary. The fraction of test words known by the individual is a good indication of the fraction of words that he or she knows in the complete dictionary. The estimated vocabulary size is the test fraction multiplied by the number of words in the dictionary. Such an experiment depends on having a predetermined body of knowledge against which to measure. For example, it would be possible to estimate how many facts in the *Encyclopaedia Britannica* were known by a given individual, but this would give no measure of facts known by the individual but not contained in the encyclopedia. The method is useful only in establishing a lower bound.

A related experiment is the game of twenty questions, in which one player identifies an object chosen by another by asking a series of twenty yes-or-no questions. Since each answer provides no more than a single bit of information, and since skillful players generally need to ask almost all of the twenty questions to correctly identify the chosen object, we can estimate that the number of allowable choices known in common by the two players is on the order of 2^{20}, or about one million. Of course, this measure is inaccurate because the questions are not perfect and the choices of objects are not random. It is possible that a refined version of the game could be developed and used to provide another lower bound.

A third approach to gauging the human brain's storage requirements for information in the symbolic portion of knowledge is to estimate the average rate of information acquisition and to calculate the amount that would accumulate over time. For example, experiments on memorizing random sequences of syllables indicate that the maximum rate of memorization of this type of knowledge is about one "chunk" per second. A chunk, in this context, can be safely assumed to contain less than 100 bits of information, so the results suggest that the maximum rate at which a human is able to commit information to long-term memory is significantly less than 100 bits per second.[2] If this is true, a twenty-year-old human learning at the maximum rate for sixteen hours a day (and never forgetting) would know less than 50 billion bits of information. I find this number surprisingly small.

A difficulty with this estimate of the rate of acquisition is that the experiment measures only information coming through one sensory channel under one particular set of circumstances. The visual system sends more than a million times this rate of information to the optic nerve, and it is conceivable that all of this information is committed to memory. If it turns out that images are stored directly, it will be necessary to significantly increase the 100-bit-per-second limit, but there is no current evidence that this is the case. In experiments measuring the ability of exceptional individuals to store eidetic (i.e., extraordinarily accurate and vivid) images of random-dot stereograms, the subjects are given about five minutes to memorize an image formed in a square array of 100×100 dots. Memorizing only a few hundred bits is probably sufficient to pass the test.

I am aware of no evidence suggesting that more than a few bits per second of any type of information can be committed to long-term memory. Even if we accept reports of extraordinary feats of memory (such as those of Luria's showman in *Mind of the Mnemonist*[3]) at face value, the average rate of commitment to memory never seems to exceed a few bits per second; experiments should be able to refine this estimate. Even if we knew the maximum rate of memorization exactly, the rate averaged over a lifetime would probably be very much less—but knowing the maximum rate would establish an upper bound on the requirements of storage.

The sketchy data cited above suggests that an intelligent machine would require 10^9 bits of storage, plus or minus two orders of magnitude. This assumes that the information is encoded in such a way that it requires a minimum amount of storage; for the purpose of processing information, this would probably not be the most practical representation. As a would-be builder of thinking machines, I find this number encouragingly small, since it is well within the range of current electronic computers. As a human with an ego, I find it distressing: I do not like to think that my entire lifetime of memories could be placed on a reel of magnetic tape. It is to be hoped that experimental evidence will clear this up one way or another.

There are a few subtleties in the question of storage requirements that involve defining the quantity of information in a way that is independent of its representation. Information theory provides a precise way of measuring information in terms of bits, but it requires a measure of the probabilities over the ensemble of possible states. That is, it requires assigning an a priori probability to each possible set of knowledge, which is the role of inherited intelligence. Inherited intelligence provides a framework in which the knowledge of acquired intelligence can be interpreted. Inherited intelligence defines what is knowable; acquired intelligence determines what of the knowable is known.

Another potential difficulty is how to count the storage of information that can be deduced from other data. In the strict information-theoretical sense, data that can be inferred from other data add no information at all. An accurate measure would have to take into account the possibility that knowledge is inconsistent, and that only limited inferences are actually made. These are the kinds of issues currently being studied on the symbolic side of the field of artificial intelligence.

One issue that does not need to be resolved to measure storage capacity is localized versus distributed representation—that is, whether each piece of information is stored in a specific place or spread "holographically" over a large area. Knowing what types of representation are used in what parts of the human brain is of considerable scientific interest, but it does not have a profound impact on the amount of storage in the system or on our ability to measure it. Nontechnical commentators have a tendency to attribute almost mystical qualities to distributed storage mechanisms such as those used in creating holograms and neural networks, but the limitations on the capacities of these storage mechanisms are well understood.

When a holographic plate is cut in two, each half contains a slightly degraded version of the entire image. Distributed representations with properties similar to holograms are often used within conventional digital computers, and they are invisible to most users except in the system's capacity to tolerate errors. The error-correcting memory system used in most computers is a good example. The system is composed of many physically separate memory chips, but any single chip can be removed without losing any data. This is because the data are not stored in any one place, but in a distributed, nonlocal representation across all of the units. In spite of this "holographic" representation, the information storage capacity of the system is no greater than it would be with a conventional representation, in which each piece of data is stored in a single chip. In fact, it is slightly less. This is typical of distributed representations.

Storage capacity offers one measure of the requirements of a humanlike emergent intelligence. Another measure is the required rate of computation. Here there is no agreed-upon metric, and it is particularly difficult to define a unit of measure that is completely independent of representation. The measure suggested below is simple and important, if not sufficient.

Given an efficiently stored representation of human knowledge, what rate of access to that storage (in bits per second) is required to achieve humanlike performance? Here, *efficiently stored representation* means any representation requiring only a multiplicative constant of storage over the number of bits of information. This is a mathematical restriction that eliminates, for example, any representation that stores a precomputed answer to every question. Such a restriction does limit the range of possible representations, but it allows most representations that we would regard as reasonable. In particular, it allows both distributed and local representations.

The question of the memory bandwidth required for humanlike performance is accessible by experiment through approaches similar to those outlined for the question of storage capacity. If the time required for a primitive operation of human memory is limited by the firing time of a neuron, then the ratio of this "cycle time" to the total number of bits indicates what fraction of the memory is accessed simultaneously. This gives an indication of whether the brain is a parallel or a serial device. In a serial device, data items are operated on sequentially, one at a time. In a parallel device, all data are operated on concurrently. Both serial and parallel behaviors are exhibited by the brain, but there is a question as to which model best describes the way that it reasons and accesses knowledge. Informed opinions differ greatly in this matter, but the bulk of the quantitative evidence favors serial computation. Memory retrieval times for items in lists, for example, depend on the position and the number of items in the list. Except for sensory processing, most successful artificial intelligence programs have been based on serial models of computation, although this may be a distortion caused by the common availability of serial machines.

My own guess is that the reaction-time experiments are misleading and that human-level performance will require that large fractions of knowledge be accessed several times per second. Given a representation of acquired intelligence with a realistic representation efficiency of 10 percent, the 10^9 bits of memory mentioned earlier would require a memory bandwidth of about 10^{11} bits per second. This bandwidth seems physiologically plausible, since it corresponds to about a bit per second per neuron in the cerebral cortex.

By way of comparison, the memory bandwidth of a conventional sequential computer is in the range of 10^6 to 10^8 bits per second. This is less than 0.1 percent of the imagined requirement. For parallel computers the bandwidth is considerably higher. For example, a 65,536-processor Connection Machine can access its memory at approximately 10^{11} bits per second.[4] It is not entirely coincidence that this fits well with the estimate above.

Another important question is, What sensory-motor functions are necessary to sustain symbolic intelligence? An ape is a complex sensory-motor machine, and it is possible that much of this complexity is necessary to sustain intelligence. Large portions of the brain seem to be devoted to visual, auditory, and motor processing, and it is unknown how much of this machinery is needed for thought. A person who is blind and deaf or totally paralyzed can undoubtedly be intelligent, but this does not prove that the portion of the brain devoted to these functions is unnecessary for thought. It may be, for example, that a blind person takes advantage of the visual processing apparatus of the brain for spatial reasoning.

As we begin to understand more of the functional architecture of the brain, it should be possible to identify certain functions as being unnecessary for thought by studying patients whose cognitive abilities are unaffected by locally confined damage to the brain. For example, binocular stereo fusion is known to take place in a specific area of the cortex near the back of the head. Patients with damage to this area of the cortex have visual handicaps but show no obvious impairment in their ability to think. This suggests that stereo fusion is not necessary for thought. This is a simple example, and the conclusion is not surprising, but it should be possible by such experiments to establish that many sensory-motor functions are unnecessary. One can imagine metaphorically whittling away at the brain until it is reduced to its essential core. Of course, it is not quite this simple. Accidental damage rarely incapacitates a single area of the brain completely and exclusively. Also, it may be difficult to eliminate one function at a time because one mental capacity may compensate for the lack of another.

It may be more productive to assume that all sensory-motor apparatus is unnecessary until proven useful for thought, but this is contrary to the usual point of view. Our current understanding of the phylogenetic development of the nervous system suggests a point of view in which intelligence is an elaborate refinement of the connection between input and output. This is reinforced by the experimental convenience of studying simple nervous systems, or of studying complicated nervous systems by concentrating on those portions most directly related to input and output. By necessity, most everything we know about the function of the nervous system comes from experiments on those portions that are closely related to sensory inputs or motor outputs. It would not be surprising to learn that we have overestimated the importance of these functions to intelligent thought.

Sensory-motor functions are clearly important for the application of intelligence and for its evolution, but these issues are separate from whether sensory-motor functions are necessary for thought to exist. Intelligence would not be of much use without an elaborate system of sensory apparatus to measure the environment and an elaborate system of motor apparatus to change it, nor would it have been likely to evolve. But much more apparatus is probably necessary to exercise and evolve intelligence than to sustain it. One can believe in the necessity of the opposable thumb for the development of intelligence without doubting a human capacity for thumbless thought. It is quite possible that even the meager sensory-motor capabilities that we currently know how to create artificially would be sufficent for the fundamental operation of emergent intelligence.

Although questions of capacity and scope are necessary in defining the magnitude of the task of constructing an emergent intelligence, the key question is one of understanding. While it is possible that we will be able to recreate the emergent substrate of intelligence without fully understanding the details of how it works, it seems likely that we would at least need to understand some of its principles. There are at least three paths by which such understanding could be achieved. One is to study the properties of specific emergent systems—to build a theory of their capabilities and limitations. This kind of experimental study is currently being conducted on several classes of promising man-made systems, including neural networks, spin glasses, cellular automata, evolutionary systems, and adaptive automata. Another possible path to understanding is the study of biological systems, which are our only real examples of intelligence and our only examples of an emergent system that has produced intelligence. The disciplines that have so far provided the most useful information of this type have been neurophysiology, cognitive psychology, and evolutionary biology. A third path would be a theoretical understanding of the requirements of intelligence or of the phenomena of emergence. Relevant examples are theories of logic and computability, linguistics, and dynamical systems theory. Anyone who looks to emergent systems as a way of defending human thought from the scrutiny of science is likely to be disappointed.

One cannot conclude, however, that a reductionist understanding is necessary for the creation of intelligence. Even a little understanding could go a long way toward the construction of an emergent system. A good example of this is how cellular automata have been used to simulate the emergent behavior of fluids. The whirlpools that form as a fluid flows past a barrier are not well understood analytically, yet they are of great practical importance in the design of boats and airplanes. Equations that describe the flow of a fluid have been known for almost a century, but except for a few simple cases they cannot be solved. In practice the flow is generally analyzed by simulation. The most common method of simulation is the numerical solution of continuous equations.

On a highly parallel computer it is possible to simulate fluids with even less understanding of the system by simulating billions of colliding particles that reproduce emergent phenomena such as vortices. Calculating the detailed molecular interactions of so many particles would be extremely difficult, but a few simple aspects of the system, such as conservations of energy and particle number, are sufficient to reproduce the large-scale behavior. A system of simplified particles that obey these two laws but are otherwise unrealistic can reproduce the same emergent phenomena as reality. For example, it is possible to use particles of unit mass that move only at unit speed along a hexagonal lattice, colliding according to the rules of billiard balls.[5] Experiments show that this model produces laminar flow, vortex streams, and even turbulence that is indistinguishable from the behavior of real fluids. Although the detailed rules of interaction are very different from the interactions of real molecules, the emergent phenomena are the same. The emergent phenomena can be created without understanding the details of the forces between the molecules or the equations that describe the flow of the fluid.

The recreation of intricate patterns of ebbs and flows within a fluid demonstrates that it is possible to produce a phenomenon without fully understanding it. But the model was constructed by physicists who knew a lot about fluids. That knowledge helped to determine which features of the physical system were important to implement and which were not.

Physics is an unusually exact science. Perhaps a better example of an emergent system that we can simulate with only a limited understanding is evolutionary biology. We understand, in a weak sense, how creatures with Mendelian patterns of inheritance and different propensities for survival can evolve toward better fitness in their environments. In certain simple situations we can even write down equations that describe how quickly this adaptation will take place.[6] But there are many gaps in our understanding of the processes of evolution. We can explain why flying animals have light bones in terms of natural selection, but we cannot explain why certain animals have evolved flight while others have not. We have some qualitative understanding of the forces that cause evolutionary change, but (except in the simplest cases) we cannot explain the rate or even the direction of that change.

In spite of these limitations, our understanding is sufficient to write programs of simulated evolution that show interesting emergent behaviors. For example, I have recently been using an evolutionary simulation to evolve programs to sort numbers. In this system, the genetic material of each simulated individual is interpreted as a program specifying a pattern of comparisons and exchanges. The probability of an individual survival in the system is dependent on the efficiency and accuracy of this program in sorting numbers. Surviving individuals produce offspring by sexual combination of their genetic material with occasional random mutation. After tens of thousands of generations, a population of hundreds of thousands of such individuals will evolve very efficient programs for sorting. Although I wrote the simulation that produced these sorting programs, I do not understand in detail how they were produced or how they work. If the simulation had not produced working programs, I would have had very little idea about how to fix it.

The fluid flow and simulated evolution examples suggest that it is possible to make a great deal of use of a small amount of under-standing. The emergent behaviors exhibited by these systems are a consequence of the simple underlying rules defined by the program. Although the systems succeed in producing the desired results, their detailed behaviors are beyond our ability to analyze and predict. One can imagine that if a similar process produced a system of emergent intelligence, we would have a similar lack of understanding about how it worked.

My own guess is that such an emergent system would not be an intelligent system itself, but rather the metabolic substrate on which intelligence might grow. In terms of the apes and the songs, the emergent portion of the system would play the role of the ape, or at least that part of the ape that hosts the songs. This artificial mind would need to be inoculated with human knowledge. I imagine this process to be not so different from teaching a child. This would be a tricky and uncertain procedure because, like a child, this emergent mind would presumably be susceptible to bad ideas as well as good. The result would be not so much an artificial intelligence, but rather a human intelligence sustained within an artificial mind.

Of course, I understand that this is just a dream, and I will admit that I am propelled more by hope than by the probability of success. But if this artificial mind can sustain itself and grow of its own accord, then for the first time human thought will live free of bones and flesh, giving this child of mind an earthly immortality denied to us.

ENDNOTES

[1]Freeman Dyson, *The Origins of Life* (Cambridge: Cambridge University Press, 1985).
[2]Allen Newell, *Human Problem Solving* (Englewood Cliffs, N.J.: Prentice Hall, 1972).
[3]A. R. Luria, *Mind of the Mnemonist* (New York: Basic Books, 1968).
[4]Daniel W. Hillis, *The Connection Machine* (Cambridge: MIT Press, 1985).
[5]Stephen Wolfram, *Theory of Applications of Cellular Automata* (World Scientific, 1986).
[6]J. B. S. Haldane, *The Causes of Evolution* (Harper & Brothers, 1932).

David L. Waltz

The Prospects for Building Truly Intelligent Machines

C AN ARTIFICIAL INTELLIGENCE be achieved? If so, how
soon? By what methods? What ideas from current AI research will in the long run be important contributions to a
science of cognition? I believe that AI can be achieved, perhaps within
our lifetimes, but that we have major scientific and engineering
obstacles to hurdle if it is to come about. The methods and perspective of AI have been dramatically skewed by the existence of the
common digital computer, sometimes called the von Neumann
machine, and ultimately, AI will have to be based on ideas and
hardware quite different from what is currently central to it. Memory, for instance, is much more important than its role in AI so far
suggests, and search has far less importance than we have given it.
Also, because computers lack bodies and life experiences comparable
to humans', intelligent systems will probably be inherently different
from humans; I speculate briefly on what such systems might be like.

OBSTACLES TO BUILDING INTELLIGENT SYSTEMS

If we are to build machines that are as intelligent as people, we have
three problems to solve: we must establish a science of cognition; we
must engineer the software, sensors, and effectors for a full system;
and we must devise adequate hardware.

*David L. Waltz, a professor of computer science at Brandeis University, is senior scientist and
director of advanced information systems at Thinking Machines Corporation.*

Establishing a Science of Cognition

We have no suitable science of cognition. We have only fragments of the conception, and some of those are certainly incorrect. We know very little about how a machine would have to be organized to solve the problems of intelligence. Virtually all aspects of intelligence—including perception, memory, reasoning, intention, generation of action, and attention—are still mysterious. However, even if we understood how to structure an intelligent system, we would not be able to complete the system because we also lack an appropriate science of knowledge. For some aspects of knowledge, any computational device will be on a strong footing when compared with a person. Machine-readable encyclopedias, dictionaries, and texts will eventually allow machines to absorb book knowledge quite readily. For such understanding to be deep, however, a system needs perceptual grounding and an understanding of the physical and social world. For humans, much of this knowledge is either innate or organized and gathered by innate structures that automatically cause us to attend to certain features of our experience, which we then regard as important. It will be extremely difficult to characterize and build into a system the kinds of a priori knowledge or structuring principles humans have.

Engineering the Software

Any truly intelligent system must be huge and complex. As Frederick Brooks argues, writing on his experience building the large operating system OS360 at IBM, it is not possible to speed up a software project by simply putting more and more people on it.[1] The optimum team size for building software is about five people. For this reason, and because of the sheer scope of a project of this sort—which dwarfs any that have been attempted in programming to date—hand coding will certainly be too slow and unreliable to accomplish the whole task. Consequently, a truly intelligent system will have to be capable of learning much of its structure from experience.

What structures must be built into a system to allow it to learn? This is a central question for current AI, and the answer depends on issues of knowledge representation: How should knowledge be represented? Out of what components (if any) are knowledge structures built?

Creating the Hardware

We must be able to build hardware that is well matched to AI's knowledge representation and learning needs and that compares in power with the human brain. No one should be surprised that the puny machines AI has used thus far have not exhibited artificial intelligence. Even the most powerful current computers are probably no more than one four-millionth as powerful as the human brain. Moreover, current machines are probably at least as deficient in memory capacity: today's largest computers probably have no more than about one four-millionth of the memory capacity of the human brain. Even given these extreme discrepancies, hardware will probably prove the easiest part of the overall AI task to achieve.

I begin with a discussion of traditional AI and its theoretical underpinnings in order to set the stage for a discussion of the major paradigm shifts (or splits) currently under way in and around AI. As an advocate of the need for new paradigms, I here confess my bias. I see no way that traditional AI methods can be extended to achieve humanlike intelligence. Assuming that new paradigms will replace or be merged with the traditional ones, I make some projections about how soon intelligent systems can be built and what they may be like.

LIMITS OF TRADITIONAL AI

Two revolutionary paradigm shifts are occurring within artificial intelligence. A major force behind the shifts is the growing suspicion among researchers that current AI models are not likely to be extendable to a point that will bring about human-level intelligence. The shifts are toward massively parallel computers and toward massively parallel programs that are more taught than programmed. The resultant hardware and software systems seem in many ways more brainlike than the serial von Neumann machines and AI programs that we have become used to.

For thirty years, virtually all AI paradigms were based on variants of what Herbert Simon and Allen Newell have presented as "physical symbol system" and "heuristic search" hypotheses.[2] (See also the article by Hubert and Stuart Dreyfus in this issue of *Dædalus*.)

According to the physical symbol system hypothesis, symbols (wordlike or numerical entities—the names of objects and events) are the primitive objects of the mind; by some unknown process, the brain mimics a "logical inference engine," whose most important feature is that it is able to manipulate symbols (that is, to remember, interpret, modify, combine, and expand upon them); and computer models that manipulate symbols therefore capture the essential operation of the mind. In this argument it does not matter whether the materials out of which this inference engine is built are transistors or neurons. The only important thing is that they be capable of a universal set of logical operations.[3] The physical symbol system hypothesis in turn rests on a foundation of mathematical results on computability, which can be used to show that if a machine is equivalent to a Turing machine—a simple kind of computational model devised by the pioneering British mathematician Alan Turing—then it is "universal"; that is, the machine can compute anything that can be computed. All ordinary digital computers can be shown to be universal in Turing's sense.*

In the heuristic search model, problems of cognition are instances of the problem of exploring a space of possibilities for a solution. The search space for heuristic search problems can be visualized as a branching tree: starting from the tree's root, each alternative considered and each decision made corresponds to a branching point of the tree. Heuristics, or rules of thumb, allow search to be focused first on branches that are likely to provide a solution, and thus prevent a combinatorially explosive search of an entire solution space.[†] Heuristic search programs are easy to implement on ordinary serial digital computers. Heuristic search has been used for a wide variety of applications, including decision making, game playing, robot planning and problem solving, natural-language processing, and the classification of perceptual objects. Heuristic search has enjoyed particular prominence, for it is at the heart of "expert systems," AI's greatest commercial success by far.

---

*There is perhaps one critical aspect in which all computers fail to match a Turing machine: the Turing machine includes an infinite tape, from which it reads its programs and onto which it writes its results. All computers (and presumably humans) have finite memories.

†Combinatorially explosive problems are problems in which the computational costs of solving each slightly more difficult problem grow so rapidly that no computer will ever be able to solve them; that is, even a computer with as many components as there are electrons in the universe and an instruction execution time as short as the shortest measurable physical event might require times greater than the age of the universe to consider all possible problem solutions.

In retrospect it is remarkable how seriously heuristic search has been taken as a cognitive model. When I was a graduate student in the late 1960s, the standard AI view was that for any intelligent system, the nature of a problem constrains the nature of any efficient solution, and that any system, human or computer, given a problem to solve, tends to evolve a similar, or at least an analogous, internal structure to deal with it. Thus, it was argued, studying efficient problem solutions on computers is a good way to study cognition.[4] Virtually everyone in AI at the time accepted the centrality and immutability of heuristic search machinery unquestioningly and assumed that learning should be accomplished by evolving, adapting, or adding to the heuristics and the knowledge structures of the search space. (The exceptions were the "neural net" and "perceptron" researchers, who had been actively exploring more brainlike models since the early 1950s. More on this later.)

It is now commonly recognized that the nature of the computers and computing models available to us inevitably constrains the problem-solving algorithms that we can consider. (John Backus introduced this idea to the broad computing community in his Turing Award lecture of 1977.[5]) As explained below, it has become clear that traditional AI methods do not scale up well and that new AI paradigms will therefore be needed. Despite this change in attitude, there have been few prospective replacements within AI for heuristic search (or for serial, single-processor digital computers) until very recently.

The reasons AI has focused almost exclusively on the physical symbol system and heuristic search views are deeply rooted in its history and in part reflect the myopic concentration on serial digital computers that has characterized all of computer science. The focus on heuristic search also reflects the influence of the psychological research of the 1950s. AI began at a time when psychologists were much enamored of protocol analysis, a way of examining human behavior by having subjects give accounts of their mental experience while they are solving problems.[6] Such psychological research was interpreted as evidence that the main human mechanism for problem solving is trial and error. AI adapted this model as its heuristic search paradigm. In this paradigm problems are solved by sequentially applying "operators" (elementary steps in a problem solution) and allowing "backtracking," a form of trial and error whereby a program backs up to an earlier decision point and tries new branches if the first ones explored prove fruitless.

It is difficult to see how any extension of heuristic-search–based systems could ever demonstrate common sense. In most AI systems, problem statements have come from users; the systems have not needed to decide what problems to work on. They have had relatively few actions or operators available, so search spaces have been tractable. Real-time performance hasn't generally been necessary. This way of operating will clearly not do in general. Eventually, AI must face the scale-up question: Given the immense range of possible situations a truly intelligent system could find itself in and the vast number of possible actions available to it, how could the system ever manage to search out appropriate goals and actions?

Moreover, as John McCarthy has pointed out, rule-based systems may be inherently limited by the "qualification problem": given a certain general rule, one can always alter the world situation in such a way that the rule is no longer appropriate.[7] For example, suppose we offered the rule:

$$bird \ (x) \rightarrow fly \ (x) \quad \text{(if } x \text{ is a bird, then } x \text{ can fly).}$$

Everyone knows that the rule must be amended to cover birds such as penguins and ostriches, so that it becomes:

> *not flightless (x) and bird (x)* $\rightarrow$ *fly (x)*, where
> "flightless *(x)*" is true of the appropriate birds.

However, we also know a bird cannot fly if it is dead, or if its wings have been pinioned, or if its feet are embedded in cement, or if it has been conditioned by being given electric shocks each time it tries to fly.[8] There seems to be no way to ever completely specify rules for such cases. There are also serious difficulties in formulating rules for deciding which facts about the world ought to be retracted and which should still hold after particular events or actions have occurred. This is known as the "frame problem." "Nonmonotonic logic," which treats all new propositions or rules as retractable hypotheses, has been proposed for dealing with these problems.[9] However, some researchers in this area[10] are pessimistic about its potential, as am I.

By objecting to traditional AI approaches, I am not disputing the notions of universal computation or the Turing machine results, which are established mathematically beyond doubt. Rather, I dispute the heuristic search metaphor, the relationship between physical symbol systems and human cognition, and the nature and "granularity" of the units of thought. The physical symbol system hypothesis, also long shared by AI researchers, is that a vocabulary close to natural language (English, for example, perhaps supplemented by previously unnamed categories and concepts) would be sufficient to express all concepts that ever need to be expressed. My belief is that natural-language–like terms are, for some concepts, hopelessly coarse and vague, and that much finer, "subsymbolic" distinctions must be made, especially for encoding sensory inputs. At the same time, some mental units (for example, whole situations or events—often remembered as mental images) seem to be important carriers of meaning that may not be reducible to tractable structures of words or wordlike entities. Even worse, I believe that words are not in any case carriers of complete meanings but are instead more like index terms or cues that a speaker uses to induce a listener to extract shared memories and knowledge. The degree of detail and number of units needed to express the speaker's knowledge and intent and the hearer's understanding are vastly greater than the number of words used to communicate. In this sense language may be like the game of charades: the speaker transmits relatively little, and the listener generates understanding through the synthesis of the memory items evoked by the speaker's clues. Similarly, I believe that the words that seem widely characteristic of human streams of consciousness do not themselves constitute thought; rather, they represent a projection of our thoughts onto our speech-production faculties. Thus, for example, we may feel happy or embarrassed without ever forming those words, or we may solve a problem by imagining a diagram without words or with far too few words to specify the diagram.

WHAT'S THE ALTERNATIVE?

Craig Stanfill and I have argued at length elsewhere that humans may well solve problems by a process much more like *lookup* than *search*, and that the items looked up may be much more like representations of specific or stereotyped episodes and objects than like rules and facts.[11]

On the Connection Machine, built by Thinking Machines Corporation,[12] we have now implemented several types of "associative memory" systems that reason on the basis of previous experience.[13] For example, one experimental system solves medical diagnosis problems with "memory-based reasoning": given a set of symptoms and patient characteristics, the system finds the most similar previous patients and hypothesizes that the same diagnoses should be given to the new patient. "Connectionist," or neural net, models, which I shall describe later, solve similar problems, though in a very different manner. While a great deal of research is still required before such systems can become serious candidates for truly intelligent systems, I believe that these architectures may prove far easier to build and extend than heuristic search models. These new models can learn and reason by remembering and generalizing specific examples; heuristic search models, in contrast, depend on rules. It has proved difficult to collect rules from experts—people are generally not even aware of using rules. We do not know how to check sets of rules for completeness and self-consistency. Moreover, a finite set of rules cannot capture all the possible conclusions that may be drawn from a set of examples any more than a set of descriptive sentences can completely describe a picture.

It is important to note, however, that some kinds of knowledge in rule-based systems are hard to encode in our memory-based model. For instance, as currently formulated, our system does not use patients' histories and is unable to figure out that medication dose size ought to be a function of a patient's weight. Recent research strongly suggests that humans reason largely from stereotypes and from specific variations of these stereotypes. Our system does not yet demonstrate such abilities.

IMPLEMENTING ASSOCIATIVE MEMORY SYSTEMS

In the short run, associative memory models can very nicely complement AI models. Associative models have been studied for quite a while but seldom implemented (except for very small problems) because they are computationally very expensive to run on traditional digital computers. One class of associative memory implementation is called the connectionist, or neural net, model. Such systems are direct descendents of the neural net models of the 1950s. In them, thousands of processing units, each analogous to a neuron, are interconnected by links, each analogous to a synaptic connection between neurons. Each link has a "weight," or a connection strength. A system's knowledge is encoded in link weights and in the interconnection pattern of the system. Some units serve as input units, some as output units, and others as "hidden units" (they are connected only to other units and thus cannot be "seen" from either the input or the output channels).

Such networks display three interesting abilities. The first is *learning*. Several methods have now been devised that enable such a system, upon being given particular inputs, to be taught to produce any desired outputs. The second interesting ability is *associative recall*. Once trained to associate an output with a certain input, a network can, given some fraction of an input, produce a full pattern as its output. The third interesting property is *fault tolerance:* the network continues to operate even when some of the units are removed or damaged. In short, connectionist computing systems have many of the properties that we have associated with brains; these systems differ significantly from computers, which have traditionally been viewed as automatons with literal minds, able to do only what they are programmed to do.[14]

These networks can now be implemented efficiently on such massively parallel hardware as the Connection Machine system or by using custom chips. While associative memory systems have been simulated on traditional serial digital computers, the simulations have been very slow; a serial computer must simulate each of the computational units and links in turn and must do so many times to carry out a single calculation. A massively parallel machine can provide a separate small processor for each of the units in the associative memory system and can thus operate much more rapidly.

Stanfill and I have been exploring a functionally similar massively parallel method called memory-based reasoning. In this type of reasoning, a Connection Machine is loaded with a large data base of situations. Each situation in the data base contains both a set of attributes and an outcome. In a medical data base, for instance, the attributes would be symptoms and a patient's characteristics, and the outcome would be a diagnosis or a treatment. Each item in the data base is stored in a separate processor. When a new example to be classified is encountered, its properties are broadcast to all the processors that hold situations; each of these processors compares its situation with the input situation and computes a score of nearness to the input. The system then finds the nearest matches to the input example and, provided they are sufficiently close, uses the outcomes of these matching items to classify the new example.

Memory-based reasoning systems also have many desirable characteristics. They are fault tolerant; they can generalize well to examples that have never been seen in their exact form before; they give measurements of the closeness of the precedents to the current example, which can serve as measures of confidence for the match. If there is an exact match with a previous example, the systems can give a decision with certainty. It is easy to teach such systems: one simply adds more items to their data bases.

The complicated part of memory-based reasoning systems is the computation of nearness. To calculate the similarity of any memory example to the pattern to be classified, each memory item must first find the distance, or difference, between each of its attribute values and the attribute values of the pattern to be classified. These distances in turn depend on the statistical distribution of attribute values and on the degree of correlation between each attribute value and the outcomes with which it simultaneously occurs. All the distances for each attribute must then be combined for each memory item to arrive at its total distance from the item to be classified. Thus, computing the nearness score involves a great deal of statistical calculation across all records in the data base.[15]

What is the role of associative memory systems in traditional artificial intelligence? While they can substitute for expert systems under certain circumstances, connectionist and memory-based reasoning systems are better viewed as complements to traditional AI than as replacements for it. In one very useful mode, associative memory systems can be used to propose or hypothesize solutions to complex problems, and traditional AI systems can be used to verify that the differences between the problems that are currently being attacked and examples in the data base are unimportant. If such differences are important, the associative memory systems can propose subgoals to attempt. Thus, the associative memory process can provide a very powerful heuristic method for jumping to conclusions, while traditional AI can be used to verify or disconfirm such conclusions. Such hybrid systems could help AI models avoid the problems of searching combinatorially large spaces. Because of the computational resources required, the bulk of the computing power in an AI system of this sort would probably reside in the associative memory portion.

In the long run, however, such models are still unlikely to provide a satisfactory explanation for the operations of human thought, though I suspect they will come much closer than AI has. To my mind, the best exposition on the ultimate architecture required is Marvin Minsky's "society of mind."[16] Minsky argues persuasively, using a very wide range of types of evidence, that the brain and the mind are made up of a very large number of modules organized like a bureaucracy. Each module, or "demon," in the bureaucracy has only limited responsibilities and very limited knowledge; demons constantly watch for events of interest to themselves and act only when such events occur. These events may be external (signaled by sensory units) or purely internal (the result of other internal demons that have recognized items of interest to themselves). Actions of demons can either influence other demons or activate effectors and can thereby influence the outside world. One can make a simple analogy between a society of mind and associative memory models: in memory-based reasoning each data base item would correspond to an agent; in a connectionist model, each neural unit would correspond to an agent.

LOGICAL REASONING

I believe logical reasoning is not the foundation on which cognition is built but an emergent behavior that results from observing a sufficient number of regularities in the world. Thus, if a society of demonlike agents exhibits logical behavior, its behavior can be described by rules, although the system contains no rules to govern its operation. It operates in a regular fashion because it simulates the world's regularities.

Consider a developing infant. In the society-of-mind model, the infant first develops a large number of independent agencies that encode knowledge of the behavior of specific items in the physical world: when a block is dropped, it falls; when the child cries, its parent comes to attend; when the child touches a flame, it feels pain. Each of these examples is handled initially by a separate small bureaucracy of agents. Each bureaucracy represents the memory of some specific event. A particular agency becomes responsible for an episode because of the initial "wiring" of the brain; shortly after an agency is first activated, it changes its synaptic weights, so that any new event that activates any part of the agency will cause the entire agency to be reactivated. When similar events reactivate these agencies, new bureaucracies encoding the similarities and differences between the new and the old events are constructed out of previously unused, but closely connected (hence activated), agents. After many such incremental additions to the society of agents, a child eventually develops agents for abstract categories and rules; cuts, pinches, and burns all cause pain, and thus other agents that happen to be activated in these cases become associated with the concept of pain. Eventually, the concepts of the constant conjunction of pain with its various causes become the specialty of particular "expert" agents responsible for certain regularities in the world. Ultimately, these agents become part of the bureaucracy for the concept of causality itself. Thus agents come to reason about very general categories, no longer necessarily rooted directly in experience, and can understand abstract causal relationships. Take pain in the abstract, for example: if one breaks a law and is apprehended, one knows one will probably be punished; if one does not keep promises, one understands that other people may be angry and may retaliate; and so on.

On the surface it might seem that what is being proposed is to replace a single expert program with many expert programs, arranged in a hierarchy. However, each of the expert agents is extremely simple, in the sense that it "knows" only about one thing. The experts are connected to a perceptual system and to each other in such a way that they are triggered only when the conditions about which they are expert are actually satisfied.

While this may be a satisfactory description of the composition of the mind, it is not yet sufficiently precise to serve as a design for a very large-scale program that can organize itself to achieve intelligence. Programs that operate on the principles of the society of mind may well be the end point of many steps in the evolution of the design of intelligent systems. I believe that hybrids of associative memory and traditional AI programs for logical reasoning show the greatest promise in the near term for AI applications. It is possible that they will also prove to be useful models of cognition.[17]

LIMITS OF TRADITIONAL COMPUTER HARDWARE

Researchers' suspicion that current AI models may not be extensible to systems with human-level intelligence is not the only force driving the paradigm shift toward massively parallel computing models. Economic considerations, which transcend AI concerns, are another. Today's serial computers have begun to reach limits beyond which they cannot be speeded up at reasonable cost. For a serial, single-processor computer to operate more rapidly than at present, its processor must execute each instruction more rapidly. To accelerate processing, manufacturers have brought new, faster-acting materials into use. They have also shrunk circuits to smaller and smaller sizes so as to shorten signal paths, since internal communication speeds, and therefore overall processing rates, are limited by the speed of light. The smaller the computer, the faster its internal communications. Because each component generates heat, and because dense chips produce more heat than others, ultradense chips of exotic materials often require the addition of elaborate and expensive cooling systems. All this means that doubling the power of a serial machine usually increases its cost by more than a factor of two— sometimes much more.

In contrast, parallel designs promise the possibility of doubling power by simply doubling the number of processors, possibly for less than two times the cost, since many system components (disk storage units, power supplies, control logic, and so on) can be shared by all processors, no matter how numerous. For example, the Connection Machine system contains up to 65,536 processors. Even in its initial version, the Connection Machine is very inexpensive in terms of the number of dollars it costs per unit of computation; its cost in relation to its performance is about one-twentieth that of serial supercomputers.* Moreover, the cost of highly parallel processors is likely to drop dramatically. Initially, any chip is expensive because of

---

*The cost/performance figure is the cost per standard computing operation. The typical standard computing operation is either a fixed-point addition or a floating-point multiplication. Fixed-point performance is measured in millions of instructions per second (MIPS). Floating-point performance is measured in millions of floating operations per second (MFLOPS— pronounced "megaflops"). Cost/performance is measured in dollars per MIPS or dollars per MFLOPS.

low yield (only a fraction of usable chips results from initial production) and the need to recover research, design, and development costs. The price of chips follows a "learning curve," a drop-off in cost as a function of the number of chips fabricated. Memory is the prime example: the cost per bit of memory storage has dropped by a factor of ten every five years for thirty-five years running, yielding a cost that is one ten-millionth that of the 1950 price—one one-hundred millionth after adjustment for inflation! Since the processors of a massively parallel computer are mass-produced, as memory chips are, the cost of a given amount of processing power for parallel machines should drop as rapidly as the cost of memory—that is, very rapidly indeed.

The cost of computer systems involves, of course, both hardware and software. How is one to program a machine with tens of thousands or perhaps millions of processors? Clearly, human programmers cannot afford the time or the money to write a program for each processor. There seem to be two practical ways to program such machines. The first, which has been in most use to date, is to write a single program and have each processor execute it in synchrony, each processor working on its own portion of the data. This method is "data-level parallelism." A second way is to program learning machines that can turn their experiences into a different code or data for each processor.

Research in machine learning has grown dramatically during the last few years. Researchers have identified perhaps a dozen distinctly different learning methods.[18] Many massively parallel learning schemes involve the connectionist, or neural net, models mentioned earlier. Connectionist systems have usually been taught with some form of supervised learning: an input and a desired output are both presented to a system, which then adjusts the internal connection strengths among its neuronlike units so as to closely match the desired input-output behavior. Given a sufficiently large number of trials, generally on the order of tens of thousands, such systems are able to learn to produce moderately complex desired behavior. For example, after starting from a completely random state and being trained repeatedly with a 4,500-word data base of sample pronunciations, a system called NETtalk was able to learn to pronounce novel English words with fairly good accuracy.[19]

The central problem to be solved in connectionist and society-of-mind learning research is the "credit assignment problem," the problem of apportioning simple rewards and punishments among a vast number of interconnected neuronlike computing elements. To show the relevance of this problem to the ultimate goals of AI, I will couch the problem in terms of the "brain" of a robotic system that we hope will learn through its experiences.

Assume a large set (perhaps billions) of independent neural-like processing elements interconnected with many links per element. Some elements are connected to sensors, driven by the outside world; others are connected to motor systems that can influence the outside world through robotic arms and legs or wheels, which generate physical acts, as well as through language-production facilities, which generate "speech acts." At any given time a subset of these elements is active; they form a complex pattern of activation over the entire network. A short time later, the activation pattern changes because of the mutual influences among processing elements and sensory inputs.

Some activation patterns trigger motor actions. Now and then rewards or punishments are given to the system. The credit assignment problem is this: which individual elements within the mass of perhaps trillions of elements should be altered on the basis of these rewards and punishments so the system will learn to perform more effectively—that is, so the situations that have led to punishments can be avoided in the future and so the system will more often find itself in situations that lead to rewards?

The credit assignment problem has at least two aspects. The simpler is the *static* credit assignment problem, in which rewards and punishments occur shortly after the actions that cause them. Such systems receive instant gratification and instant negative feedback. The static credit assignment problem has been found reasonably tractable: units that are active can be examined, and those that have been active in the correct direction have their connections with action systems strengthened, while those that have been inappropriately active have their connection strengths reduced. If the reward or punishment occurs substantially after the fact, however, we have a *temporal* credit assignment problem, which is significantly more difficult. To solve this problem, a system must keep memories of the past states through which it has passed and have the capacity to analyze and make judgments about which earlier states were responsible for the rewards and punishments. Progress on the temporal credit assignment problem has been promising, but much remains to be done before it can be considered solved.[20]

In my estimation, these learning methods will only be suitable for producing modules of an overall intelligent system. A truly intelligent system must contain many modules. It seems very unlikely that the organization of an entire brain or mind could be automatically learned, starting with a very large, randomly interconnected system. Infants are highly organized at birth. They do not, for instance, have to learn to see or hear in any sense that we would recognize as learning. Their auditory and visual systems seem already organized to be able to extract meaningful units (objects, events, sounds, shapes, and so on). Elizabeth Spelke and her research associates have found that two-month-old infants are able to recognize the coherence of objects and that they show surprise when objects disappear or apparently move through each other.[21] At that age they cannot have learned about the properties of objects through tactile experience. It is not too surprising that such abilities can be "prewired" in the brain: newborn horses and cattle are able to walk, avoid bumping into objects, and find their mother's milk within minutes of birth. In any case, the necessity for providing intelligent systems with a priori sensory organization seems inescapable. On what other basis could we learn from scratch what the meaningful units of the world are?[22]

THE FUTURE OF ARTIFICIAL INTELLIGENCE

Any extrapolation of current trends forces one to conclude that it will take a very long time indeed to achieve systems that are as intelligent as humans. Nevertheless, the performance of the fastest computers seems destined to increase at a much greater rate than it has over the last thirty years, and the cost/performance figures for large-scale computers will certainly drop.

The effect of a great deal more processing power should be highly significant for AI. As claimed earlier, current machines probably have only one four-millionth the amount of computing power that the human brain has. However, it is quite conceivable that within about twenty-five years we could build machines with comparable power for affordable prices (for the purposes of this argument, let an affordable price be $20 million, the cost of today's most expensive supercomputer).

The Connection Machine system, currently probably the fastest in the world, can carry out the kinds of calculations we think the brain uses at the rate of about 3.6×10^{12} bits a second, a factor of about twenty million away from matching the brain's power (as estimated by Jack Schwartz in his article in this issue of *Dædalus*). One may build a more powerful Connection Machine system simply by plugging several of them together. The current machine costs about $4 million, so within our $20 million budget, a machine of about five times its computing power (or 1.8×10^{13} bits per second) could be built. Such a machine would be a factor of four million short. The stated goal of the DARPA (Defense Advanced Research Projects Agency) Strategic Computing Initiative is to achieve a thousandfold increase in computing power over the next ten years, and there is good reason to expect that this goal can be achieved. In particular, the Connection Machine system achieves its computation rates without yet using exotic materials or extreme miniaturization, the factors that have enabled us to so dramatically speed up traditional computers. If a speedup of one thousand times every ten years can be achieved, a computer comparable in processing power to the brain could be built for $20 million by 2012.

Using Schwartz's estimates, we find that the total memory capacity of the brain is 4×10^{16} bytes. The current Connection Machine can contain up to two gigabytes (2×10^9 bytes). In today's computer world, two gigabytes of memory is considered a large amount, yet this is a factor of twenty million short, or a factor of four million short for a system with five Connection Machines.

At today's prices, two gigabytes of memory costs roughly $1 million, so to buy enough memory to match human capacity would cost on the order of $20 trillion, roughly ten times our current national debt. Given its long-term price decline of roughly a factor of ten every five years, the cost of 4×10^{16} bytes of memory will be in the $20 million range within thirty years, so that the time at which we might expect to build a computer with the potential to match human intelligence would be around the year 2017.* As suggested earlier,

---

*Well before the 2017 date, however, mass storage devices (disk units and other storage media) will certainly be capable of storing this much material at an affordable price.

however, building the hardware may be the easiest part; the need to untangle the mysteries of the structure and functioning of the mind, to gather the knowledge both innate and learned, and to engineer the software for the entire system will probably require time that goes well beyond 2017. Once we have a piece of hardware with brain-level power and appropriate a priori structure, it still might take as long as the twenty years humans require to reach adult-level mental competence! More than one such lengthy experiment is likely to be required.

What could we expect the intelligence of such powerful machines to be like? Almost certainly they will seem alien when compared with people. In some ways such machines will eclipse maximum human performance, much as pocket calculators outperform humans in arithmetic calculation. The new machines may have perfect recall of vast quantities of information, something that is not possible for people. (While humans apparently have vast amounts of memory, we are quite poor at the literal memorization of words, images, names, and details of events.) Unless deliberately programmed in, such machines would not have a repertoire of recognizable human emotions. Nor would they have motivation in any ordinary human sense. Motivation and drive seem to be based on innate mechanisms developed over eons of evolution to ensure that we make species-preserving decisions—to avoid pain, continue to eat and drink, get enough sleep, reproduce, care for our young, act altruistically (especially toward relatives and friends)—without requiring that we understand that the real reason for carrying out these actions is species preservation.[23] (It is, however, quite possible that it will prove useful to endow machines capable of problem solving and learning with the ability to experience some analogues of frustration, pleasure at achieving a goal, confusion, and other such emotion-related attitudes toward emergent phenomena in order that they can generate useful abstractions for deciding when to abandon a task, ask for advice, or give up.)

AI researchers can grasp the opportunity to build human-level intelligent machines only if they find ways to fill prodigious quantities of memory with important material. They will be able to do so only if AI can produce adequate sensory systems (for hearing, vision, touch, kinesthesia, smell, and taste). With sensory systems, AI systems will for the first time be able to learn from experience. Such experience may initially be little more than rote memory—that is, storing records of the partially digested sensory patterns seen by the system. Yet, as argued earlier, the storage of vast amounts of relatively literal material may be a key to intelligent behavior. The potential for artificial intelligence depends on the possibility of building systems that no longer require programming in the same sense that it is now required. Then we could overcome the tendency of systems development to be very slow because of software engineering difficulties.

There is also the question of what kind of "body" such an intelligence must be embedded in for it to really understand rather than to merely simulate understanding. Must the machine be wired to have emotions if it is to understand our human emotional reactions? If a machine were immortal, could it understand our reactions to our knowledge of our own mortality? Intelligent machines might be cloned by simply copying their programming or internal coding onto other identical pieces of hardware. There is no human analogue to a machine that would have experience as a unitary entity for an extended period and then, at some point during its "lifetime," suddenly become many separate entities, each with different experiences. Exactly what kind of intelligence this would be is therefore an open question.

SUMMARY

We are nearing an important milestone in the history of life on earth, the point at which we can construct machines with the potential for exhibiting an intelligence comparable to ours. It seems certain that we will be able to build hardware that is a match for human computational power for an affordable price within the next thirty years or so. Such hardware will without doubt have profound consequences for industry, defense, government, the arts, and our images of ourselves.

Having hardware with brain-level power will not in itself, however, lead to human-level intelligent systems, since the architecture and programs for such systems also present unprecedented obstacles. It is difficult to extrapolate to future effects from the rate of progress that has been made to date. Progress has been very slow, in part because the computational models that have been used have been inappropriate to the task. This inappropriateness applies most critically to the problem of learning. Without learning, systems must be handbuilt. We don't know how closely we must match human brain details to foster appropriate learning and performance. With the right architectures, it is likely that progress, both in the building of adequately powerful hardware and in programming such hardware (by teaching), will accelerate. I believe that the construction of truly intelligent machines is sufficiently likely to justify beginning study and policy planning now. In that way we can maximize their benefits and minimize their negative effects on society.

ENDNOTES

[1] Frederick P. Brooks, *The Mythical Man-Month: Essays on Software Engineering* (Reading, Mass.: Addison-Wesley, 1974).

[2] Allen Newell and Herbert Simon, *Human Problem Solving* (Engelwood Cliffs, N.J.: Prentice-Hall, 1972).

[3] The Boolean operations AND, OR, and NOT constitute a universal set. NAND (NOT AND) also is universal by itself, as is NOR (NOT OR). For a derivation of this result see Marvin L. Minsky, *Computation: Finite and Infinite Machines* (Cambridge: MIT Press, 1967).

[4] Herbert A. Simon, *The Sciences of the Artificial* (Cambridge: MIT Press, 1965).

[5] John Backus, "Can Programming Be Liberated from the von Neumann Style? A Functional Style and its Algebra of Programs," *Communications of the ACM* 21 (8) (August 1978):613–41.

[6] George A. Miller, Eugene Galanter, and Karl Pribram, *Plans and the Structure of Behavior* (New York: Holt, Rinehart, and Winston, 1954).

[7] John McCarthy, "Epistemological Problems in Artificial Intelligence," in *Proceedings of the Fifth International Joint Conference on Artificial Intelligence* (Los Altos, Calif.: Morgan-Kaufmann, August 1977), 1038–44.

[8] Example from Marvin Minsky, personal communication.

[9] John McCarthy, "Circumscription—A Form of Nonmonotonic Reasoning," *Artificial Intelligence* 13 (1) (1980):27–39; and Drew V. McDermott and Jon Doyle, "Nonmonotonic Logic I," *Artificial Intelligence* 13 (1) (1980):41–72.

[10] Steve Hanks and Drew V. McDermott, "Default Reasoning, Nonmonotonic Logics, and the Frame Problem," in *Proceedings of the Fifth National Conference on Artificial Intelligence* (Los Altos, Calif.: Morgan-Kaufmann, August 1986), 328–33.

[11] Craig Stanfill and David L. Waltz, "Toward Memory-Based Reasoning," *Communications of the ACM* 29 (12) (December 1986): 1213–28.

[12] W. Daniel Hillis, *The Connection Machine* (Cambridge: MIT Press, 1986).

[13] David E. Rumelhart, James L. McClelland, and the PDP Research Group, eds., *Parallel Distributed Processing: Explorations in the Microstructure of Cognition*, vols. 1, 2 (Cambridge: MIT Press, 1986).

[14] For extended treatment of such systems, see Rumelhart and McClelland, *Parallel Distributed Processing*, and the special issue on connectionist models of *Cognitive Science* 9 (1) (1985).

[15] For details, see Stanfill and Waltz, "Toward Memory-Based Reasoning."

[16]Marvin L. Minsky, *The Society of Mind* (New York: Simon and Schuster, 1986); *The Hedonistic Neuron: A Theory of Memory, Learning, and Intelligence*, by A. Harry Klopf (Washington, D.C.: Hemisphere, 1982), presents a compatible neural theory.

[17]There is also a fairly extensive literature on learning and knowledge acquisition. It is based on the heuristic search and physical symbol system paradigms. Broadly speaking, these learning algorithms fall into three categories. The first type is statistical and uses a large number of processors to find patterns or regularities in data bases of examples—in medical diagnosis, weather forecasting, and decision making, for example. Three systems that fall into this category are the ID3 system of Ross Quinlan and the systems built by Ryszard Michalski, both of which are described in Ryszard S. Michalski, Jaime Carbonell, and Thomas Mitchell, eds., *Machine Learning: An Artificial Intelligence Approach* (Los Altos, Calif.: Tioga Publishing Company, 1983), and the "memory-based reasoning" system of Craig Stanfill and David Waltz (see Stanfill and Waltz, "Toward Memory-Based Reasoning"). A second type of learning algorithm uses "production rules" (sometimes termed "if-then rules") and learns by adding to and modifying an existing set of such rules. The rules are changed by providing "experience," which may include "rewards and punishments." Such systems can also be taught by giving them correct examples from which they can learn rules by rote. Two systems of this sort are the genetic algorithms of John Holland (see John H. Holland, *Adaptation in Natural and Artificial Systems: An Introductory Analysis with Applications to Biology, Control and Artificial Intelligence* [Ann Arbor: University of Michigan Press, 1975]) and the SOAR system of Allen Newell and Paul Rosenbloom (see John E. Laird, Paul S. Rosenbloom, and Allen Newell, "Chunking and SOAR: The Anatomy of a General Learning Mechanism," *Machine Learning* 1 [1] [1986]:11– 46). The third branch is "explanation-based learning" (see Gerald F. DeJong and Raymond A. Mooney, "Explanation-Based Learning: An Alternative View," *Machine Learning* 1 [2] [April 1986]:145–76). An explanation-based learning system attempts to build causal structures, or "schemata," as explanations of new phenomena and as elements for building new schemata.

[18]One of the most successful learning methods is the centerpiece of McClelland and Rumelhart's *Parallel Distributed Processing*. Other systems include Stephen Grossberg's, Andrew Barto's, and Geoffrey Hinton's. See Stephen Grossberg, "Competitive Learning: From Interactive Activation to Adaptive Resonance," *Cognitive Science* 11 (1) (January-March 1987):23–64; Andrew G. Barto, "Learning by Statistical Cooperation of Self-Interested Neuron-like Computing Elements," *Human Neurobiology* 4 (1985):229–56; and Geoffrey Hinton, "The Boltzmann Machine," in Geoffrey E. Hinton and John A. Anderson, eds., *Parallel Models of Associative Memory* (Hillsdale, N.J.: Lawrence Erlbaum Associates, 1981).

[19]Terrence J. Sejnowski and Charles R. Rosenberg, "NETtalk: A Parallel Network that Learns to Read Aloud," Technical Report JHU/EECS-86–01 (Baltimore, Md.: Johns Hopkins University, Electrical Engineering and Computer Science, 1986).

[20]Ronald J. Williams, "Reinforcement-Learning Connectionist Systems: A Progress Report" (unpublished manuscript, College of Computer Science, Northeastern University, November 1986).

[21]Elizabeth Spelke, "Perceptual Knowledge of Objects in Infancy," in Jacques Mehler, Edward C. T. Walker, and Merrill Garrett, eds., *Perspectives on Mental Representation: Experimental and Theoretical Studies of Cognitive Processes and Capacities* (Hillsdale, N.J.: Lawrence Erlbaum Associates, 1962).

[22]In the *Critique of Pure Reason* Immanuel Kant argues essentially this point: that "the innate forms of human perception and the innate categories of human understanding impose an invariant order on the initial chaos of raw sensory experience." This is quoted from Paul M. Churchland in *Matter and Consciousness* (Cambridge: MIT Press, 1984), 84.

[23]See Isaac Asimov, *I, Robot* (New York: The New American Library of World Literature, 1950), 6, for an early exploration of the need for a kind of ethics for robots, embodied in three laws of robotics:

1. A robot may not injure a human being, or, through inaction, allow a human being to come to harm; 2. A robot must obey the orders given it by human beings except where such orders would conflict with the First Law; 3. A robot must protect its own existence as long as such protection does not conflict with the First or Second Law.

Ironic, alas, for the first highly intelligent mobile robot will probably be embedded in tanks and fighter aircraft.

Anya Hurlbert and Tomaso Poggio

Making Machines (and Artificial Intelligence) See

VISION IS MORE THAN A SENSE; it is an intelligence. Imagine watching television: from the flickering light on a two-dimensional screen you create a three-dimensional world of people, places, and things. The mental processes that lead from the pattern of light on your retina to an internal picture of the world are as "intelligent" as the analyses and interpretations that lead a doctor from symptoms to diagnosis. Yet when we marvel at the human brain, we are more apt to prize the deductive powers of a logician than the skill of the average person in recognizing a face.

We humans are highly visual animals. Almost fifty percent of our neocortex—the part of the brain that arrived latest in evolution and hence is most characteristic of primates—is dedicated to vision. Vision is so integral to our understanding of the world that the ability to "see" means not only to decode light signals but also to comprehend the thrust of a verbal argument. Why, then, have we balked at calling vision intelligence?

This question has special relevance for researchers in artificial intelligence (AI). The declared goal of AI research is to recreate intelligence on machines and, at the same time, to understand what

Anya C. Hurlbert is an M.D. / Ph.D. student in the Harvard Medical School / Massachusetts Institute of Technology Health Sciences and Technology Program and the MIT Department of Brain and Cognitive Sciences.

Tomaso Poggio is a professor in the Department of Brain and Cognitive Sciences at MIT. Professor Poggio directs research in computational vision in the Artificial Intelligence Laboratory at MIT, where he is also codirector of the Center for Biological Information Processing.

intelligence is. Traditionally, AI research has tackled such blatantly advanced abilities as reasoning, problem solving, and language. Yet an undisputed assumption underlying AI research is that the goal of intelligence is to enrich our interaction with, and enhance our control of, the outside world. A disembodied intelligence, however clever at solving math problems, could not attain that goal if unable to sense or affect the world. Robotics, the study of how to join perception with action, is therefore a crucial adjunct to AI.

Research in robotics naturally segments into two major efforts: machine vision and robot movement. The goal of machine vision research is to build machines that can see, and at the same time, to understand vision. Similarly, robot movement research seeks not only to build robots that can manipulate things and move about but also to understand motor control. The obvious temptation in AI research is to assign machine vision the task of supplying input to an intelligent machine and to assign robot movement the task of performing its output. In its beginnings, AI research did just that, and in doing so excluded both vision and motor control from the realm of intelligence.

The reason for the early exile of machine vision was in part the same reason that we so readily take vision for granted and underestimate its everyday powers: seeing seems easy and immediate. But progress in machine vision in the past twenty years has exploded that delusion and revealed a humbling irony. Vision is not only "intelligent," but also harder to understand or recreate than the most sophisticated mathematical reasoning. In fact, vision poses such difficult problems that AI today is much closer to developing systems that could serve as physicians or lawyers than to building robots that could replace gardeners or cooks.

THE PROMISE OF VISION

Today machine vision is integral to the entire AI effort, not only for its power, complexity, and sheer utility, but also for a salient message that its approach to studying intelligence bears. Recently, traditional AI (the term we use for AI research that excludes machine vision and robotics) has been challenged by an old charge under a new name, "connectionism." The challenge comes from modern Gestaltists who believe that traditional AI's logical dissection of intelligence can never reveal the true structure or capacity of the mind's deepest powers.

The dispute is aimed at a tradition that has taken to heart the physical symbol system hypothesis of Newell and Simon. The hypothesis states that "a physical symbol system has the necessary and sufficient means for general intelligent action."[1] A physical symbol system is a "machine," born or built in the real world, that deals in physical symbols—"physical patterns" that designate things in the real world. The system must be able to construct new symbols from old symbols. In turn, new symbols may instruct the system to create, change, or destroy other symbols. Ultimately the system must be able to influence real things through its symbols for them. The hypothesis vindicates the study of what computers can do: computers are physical symbol systems and are therefore intelligent.

For traditional AI, studying what computers can do means programming them to do things. The uprising against traditional AI is partly against the way it programs. The AI approach has been to break problems down into their smallest discrete tasks and to tackle each task in turn, following explicit rules that prune a tree of branching solutions. Expert systems, which follow tailor-made rules to draw inferences from a tailor-made data base, are the marketable fruit borne by this approach. MYCIN, a knowledge-based system for medical diagnosis, reasons from symptom to differential diagnosis by following "if–then" rules stored in its knowledge base. Cued by the results of a lab test to search through its data base for all possible pathogens, MYCIN would take its next instruction from an appropriate "if–then" statement: "If you find a bug, then look for a drug." Although much of the fruit has not ripened—physicians have yet to employ any medical expert system as more than a computerized reference library—expert systems in a few specialized areas such as configuring computers and repairing telecommunication lines have proved useful.

The flip side of the hypothesis says that because humans are intelligent, they are physical symbol systems. Part of the new rage against traditional AI is against calling man a physical symbol system; the cathexis is on the word *symbol*. In a strict sense, a physical symbol could be text on a screen, a set of electronic switches, a mesh of neurons, or an electrical current across a cell membrane. But traditional AI research has taken an even stricter definition:

symbols are abstract terms that denote known things and obey a circumscribed grammar. Like logical symbols in mathematics or words in the Latvian language, symbols should behave according to formal rules. Newell and Simon listed the computer language LISP as one example of a physical symbol system, yet traditional AI seems to have considered it the only one. For traditional AI, engineering intelligence has come to mean manipulating the symbols of LISP-like languages to create systems whose every cog turns according to the rules of logic.

The authors of the physical symbol system hypothesis meant it as a benediction on computer science. But some see the blessing as a curse on human intelligence if all that physical symbol systems can do is wield computer commands. The grandly named General Problem Solver (GPS), one of the first programs to seek out universal mechanisms for solving puzzles, was derived by listening to people solve problems out loud. How, asks the offended human, could even the best such GPS drive a car? An experienced driver does not consciously apply rules such as "when traveling above a speed of thirty miles an hour, shift into third gear," or "when shifting gears, depress the clutch pedal," or "when approaching a toll booth, let up on the accelerator pedal." She simply drives, performing the necessary actions automatically. Or consider a mechanic reaching for a wrench to loosen a bolt. He decides on the right tool for the job by quick intuition, not by systematic search through the available implements. No expert system, argue traditional AI's opponents, could maneuver chess pieces as cleverly and as quickly as a chess master could unless it were infinitely large and infinitely fast.

The complaint against traditional AI's model of intelligence crystallizes in connectionism. Connectionists argue that the supremely characteristic features of human intelligence are, among others, associative thinking and the ability to learn and generalize from examples. They argue that these features are not captured by the serial search procedures and the dendriform structure of AI's expert systems. Instead, they argue, intelligence will emerge only from a special hardware that reproduces the massive parallelism of the human brain, in which huge numbers of interconnected cells tackle different parts of the same task at the same time.

Yet what we must remember before succumbing to arguments against the traditional AI approach is where and why it *does* succeed.

The very things that AI, in its beginnings, so eagerly labeled intelligent—mathematical reasoning, language understanding, abstract logic—are the things that expert systems do best. We would go so far as to argue that the things that we consider most mentally challenging are simply the things of which we are most conscious, and that we are most conscious of them because they are the things that we learned latest in evolution and consequently do least well. Expert systems stand a good chance of surpassing us in these consciously difficult tasks and should not be faulted prematurely for the finitude of technological progress. The intrinsic weakness of medical expert systems lies not in their present inability to encompass the enormous domain of medical knowledge—in time, they probably will do it—but in their inability to reproduce the art of medicine. Although even a present-day medical expert system can probably outdo a sleep-deprived medical intern in calling up a full list of prescribed laboratory tests, the intern always has an edge on the computer in sensing unhappiness as the cause of a patient's loss of appetite.

Leaps of intuition and instant insights at one extreme, ordinary perceptual skills such as speech recognition at the other: these are the powers of the mind that traditional AI is hard put to model. They are the mental activities of which we are least conscious and most capable. Evolution has spent millennia perfecting such unconscious talents, and it is more than logical to suggest that to reproduce those talents, tactics other than those used exclusively (and relatively poorly) by our most conscious mind must be deployed.

Vision is possibly the most intelligent of the mental machinations hidden from consciousness. Yet the methods of studying intelligence that machine vision has developed are neither recondite nor magical, and shun neither logic nor intuition. In machine vision, the best of traditional AI meets the best of connectionism to build a science that stands apart from both.

Machine vision has distilled its guiding philosophy from the same source as traditional AI. At the core of the physical symbol system hypothesis is the idea that symbols should be arbitrary things, independent of the underlying machines and meaningless until made otherwise. Machine vision turned that idea into what we call its central dogma: intelligence may be studied as an abstract information-processing system, independent of the machinery on which it runs. Machine vision has followed the dogma onto a unique path, the computational approach. The computational approach describes exactly what information a system receives and what information it puts out, and seeks a computation that will transform the input into the output. For natural or artificial visual systems, any such computation is necessarily constrained by the properties of the environment, the eye, and the light that travels between them. The key to the right computation is in discovering and respecting those constraints. Machine vision has turned the search for constraints into a science of the natural world.

THE PROBLEM OF VISION

To understand the strength of the machine vision approach, one must first appreciate the difficulty of the problems it attacks. A cherished bit of apocrypha about Marvin Minsky, a founding father of AI, illustrates the difficulty of the appreciation itself. About twenty years ago, he assigned a graduate student a seemingly tractable problem for a summer project: connect a camera to a computer and make the computer describe what it sees. The summer project has expanded into a research industry, and despite machine vision's enormous progress, that problem has still not been solved.

Much of the progress has resulted from painstaking research into how to formulate the problem: What does vision do? The plain answer is that vision transforms light signals into internal representations of the things that transmit them. Human vision starts with a two-dimensional pattern of light (an image) on each retina and ends with a description of three-dimensional objects in terms of their shape, color, texture, size, distance, and movement. The first obstacle in vision is the retinal image itself: it contains an enormous, almost unimaginable amount of information. More than 100 million photoreceptors are arrayed on the retina. The eye's lens focuses light onto the retina in such a way that the three-dimensional world is flattened and mapped directly onto the photoreceptor mosaic, each photoreceptor corresponding to a particular spot in the field of view. The amount of light falling onto a single photoreceptor is determined by the amount of light reflected by whatever object occupies the corresponding location in the field of view. In turn, the amount of light an object reflects depends on the amount of light that falls on it (which depends, for instance, on how close it is to a lamp, or whether it lies in the shadow of another object) and on the stuff of which it is made (shiny metal, matte black velvet, transparent gossamer, lustrous vegetable skin), among other things.

If, for each photon it captured, each photoreceptor deposited a dark grain of silver onto photographic paper behind the eye, we could peel off snapshots of the world from our built-in Polaroid cameras. But the retina is not so obliging, and the picture it sends to the brain is abstruse. At any one instant, the image is an array of electrochemical signals, the size of each signal proportional to the amount of light striking the photoreceptor that conveys it. Over each second, the brain must process about a hundred such images as the eye roves over a constantly changing world. Thus, far from recording static photographs, the retina transmits a stream of dynamic visual information.

In machine vision the retinal image is translated into a two-dimensional array of pixels. Each pixel is a tiny subdivision of the picture and contains a number that represents the size of the signal transmitted by a single light sensor (or, equivalently, the intensity of the light striking the sensor). The machine's task is to perform mathematical manipulations on the array of numbers to convert it into more telling arrays: for example, arrays that explicitly encode the distances of objects from the camera, or arrays that assign one color to each distinct material.

A typical image in machine vision might be composed of one million pixels. Each pixel holds an eight-bit number. The total amount of information, although far less than in a human retinal image, is still a staggering eight million bits. Multiply that number by the number of images per second that a camera must deliver in order to mimic the human eye, and the information transmission rate climbs to at least several hundred million bits per second. Thus even the simplest mathematical operation the machine performs on the flow of images requires billions of multiplications and additions per second. A million or more personal computers working together could just do the job.

Ironically, the real problem in vision is that all the information in an image is never enough. Too much information is lost in the projection of the three-dimensional world onto a two-dimensional surface, making each pixel value in the huge array highly ambiguous. Consider a typical beginning photographer's mistake: she positions her subject in front of a telephone pole to capture the greenery on either side, but in the photo the pole appears to pierce the subject's head. In the projection of the three-dimensional scene onto the two-dimensional film, crucial information about depth has been lost. The size of the telephone pole is a clue that can be interpreted in at least two ways: either it is a thick telephone pole far away or a thin wooden rod protruding straight from the subject's head. The ambiguity of depth is the most obvious one; another ambiguity lies in the interpretation of brightness and darkness. If the intensity values in one cluster of pixels are much higher than those in a neighboring cluster, the rift between them could be caused in several different ways. Perhaps a shadow falls across a single piece of paper, creating the illusion of a border between light and dark papers, or perhaps a sheet of white paper lies next to a sheet of black. The numbers themselves do not tell.

Machine vision formulates its problem as follows: given a two-dimensional array of intensity values, find the three-dimensional arrangement of objects and surfaces that produced it. As stated, the problem appears to be impenetrable. The features that must be recovered—the colors, textures, and spatial relationships of objects, the position and color of the light source—are hopelessly entangled in a matrix of numbers. Yet machine vision has come a long way since Minsky's graduate student grappled with the problem. What has emerged in the past fifteen years is a sense of the structure of vision that enables us to break down the problem into independent, manageable sections. First, vision can be cleanly divided into at least two stages: *early vision* (which determines where things are) and *high-level vision* (which determines what things are). Second, early vision itself may be studied as a set of separate visual modules, each extracting a distinct type of visual information from the image. In finding the right perspective, machine vision has gone beyond the bounds of traditional AI and constructed a solid science of its own: the science of inverse optics.

A GLIMPSE OF MACHINE VISION

A sense of the structure of vision did not emerge immediately. Vision scientists' first attempts were, in effect, to solve the problem by hook or by crook: any tactic that could resolve the ambiguity in the image was exploited, no matter how narrowly restricted it was to the task at hand. This approach produced *expert systems* in vision: image-interpretation programs that called upon a store of specific, custom-made knowledge to fuel the application of custom-made rules. An exaggerated example of such a program undertakes the task of locating the telephone in a picture of a cluttered office desk. Among the assumptions the program makes to constrain its search are that the telephone is black and that it sits at a fixed height and a fixed distance from the camera taking the picture. The search the program executes is relatively easy: it scans the appropriate row of pixels for a cluster of low pixel values signifying a dark object, then checks that the size of the cluster matches the size that a telephone should be when seen from the specified distance. If the assumptions hold true, the program performs well. But it fails miserably if the telephone is white or if it has moved from the desk to the floor.

The *ad hoc* solutions (or "hacks") generated by this approach left little room for the development or application of general scientific principles. Instead of clearly outlining the steps a visual system must follow in going from image to object representations, the first vision programs mixed levels haphazardly, exploiting high-level decisions to deal with the low-level information registered by the array of pixel values. Like many infant expert systems in other domains, the first machine vision systems could function only in restricted, artificial environments. Their techniques for coping with circumscribed mini-worlds could not be generalized to deal with the unpredictable surroundings in which humans and more primitive animals exploit vision so efficiently.

Early Vision

The weakness of the first stabs at the problem of vision provoked a movement toward early vision. What the pioneers of the move realized was that without a theory of image understanding general enough to instruct the interpretation of any image, machine vision would be doomed to the endless perpetration of hacks, each more cleverly conceived than the last, but no single one able to touch the all-purpose flexibility of the human visual system. The way to that general theory was through a science of the world, not a science of the mind: a thorough analysis of the physics of the interaction between light, eye, and object.

Concentrated efforts in the past fifteen years have produced a scheme for early vision whose first goal is to construct a map of the scene that records for each opaque surface in the image its distance and orientation relative to the viewer. That is, early vision seeks to transform the initial array of pixel values into another array of numbers that explicitly groups together parts of the image that are all part of one thing and tells *where* each thing is, relative to the viewer. The "things" of early vision are themselves only parts of objects, the visible faces and sides of larger, still unrecognized, wholes. This map, termed the "$2\frac{1}{2}$-D sketch" by David Marr, provides the springboard from which the next goals of early vision can be pursued: to assign shape, color, texture, speed, and direction of motion to each thing in the image. Separate maps could then be drawn up, each recording a distinct type of visual information, and each could be superimposed in register with the $2\frac{1}{2}$-D sketch. By thus aligning the color map with the $2\frac{1}{2}$-D sketch, for example, an imaginary overseer could read out the distance, orientation, and color of each distinct surface in the image.

Early vision must accomplish two tasks on the way to computing distinct visual properties for each solid surface in the image: (1) compress the abundant information of the image into just its important features, and (2) reduce the ambiguity of that information.

Edge Detection

The first step in making the first map is to delineate the boundaries between distinct regions in the image. *Edge detection,* the most thoroughly studied process of early vision, takes on that task. It does so by marking the borders that separate clusters of significantly different pixel values. The fact that edge detectors exist at the lowest level of the human visual system is easy to accept, given the tendency of our senses to prefer changes over steady states. In fact, our visual system seems designed primarily to detect changes in, rather than absolute values of, light signals. Imagine what you would see in a uniform white expanse spanning your field of view: not much. The image is boring because there are no changes in the intensity signal across space. But spatial changes in intensity are not the only kind of changes for which our visual system is on the lookout. If the projection of the complex scene you see upon lifting your eyes from this page were to stay perfectly still on your retina, within an instant it would become as featureless as the white expanse. It would disappear because there would be no *temporal* changes in the light signal registered by each photoreceptor.

The retinal cells to which the photoreceptors send their signals are specially designed to detect changes in light intensity across time and space. The cells continually compare intensity values now to intensity values registered an instant ago and send out transient responses that encode changes in intensity values rather than the intensity values themselves. If the intensity values stay the same, the cells' response falls to zero and the image fades. The spatial and temporal intensity changes are intertwined; as the eye flickers restlessly in its socket, edges in space move across photoreceptors and are converted into edges in time.

In machine vision, edge detection seeks out intensity changes as the most important, most primitive features, and so performs the first task in paring down the massive amount of information in the image. The difficulty in edge detection lies not in finding intensity changes but in discarding the unimportant ones. Small intensity changes between pixel clusters are rife in any image. Even an image of a single sheet of white paper would not carry the same value for every pixel unless the white of the paper were absolutely uniform, the light shining on the paper were exactly the same at every point, and the sensors recording the image faithfully registered the amount of light that struck them. These conditions are not met in reality: the white of the paper is flecked with impurities, the light strikes the paper at an angle, shading it, and the sensors, continually bombarded by random photons, transmit a noisy signal. A good edge detector should discount the miscellaneous ups and downs of the intensity signal arising from the surface of the paper and detect only the actual edges of the paper. Ideally, edge detection should deliver a line drawing of the scene, capturing the physical contours and boundaries of objects and leaving blank the surfaces in between. Yet designing an edge detector to do that is no simple task.

Tremendous effort has gone into constructing efficient edge detectors. The problem in devising them is the trade-off between smoothing the noise in the intensity signal while catching all the significant edges. Successful edge detectors copy the way human retinal cells do both of these things by performing two steps. First, the detector blurs the entire image by adding to each pixel value the average of the pixel values in a cluster surrounding it. Second, it takes the difference between that new pixel value and an average of the new pixel values in a larger surrounding cluster, and assigns the value of that difference to the central pixel.[2] These two operations, *blurring,* or *filtering,* and *differentiating,* insure that small changes in the intensity signal are smoothed away (small changes become even smaller difference values after filtering) and large changes are enhanced. The effect of these actions on the following scan line across an image

would be to transform it into the following clearer signal.

The cutoff below which intensity changes are discarded and above which they are retained can be controlled in several ways: by changing the size of the pixel cluster from which the average is calculated, by changing the weights the pixel values carry in the average, and by keeping only those blurred, differentiated values that are above a set threshold. If the cutoff is too low, intensity edges might be detected that do not represent physical edges in the scene, but if it is too high, some real edges might get thrown out with the noise. The developers of edge detectors for machine vision have put great effort into contriving filters and differentiators that most effectively enhance edges and make surfaces smooth. No single edge detector can be perfect, though; the line drawings produced by this first stage of early vision contain many miscellaneous lines.

Natural Constraints

Early vision's goal of reducing the ambiguity of images inspired the idea of *natural constraints.* It was obvious from the start that constraints were necessary to reduce the number of possible interpretations of a single image, but not obvious from what realm the constraints should arise. Hence, *unnatural constraints* like those in the telephone-recognition program were considered as good as any. Turning to the physics of images led vision scientists to turn to the physical world for constraints—to make assumptions about the properties of lights, surfaces, and geometries that would almost always be true: natural constraints. Natural constraints reduce the number of interpretations of an image by ruling out some of them as physically impossible.

A stereo algorithm. The task of finding and precisely formulating the right natural constraints has proved to be the most difficult one in early vision. Natural constraints figure prominently in the solution to the problem of depth perception.

You can appreciate the problem of depth perception, and how humans make it easier by using two eyes, with a simple experiment. Hold up one finger several inches from your face and look at it with your right eye closed. Now open the right eye and close the left. Your finger appears to jump to the left. Now hold your finger as far from your face as you can and alternate between the views in your two eyes in the same way. Your finger now makes a smaller jump to the left. The explanation: because your two eyes are in slightly different positions in your face, the image of the world falls on each eye in a slightly different way.

The difference in the position of your finger in your eyes' two images is its binocular disparity and, as your experiment showed, is directly related to the distance between the finger and your face. The farther away your finger, the smaller its disparity. Stereoscopic vision capitalizes on this fact by using disparity to estimate the relative depths of surfaces in a scene and thus to recreate solid, three-dimensional objects. To calculate the binocular disparity of a particular point in the scene, the visual system must first identify which pixels in the two images correspond to that same point. This correspondence problem has too many solutions: each pixel in the left image could correspond to any one of many pixels with similar pixel values in the right image. Enter natural constraints, which eliminate all but the physically correct match.

In the search for constraints that are both powerful and general enough to solve the problem, two assumptions about the everyday world stand out. The *uniqueness* constraint embodies the fact that most surfaces are not transparent; it rules that each pixel in, say, the left eye's image can be assigned one and only one depth (this constraint would not hold if most scenes were viewed through many layers of glass). The *continuity* constraint expresses the fact that most surfaces are smooth, so that if one point in an image is assigned a certain distance from the eye, nearby points will be assigned similar distances. Only if the world were composed of blizzards of disconnected points at random depths would we expect to see wildly different disparities for neighboring pixels.

Having found the constraints, what does one do with them? Marr and Poggio[3] incorporated them into a stereo algorithm that, in its latest version, starts with a left and a right image, each having been filtered and differentiated by an edge detector, and produces a final image in which each pixel value represents one depth. For each pixel in the left image, the algorithm computes the disparity for each of its possible matches with the right image. For each disparity for each pixel, the algorithm then counts the number of matches for nearby pixels that yield that same disparity. The disparity with the highest number of "votes" wins. The continuity constraint insures that the method of voting is fair—if one disparity is supported by many neighboring matches, it is likely to be the right one for a smooth surface—and the uniqueness constraint dictates that there be only one winner.

This simple method of implementing natural constraints yields realistic results on most images. Unlike its predecessors in the days of hacks, it does not rely on high-level clues that point out, say, the tip of the nose in the left image, and then solve the correspondence problem by recognizing the tip of the nose in the right image. We can see depth in random dot stereograms,* proving the remarkable fact that we, like this stereo algorithm, do not need to recognize objects before we can see them in depth.

---

*Random dot stereograms are three-dimensional pictures created by showing the right eye one display of random black dots on a white background and the left eye another display. The patterns of dots in the two displays are identical except that a central patch of dots is slightly displaced in the left image relative to its position in the right image. The eye interprets that slight displacement as a difference in depth between the central patch and its background, so the patch appears to float above or below the surrounding dots.

Inverse Optics

For early vision, exploring the properties of the environment that interact with vision and pursuing natural constraints meant developing a new science of the world: *inverse optics.* Just as optics is the physics of the formation of two-dimensional images from three-dimensional scenes, so inverse optics is the physics of the recovery of three-dimensional scenes from two-dimensional images. Just as Renaissance artists reproduced three-dimensional contours and boundaries on two-dimensional paper by following the rules of linear perspective, so modern-day vision scientists are learning to decode two-dimensional images by discovering the new rules of inverse optics.

Inverse optics is a science of impossible problems. The information provided in the image data is insufficient, and the solution might be neither unique nor well-defined. Traditional AI might struggle to define a problem precisely, but once the problem is defined, its solution is unique and straightforward (although time-consuming) to find. In inverse optics the opposite is true: problems are easy to state but very hard to solve. One of the major advances in early vision has been the realization that these impossible problems fall into a class of problems—technically called ill-posed problems—that has been extensively studied in mathematics. Because mathematicians have already developed useful techniques to deal with the general form of ill-posed problems, vision scientists can call upon the same techniques to solve the particular problems of inverse optics. These techniques fall under the heading of *regularization theory.*[4]

Regularization theory provides a framework into which natural constraints, once discovered, can be slotted. The framework is the same for all problems in early vision, and it points to a general solution that can be tailored to each problem. Thus the difficulty of the not-quite-so-impossible problems in vision lies almost solely in finding the right natural constraints, since one way to exercise them has now been formally prescribed.

Early vision's tactics can be characterized as three general activities. The first is to segregate the problem from other problems in vision; that is, if the goal is to recover the color map of the surfaces in the image, there is no need to compute binocular disparity (our own neurons divide duties similarly: a color-selective neuron generally cares little for disparity). The second is to identify the natural constraints that govern the problem. The last task is to fit the natural constraints into an algorithm that works, perhaps by using the framework of regularization theory.

High-Level Vision

A "mobot" trundles along a hallway of MIT's AI Lab, halting when it suspects that something solid is too close for comfort. It can follow a wall or reverse its path, making its way as if it can see. But its bank of infrared sensors transmits only the most basic of messages: something's there, or not. It cannot tell what that something is.

Although far more advanced than the mobot's images of the world, the $2\frac{1}{2}$-D sketch produced by early vision also stops short of telling what things are. Its goal is to tell where things are. Determining what things are is the goal of high-level vision. If the $2\frac{1}{2}$-D sketch segregated each object from others in the image, the task of recognizing the objects by such characteristics as color, shape, texture, and so forth would not be too difficult. But drawing boundaries between separate objects is exactly what early vision—at least as reproduced on machines—cannot yet do. The things in the image that early vision picks out are at best parts of objects—unbroken surfaces of one color, small dark blobs on an otherwise uniform surface—not the objects themselves. The difficulty lies not in finding edges between regions of the image that are different from each other, but in determining which regions are the significant ones for distinguishing and labeling objects.

The tasks of image segmentation (carving up the image into regions likely to correspond to separate objects) and object recognition (matching these significant regions with labeled objects in memory) have been the focus of intense study in high-level vision. Yet even the most sophisticated object recognition programs today make an unfair demand on the images they process. The programs require that the objects they recognize must first be pinpointed in the image. Thus told where to look, such a program can match each feature of a pinpointed object to a virtually identical image in its memory. But faced with just the $2\frac{1}{2}$-D sketch of a scene, the program does not know where to start. The problem that vision scientists now avidly address is how to make the two approaches to vision—early and high-level—meet in the middle. How does one get from edges to objects?

Although that question is still unanswered, machine vision has made remarkable progress since its birth as a science. Five years ago, extracting edges from an image took thirty minutes of computer time; now it takes less than a tenth of a second and produces a clean image that aircraft makers, among others, use profitably. Algorithms that recover the color, depth, motion, and shape of surfaces from two-dimensional images of the world work faster than ever. They already aid the military's experimental autonomous vehicles in navigating over land and assist industry's robots in inspecting factory products. The next hurdle is to integrate distinct algorithms into one visual system that can see in real time. The Vision Machine at the MIT AI Lab is a first version of such a system. Machine vision has also built bridges to biology and psychology and shown that making machines see can mean seeing into the human mind.

LEVELS OF UNDERSTANDING

Machine vision's commitment to understanding vision on all levels arises from the nature and difficulty of the problems it faces. Vision is a hard problem, and trying to solve it just by constructing telephone-recognition programs won't work. The solid successes of machine vision research stem from its singular practice of the central dogma (that intelligence may be studied as an abstract information-processing system, independent of the machinery on which it runs), which has grown into a philosophy and science of its own. The science is inverse optics, grounded in the physics of the real world and formalized in terms of rigorous mathematics. The philosophy at the heart of machine vision (especially as practiced at the MIT AI Lab) is underpinned by a belief in levels of understanding and analysis, which dictates that information-processing problems be probed on three levels: computation, algorithm, and hardware. Machine vision's creed is to find its first and firmest footing for every problem on the computational level.

The computational approach maintains that the problems of vision can be studied as problems of mathematics and physics, constrained by the properties of the world being imaged and of the eye making the images. The solutions must be fully characterized independently of the machinery that will implement them; the natural constraints that enable a unique solution to exist are the same, whether neurons or switches exploit them. As David Marr wrote, "Once a computational theory has been established for a particular problem, it never has to be done again."[5] It becomes a pillar of AI, just as a theorem is a basic principle of mathematics. The computational theory underlying edge detection, which states that the most meaningful primitive features in an image are edges, is not tied to the way any piece of hardware might find edges. Instead, the theory supplies firm facts about visual information.

The algorithm is the step-by-step procedure that executes the commands of the computation: in edge detection, it is the set of instructions to calculate the sum of a group of pixel values, to divide that sum by the number of pixels in the group, to add that number to the central pixel value, and so forth. The hardware is the gadgetry that implements the algorithm: in the human visual system, retinal cells are vastly interconnected with each other, enabling neighboring cells to feed the sum of their activity into a central cell. On the computational level, machine vision determines what it wants to compute; on the levels of algorithm and hardware, it prescribes how to do the computation.

When Marr and Poggio first advocated the use of the computational level in the pursuit of solutions,[6] they stressed its independence from the other levels in order to lift it from a throng of AI algorithms. Yet in practice the levels must interact. The algorithm is dictated by the computation it must perform and is often constrained by the properties and limitations of the hardware. Yet it has reciprocal influence on both the computation and the hardware. To alter the exact procedure that an algorithm follows—for instance, to increase its speed or improve its reliability—is often to modify the computation that it performs. Fiddling with an algorithm may therefore lead to the invention of a new computation or an insight into what the problem to be solved really is. Similarly, the algorithm may require certain manipulations—multiplying together huge arrays of numbers, for example—that existing hardware simply cannot perform efficiently, so it may spur the evolution or discovery of new machinery. Efforts in machine vision over the past fifteen years demonstrate a firm commitment to tackling vision on all levels, and a belief that the levels are so intrinsically intertwined that such a commitment is needed if vision is ever to be understood.

POLAR OPPOSITES

Before it became obvious that vision was one of the toughest problems AI could tackle, some AI researchers responded to Marr's exhortation to build solid computational theories rather than rickety algorithms with the retort that that was all very well for easy things like vision but not for hard things like higher intelligence. Today the impact that machine vision's philosophy could have on traditional AI research is strengthened by AI's conflict with connectionism. Yet we find that connectionism can learn something from machine vision as well.

Traditional AI and connectionism are two branches of the same enterprise, and can be viewed as representing the two poles of intelligence. The connectionist philosophy is inspired by our *associative* powers (awed by the way we wade through the quicksand of multiple constraints, talking, humming, driving cars, reaching for coffee cups, recognizing faces in the crowd), whereas AI is inspired by our *deductive* powers (impressed by logic, mathematical proofs, legal debates, and the systematic elimination of all possible bugs in computer codes). Their different views on intelligence lead to different plans for recreating it.

- AI revels in algorithms; connectionism insists on hardware. Connectionism maintains that algorithms alone cannot recreate intelligence and that AI's emphasis on algorithms gives inappropriate primacy to symbolic processing, which can never capture the "fluidity and adaptability"[7] of human intelligence.

- Hardware is the essence of intelligence, says connectionism, and not only does traditional AI miss out on this fact, but it uses the wrong hardware. AI has thrived on the rapid development of ever more powerful serial computers, "von Neumann machines," that carry out instructions one after another. Connectionists believe that hardware should perform operations not in series, but in parallel, and that the quantities it works with should be numbers, not symbols, and analog, not digital.*

- Connectionists further believe that the right hardware is a highly interconnected network of simple units that simultaneously process mutually interacting parts of the same problem. The output of the system is determined by the sum total of the activity of all the units in the network, not just the "yes" or "no" value of a single predicate terminating a series of logical deductions.

- The ultimate dream of connectionists and AI researchers alike is to build a machine that can learn. Connectionists predict that the right hardware will spontaneously—perhaps magically—organize itself into a system that is intelligent, not simply by virtue of what it has been told to do, but because it can learn and generalize from examples. It will contain the very elements of the mind that in aggregate—just like water molecules coalescing into snowflakes—will display emergent properties such as intelligence. Feed the right kind of network a list of written words and their correct pronunciations, and that network will figure out the state it ought to be in to pronounce words that are not on its training list. The computation that the network performs to get from text to speech does not need to be explored.

Rather than questions of hardware versus software, symbols versus numbers, or serial versus parallel operations, the debate really boils down to a single question: What is the final goal of the enterprise? Or, phrased another way, What is the goal of studying intelligence: to build intelligent machines? to understand how the brain is put together? or to describe the structure and powers of intelligence as a free-floating entity, tied to neither brain nor machine?

If we invent an ideal connectionist and an ideal AI hacker and ask each of them this question, we get sharply differing answers. The ideal connectionist replies that her aim is to make a model of the brain by simulating its neural networks. The model should capture enough of the brain's natural power to be commercially viable. Yet

---

*In a digital computer the data are represented and operated on as strings of zeros and ones (binary digits). In an analog computer the data are represented as physical quantities, such as voltages, that can take on a continuous range of values.

she would shy away from a free-floating theory of intelligence in order to avoid the "middlemen" of symbols that intrude on the transaction between data and solution. In practice, the units in most connectionist networks have been simplified to the point where they look nothing like real neurons, which are biophysically and computationally very complex devices. A real connectionist would admit that the only true resemblance between artificial networks and the brain is on the abstract level of lots of connections and lots of simultaneous operations.

The ideal AI hacker, on the other hand, could claim to be the first to want to build an intelligent machine, but would probably demur on whether it was essential to delve into a wet brain. That is not to say that the hacker would reject the insights offered by scientists who do delve into brains. Yet although the hacker says he takes to heart the lofty goal to understand intelligence purely as an abstract information-processing system, as proof he produces only task-specific computer programs.

In terms of levels of understanding, AI professes to be on the computational level, while in reality it is stuck on the algorithmic level.[8] Connectionism professes to ignore the computational level and just tries to build hardware like the brain's. But the hardware of connectionists' networks is a far cry from the brain's, and many of the networks work only because the necessary computational analysis has been done first." Machine vision's message to both connectionism and AI is that no one of its goals can be attained without the simultaneous pursuit of the others.

VISION: A SYNTHESIS

In reality, the boundaries between traditional AI and connectionism are not so boldly drawn. Although their doctrines and techniques seem as diametric as the poles of intelligence that inspire them, they converge in machine vision. As the ideal connectionist and the ideal

---

*For example, John Hopfield's network is simply a minimization machine. That is, before using it to solve a problem, one must express the problem, if possible, as a mathematical quantity that must be minimized. This preliminary analysis is at the computational level and has little to do with the network itself.

AI hacker face off, the machine vision scientist follows a steady course that coincides with parts of each approach.

The ease, immediacy, and inscrutability of vision places it on the associative pole of intelligence. With the coarse resolution of our consciousness, that is how we see it. Yet on the fine scale viewed by computational theories, vision often operates in a very deductive fashion. In turn, machine vision embraces contrasting methodologies inspired by the two poles of intelligence: it develops highly parallel algorithms, deals heavily in raw numbers, relies on abstract information-processing theories, and assembles expert visual systems.

Machine vision is the most numerical and parallel game in town. The goal of most procedures in machine vision is to transform an enormous array of numbers into yet another enormous array of numbers, not to evaluate the logical truth of a single statement. Because of the enormity of the initial array, and because all points in it often must be transformed in the same way (for example, an edge detector performs exactly the same operation regardless of which particular pixel cluster is involved), the most natural way to do the transformation is simultaneously, in parallel, on each pixel. Most early vision algorithms have been developed with the idea of parallel processing in mind, using the retina and the brain (prototypically "parallel" organs) as models.* Many of these algorithms, although first tested on digital computers, can readily and more efficiently be implemented in a highly parallel way on networks whose units' activities are expressed in analog quantities; regularization theory, which unifies many early vision algorithms, shows a natural way to do so.[9] The Connection Machine, a powerful computer that consists

---

*Marr and Poggio's first paper on stereo vision (1976)[10] begins: "Perhaps one of the most striking differences between a brain and today's computers is the amount of 'wiring.' In a digital computer the ratio of connections to components is about 3, whereas for the mammalian cortex it lies between 10 and 10,000. Although this fact points to a clear structural difference between the two, this distinction is not fundamental to the nature of the information processing that each accomplishes, merely to the particulars of how each does it. In Chomsky's terms, this difference affects theories of performance but not theories of competence, because the nature of a computation that is carried out by a machine or a nervous system depends only on a problem to be solved, not on the available hardware. Nevertheless, one can expect a nervous system and a digital computer to use different types of algorithms, even when performing the same underlying computation. Algorithms with a parallel structure, requiring many simultaneous local operations on large data arrays, are expensive for today's computers but probably well-suited to the highly interactive organization of nervous systems. . . . "

of many thousands of simple processors densely interconnected, was originally conceived, in part, for vision research.

Machine vision has also stayed close to the brain. Vision researchers have realized that artificial machines can gain much by emulating the biological ones that perform so extraordinarily well in vision and other senses. Accordingly, they have modeled edge detectors on retinal cells and taken other cues from the brain. Meanwhile, brain biologists increasingly look to machine vision for insights into what operations neurons must perform to solve the perceptual problems they face.

Yet machine vision does not just implore AI to turn to numbers and parallelism. After all, AI cannot simply and instantly transform the data bases and inference engines of expert systems into huge arrays of numbers.[11] Nor does machine vision just instruct connectionism to be more faithful to the brain. Most importantly, it tells both connectionism and traditional AI to seek out solutions on the computational level.

A connectionist's solution to the problem of stereo vision might be to feed sets of three images into an artificial network of neurons, one input image for each eye (which gives the light intensity at each pixel) and one output image, the solution (which gives the distance from the viewer at each pixel). For each set, the network would produce its own output image from the two inputs, compare that with the correct solution, and adjust the strengths of connections between its units to make the two output images match. Given enough training sets, the network might eventually settle on a pattern of strengths that would produce an accurate depth image when fed an entirely new pair of input images. Looking into the network might reveal a mesh of excitatory and inhibitory connections very similar to the ones that the Marr-Poggio algorithm sets up to solve the same problem. Yet whereas the Marr-Poggio algorithm springs from a computational analysis of depth perception and therefore works within a domain that is fully described, one can only guess what and how much the connectionist's network might do.

How might traditional AI benefit from the computational approach? Take the cruising habits of the ordinary housefly. The fly has simple tastes in targets owing to its coarse vision. Any small black-and-white pattern (a crumb on a tablecloth) or moving black dot (another fly, possibly of the opposite sex) might alert the fly to follow.

A traditional AI hacker would be tempted to construct explicit rules telling the fly how to track a potential mate: *If dark spot veers right, turn right. If dark spot hovers, head for it.* The scheme beneath the rules would be to compare continually the target's direction to the fly's direction, and make movements to match the two. The computational approach might develop a similar scheme, but not by packaging a set of rules that cover only a finite list of maneuvers.

The Poggio-Reichardt theory[12] of how flies fly is a classic computational theory. It takes apart the rules, exposing their underlying structures. It embodies the rules in a single mathematical statement that shows how visual input is transformed into motor output, constrained by the physics of flight and the biology of sight. The statement equates the torque exerted by the fly's wings (which in turn controls its position and velocity) with the difference between the actual and desired position of the target's image on the retina. How fast that difference changes determines how fast the torque changes. A single equation sums up the fly's flight pattern on a chase.

Although a connectionist might find the fly's behavior grossly unsophisticated, a human's reflexive act of stepping on the brakes when a car skids to a halt in front of his own might prove to be governed by a similar equation. But the major hitch in the AI hacker's fly program is more telling than the connectionist's denigration of the fly: the traditional AI program assumes that the hard work of pinpointing the target has already been done. Its rules apply only when supplied with high-level information about the location and speed of black spots. If it were a truly intelligent program, it would start with the raw picture produced by the fly's primitive eye, find the prominent spots in it, and track those spots continuously over time. The labor is in deciphering the errors in target retinal position and in discovering that wing torque is the relevant output. Similarly, the connectionist's stereo vision network would have a hard time settling into a productive state if it were supplied only with raw images. The mass of information in the raw images would prove too much for an artificial network unless it were impractically vast and complex. The stereo vision network would do much better with the edge-detected images that the Marr-Poggio algorithm uses to pare down the number of possible matches between pixels in the two images. The fly's program and the stereo vision network both require the right representation of the input data to work.

Finding the right representation is what a computational theory does. It tells how to get from input to output by finding the right input and output. It specifies both the information and how to process it. In the search for the basic elements of cognition, AI has looked for the smallest steps of deduction in the most global rules of thought, while connectionism has looked for the most recondite links of association. Machine vision has turned its gaze outside. It looks for generalizations about the world that are almost always true (objects are rigid, surfaces are smooth, boundaries are continuous) and translates them into constraints on the basic elements of information.

Machine vision shares the dream of building a machine that can learn. But there are questions to be answered first. Is it possible to learn any computation from a set of examples, starting with a tabula rasa? We think probably not. For most problems, the framework that guides data to a solution must first exist before learning can act upon it, streamlining and improving the solution. Certain transformations of data into solution probably cannot be learned at all except by exhaustive search through all possible solutions. But regardless of its answer, the question represents a lode in the research mine. What must be dug out are characterizations of the computations that can be learned, and how well and by what general classes of networks they can be learned.[13] Currently too little digging is going on. Yet some machine vision scientists are exploring the implications of regularization theory, which shows that under certain conditions, some vision algorithms can be learned from examples.

Will we be satisfied with simply building machines that can learn? From a practical standpoint, the answer will probably be yes; the machines will certainly be very useful. But if the goal is to understand intelligence, the reply is no. Simply reproducing an ability doesn't explicate its underlying strategies. Humans can learn, yet we don't know how. The theory of evolution provides a self-consistent and complete description of how life—and brains—developed. It tells us how to construct a nervous system, although the procedure is unfortunately too time-consuming to be practical. Yet this theory of life and intelligence, like the view that it is enough just to build an intelligent machine, is not sufficient for those who want to understand what intelligence is. In the same way, even if the magic network is discovered that can learn to solve any problem, a true believer in levels of understanding would still insist on asking: What has the network learned?

Humans should not be insulted that they are used as existence proofs for information-processing machines just because they recoil from the symbolic manipulation in traditional AI programs. Although that style of programming is still best suited to the questions it has traditionally tackled in reasoning, problem solving, and logic, it cannot stand alone. Just as thinking has two flavors and intelligence two poles, the study of intelligence must draw on two philosophies. Such deeply intelligent acts as perception, speech recognition, and motor control need a more numerical, parallel, analogical approach. We humans should not forget that those who aim to build intelligent machines have the whole future to disprove their starting hypothesis: that intelligence can be reproduced on a machine. Today human intelligence far exceeds the capabilities of expert systems or connectionist networks, but in the future, more sophisticated machines might take offense at such a claim. Those machines might look fondly back to the days when machine vision, which combines all levels of understanding human intelligence, brought their parents together.

ENDNOTES

[1] For more extensive definitions of symbols, symbol structures, designation, and interpretation, see Allen Newell and Herbert A. Simon, "Computer Science as Empirical Inquiry," in *Mind Design*, ed. John Haugeland (Cambridge: Bradford Books, MIT Press, 1981).

[2] Actually, the way the difference is determined is slightly more complicated, but the effect is similar. For a more lengthy description of edge detection, see Berthold K. P. Horn, *Robot Vision* (Cambridge: MIT Press; New York: McGraw-Hill Inc., 1986).

[3] David Marr and Tomaso Poggio, "Cooperative Computation of Stereo Disparity," *Science* 194 (1976):283–87.

[4] Tomaso Poggio, Vincent Torre, and Christof Koch, "Computational Vision and Regularization Theory," *Nature* (1985): 314–19.

[5] David Marr, "Artificial Intelligence: A Personal View," in *Mind Design*, ed. Haugeland.

[6] David Marr and Tomaso Poggio, "From Understanding Computation to Understanding Neural Circuitry," in *Neuronal Mechanisms in Visual Perception*, ed. E. Poppel, R. Held, and J. E. Dowling, *Neuroscience Research Progress Bulletin* 15 (1977):470–88.

[7] David E. Rumelhart, James L. McClelland, and the PDP Research Group, *Foundations*, vol. 1 of *Parallel Distributed Processing: Explorations in the Microstructure of Cognition* (Cambridge: MIT Press, 1986), 3.

[8]Daniel Dennett makes a similar point in his paper "The Logical Geography of Computational Approaches: A View from the East Pole," presented at the Conference on Philosophy and Cognitive Science at MIT, 17–20 May 1984.

[9]Berthold Horn was probably the first (in 1974) to use analog networks to solve a vision problem, the computation of lightness (see Horn, *Robot Vision*). For the connection between analog networks and early vision algorithms see Poggio et al., "Computational Vision and Regularization Theory."

[10]Marr and Poggio, "Computation of Stereo Disparity."

[11]Some connectionists are trying to do just that—witness James Anderson's creation of medical data bases encoded in networks.

[12]Werner Reichardt and Tomaso Poggio, "Visual Control of Orientation Behaviour in the Fly," *Quarterly Review of Biophysics* 9 (1976):311–438.

[13]There are several basic questions that arise from, but have not been answered by, the connectionist approach to learning. Do connectionist learning techniques (typified by the stereo vision example) work only for small-size problems? Do they scale appropriately for larger-size problems? More fundamentally, which types of learning are likely to work on which classes of problems? Finally, are the connectionist learning algorithms significantly different from classical regression and clustering techniques? We venture the answer that they might not be.

READING LIST

Ballard, Dana H. and Christopher Brown. *Computer Vision*. Englewood Cliffs, New Jersey: Prentice-Hall, Inc., 1982.

Barrow, Harry G. and Jay M. Tenenbaum. "Computational Vision." *Proceedings of the IEEE* 69 (5)(1981).

Charniak, Eugene and Drew McDermott. *Introduction to Artificial Intelligence*. Reading, Mass.: Addison-Wesley Publishing Co., 1985.

Grimson, W. Eric L. *From Images to Surfaces: A Computational Study of the Human Early Visual System*. Cambridge: MIT Press, 1981.

Horn, Berthold K. P. *Robot Vision*, Cambridge and New York: MIT Press and McGraw-Hill, Inc., 1986.

Marr, David. *Vision*. San Francisco: Freeman, Cooper & Co., 1982.

Rumelhart, David E., James L. McClelland, and the PDP Research Group. *Parallel Distributed Processing: Explorations in the Microstructure of Cognition*. Cambridge: MIT Press, 1986.

Ullmann, Shimon. *The Interpretation of Visual Motion*. Cambridge: MIT Press, 1979.

Winston, Patrick. *Artificial Intelligence*. Reading, Mass.: Addison-Wesley Publishing Co., 1984.

Sherry Turkle

Artificial Intelligence and Psychoanalysis: A New Alliance

RTIFICIAL INTELLIGENCE and psychoanalysis appear to be worlds apart. Psychoanalysis looks for what is most human: the body, sexuality, what follows from being born of a woman and raised in a family. Artificial intelligence looks deliberately for what is least specifically human: the foundation of its theoretical vision is the thesis that the essence of mental life is a set of principles that could be shared by people and machines.[1]

There is another way in which they appear worlds apart. Artificial intelligence seems scientifically ascendant and has increasingly determined the agenda for academic psychology through its influence on cognitive science. In contrast, psychoanalysis is rejected by academic psychology and in conflict with dominant biological trends in psychiatry. Although there have been recent flurries of interest in Freudian theory, they have come from the worlds of literary analysis and philosophy. To scientific circles, psychoanalysis appears a frozen discipline—frozen in the scientific language of another time, frozen in the psychological assumptions of another culture.

In this essay I propose that if psychoanalysis is in trouble, artificial intelligence may be able to help. And I suggest the nature of this help by arguing that one of the ways computers influence psychological thinking is through a route that is not essentially technical. Rather, computers provide sciences of mind with a kind of theoretical

Sherry Turkle is associate professor of sociology in the Program in Science, Technology, and Society at the Massachusetts Institute of Technology. She is the author of Psychoanalytic Politics: Freud's French Revolution *and of* The Second Self: Computers and the Human Spirit.

legitimation that I call sustaining myths. Indeed, the early impact of the computer on psychology was clearly of this nature.

SUSTAINING MYTHS

As recently as the 1950s, behaviorism dominated American academic psychology, its spirit captured by saying that it was permissible to study remembering but considered a violation of scientific rigor to talk about "the memory." One could study behavior but not inner states. The study of mind had to be expressed in terms of stimulus and response. In today's jargon, what lay between was a black box that must not be opened even speculatively.

By the end of the 1960s, the behaviorist hegemony was broken, as were inhibitions about the study of memory and the inner processes of mind. Indeed, within academic psychology scarcely a trace remained of behaviorist methodology. Behaviorism had not been refuted by a critical experiment. There had been many factors influencing this scientific revolution, including the political and cultural climate of the 1960s. And one of the most central was the computer.

The computer's role in the demise of behaviorism was not technical. It was the very *existence* of the computer that provided legitimation for a radically different way of seeing mind. Computer scientists had of necessity developed a vocabulary for talking about what was happening inside their machines, the "internal states" of general systems. If the new machine "minds" had inner states, surely people had them too. The psychologist George Miller, who was at Harvard during the heyday of behaviorism, has described how psychologists began to feel embarrassed about not being allowed to discuss memory now that computers had one:

The engineers showed us how to build a machine that has memory, a machine that has purpose, a machine that plays chess, a machine that can detect signals in the presence of noise, and so on. If they can do that, then the kind of things they say about the machines, a psychologist should be permitted to say about a human being.[2]

The computer presence relegitimated the study of memory and inner states within scientific psychology. Many technical concepts that psychologists picked up from computation—ideas from cybernetics and automata theory—had existed before real computers but became more compelling because of them. "Suddenly," says Miller, "engineers were using the mentalistic terms that soft-hearted psychologists had wanted to use but had been told were unscientific."[3] Computational ideas, computational language, and the physical presence of the machines all created an intellectual climate in which it was permissible to talk about mental processes banned by behaviorism. The computer presence served as a sustaining myth for a new psychology of inner states that came to be known as cognitive science.

Computer programs provided a way to discuss beliefs and rules as causing behavior. Why did pawn take pawn? Earlier psychologies would have rejected "because the pawn blocked the bishop" as a causal explanation. It would merely be giving the chess player's "reasons." But if mind is program, reasons become explanations. A large part of the computer's appeal for psychologists is that it allows them to open the black box that is the mind. Once that box is open, the computer suggests ways to fill it with concepts that are close to commonsense understandings.

Indeed, the crux of Miller's story about memory is that computers gave psychologists permission to investigate something that "everyone knows" but that had been banished from science—the idea that people have memories. In the past two decades, cognitive science has been dominated by the computer legitimating the study of something else that "everyone knows," this time the idea that people have information and use rules, and that much of this information can be formulated in words. In the late 1950s Allen Newell and Herbert Simon built a computer program called the General Problem Solver (GPS), which was guided by something very close to verbal reasons recoded as computational rules. Questions such as "Why did GPS do such and such?" could be answered by reference to whatever rules it had been given. Why should references to rules not be used to answer questions about what people do when faced with similar problems? The existence of GPS gave credibility to the question.

There is a widespread view that the computer presence tends to move psychology toward more rigorous and quantifiable theories, arguing that the computer, by its nature, requires rules, rigor, and formalism. But the story of the computer's influence on psychology is not so simple. For example, its "first act"—the attack on behaviorism—went in the direction of creating a less rather than a more constrained, a "softer" rather than a "harder" science of mind.

Artificial intelligence is the most explicit channel for the computer's influence on psychology. It asserts a global materialism and also offers particular theories about how mind works. Its dual agenda is to build "machines that think" and to use machines to think about thinking. Its methodological premise is that if one builds a machine that can do something intelligent, the way one gets the machine to do it is relevant to thinking about how people do it as well.

Artificial intelligence is usually seen as having its strongest affinities with rationalist philosophies, defining knowledge as information and devaluing ambiguity when it offers a view of mind as program. But this view, commonplace within the literary culture, is only partial. One might call it the literary stereotype of the field. But AI has other dimensions that give it a far wider range of intellectual connections and implications for psychology.

This essay is interpretive, attempting to identify actual trends and influences of the computer on psychological thinking, and it is speculative, predicting a new alliance between AI and psychoanalysis, the latter being an intellectual companion far removed from rationalism, quantification, and formal propositions. This does not mean that there is an identity of spirit between computational and psychoanalytic models or even that there are not fundamental incompatibilities between them. But in addition to a list of traditional affinities between psychoanalysis and AI, they have something new in common. In recent years, computer scientists and psychoanalysts have talked a strikingly similar language about inner agents that construct the thinking and feeling self. Behind the language are shared concerns that suggest new theoretical linkages and a new source of vitality for psychoanalytic ideas.

Predictions are always dangerous. The point of making one here is what is gained from thinking it through: insight into how the computer's presence can act as a sustaining myth to support not one psychological culture but a range of them.

TRADITIONAL AFFINITIES

The very idea of AI—to create mind in machines—subverts traditional notions of the autonomous self in a way that parallels the psychoanalytic enterprise. Most people see the autonomous self as an unproblematic idea because they have a day-to-day experience of having one. Our everyday language captures that experience and expresses the idea of free will; we say, "I act," "I do," "I desire." And even when people have learned through theology or philosophy to question the idea of free will, what they tend to do is make small modifications in their notion of the autonomous self; it becomes a self whose decisions are constrained. Inherent in psychoanalysis is a more radical doubt. The unconscious does not constrain; it constitutes a decentered self. Inherent in AI is an even more threatening challenge: If mind is program, where is the self? It puts into question not only whether the self is free, but whether there is one at all.

Traditional humanism is committed to the notion of an acting, intentional subject. In its challenge to the humanistic subject, AI is subversive in a way that takes it out of the company of rationalism and puts it into the company of psychoanalysis and radical philosophical schools such as deconstructionism. The psychoanalytic subject is decentered in the web of the unconscious; the deconstructionist subject is decentered in language; the computational subject is decentered—indeed, perhaps dissolved—in the idea of program.

These affinities will not reassure the traditional humanist who has gotten used to seeing AI as an enemy. They do not make AI any less of an assault on the idea of the self. But the attack comes from the left, so to speak, rather than from the right. Artificial intelligence is to be feared as are Freud and Derrida, not as are Skinner and Carnap.

The computational "explanation" of the chess move points to another way in which AI is more like Freud than Skinner. Within traditional science, and certainly for behaviorism, the line between subject and object is taken as sacred. But for Freud, his self-analysis, his technique of self-understanding, was indissociable from the development of his general theory. Like psychoanalysts, AI theorists have made a profession of dissolving the line between subjective and objective reflection. The intelligence embodied in the chess move is intelligence derived from personal knowledge of chess. "There's only one place to get ideas about intelligence, and that's from thinking about myself," says AI scientist Roger Schank. "In the end, I have just myself, and if it feels right, that's what I have to trust," says Donald Norman, an AI-influenced cognitive psychologist.[4]

Marvin Minsky, one of the founders and theoretical leaders of AI for the past quarter of a century, has always made it clear that as far as he is concerned, you can make a machine do only what you yourself know how to do. In order to build a program, you have to engage in self-analytic activity. In the early 1960s Minsky worked with a student, Thomas Evans, on an AI program that could pass the familiar visual-analogy tests: *A* is to *B* as *C* is to *D, E,* or *F,* where each letter stands for a geometrical drawing. His method was psychological: Think about yourself. And its reference point was psychoanalysis: "What you had to do was something like what Freud did. Tom Evans and I asked ourselves, in depth, what we did to solve problems like this, and that seemed to work out pretty well."[5]

Behaviorism rigorously forbids any reference to personal experience, and most other psychological schools try to ignore the issue. But AI and psychoanalysis have each articulated the need to integrate personal reference into theoretical construction. Each, in its own way, is a science of self-reflection.

But are such affinities superficial? After all, psychoanalysis explores the mind to discover the irrational; artificial intelligence invents machines through the exploitation of the rational. In fact, what stands between psychoanalysis and AI is not AI's "materialism." In the past quarter of a century, psychoanalysts have learned the necessity and the productivity of an intensified dialogue with psychopharmacology and neuroscience. And Freud himself hoped that someday his science of mind would be tied to its physical substrate, even if his own first efforts to make the connection had led to an impasse.[6] What stands between psychoanalysis and AI is the view that AI is synonymous with rationalism, or rather with the kind of rationalism embodied in the idea of information processing.

If AI has seemed somewhat unitary in its implications for thinking about people, it is because what many observers know as AI is really information processing, a rule-driven, hierarchical approach to creating intelligence. But information processing is only one part of a larger picture.

THE TWO AIs

In the mid-nineteenth century George Boole formalized rules of logical inference in an algebraic form systematic enough that he felt entitled to call his work "The Laws of Thought."[7] Of course, Boole's title reached beyond his achievement, which is far from an all-inclusive model of mind. For one thing, Boole's laws need an external agent to operate them.

Boole's laws are something a person could use, but a computational version of Boole breathes life into his equations. An operator in the form of a computer program is placed within the system. Once there, the operator and the laws can be seen as a functioning model, if not of the mind, at least of a part of the mind.

One major branch of AI research can be described as doing just this—pursuing Boole's project in computational form. Information-processing AI gives active shape to formal propositions to create an embodiment of intelligence as rules and reason. Boole formulated algebraic rules for the transformation of logical propositions. Modern computer science has enlarged the logical and propositional to a more general notion of what it calls information, and it has enlarged algebraic transformation to a more general notion of computational processing. Boole would recognize a kinship between his project and Newell and Simon's way of putting these two advances together in GPS and other programs that laid the foundation for information-processing AI.

But artificial intelligence is not a unitary enterprise. Computation is a stuff out of which many theories can be fashioned. It is true to say that there is not one AI but many. And it is helpful to say that there are essentially two. The first is information processing, its roots in logic, the manipulation of propositions to obtain new propositions, the combination of concepts to obtain new concepts. The second comes from a very different style of work, present from the earliest days of the field but now having increasing influence, to the point of being the focus of attention wherever AI is discussed, from research seminars to popular articles. This second is "emergent AI."

Emergent AI has not been inspired by the orderly terrain of logic. The ideas about machine intelligence that it puts forward are not so much about teaching the computer as about allowing the machine to learn. This AI does not suggest that the computer be given rules to follow but tries to set up a system of independent elements within a computer from whose interactions intelligence is expected to emerge. From this perspective, a rule is not something you give to a computer but a pattern you infer when you observe the machine's behavior, much as you would observe a person's. Its sustaining images are not drawn from the logical but from the biological.

Information processing breathes life into Boole by putting an operator into his system, but what it operates on shares the static nature of Boole's propositions. In traditional computers, millions of units of information sit in memory doing nothing as they wait for the central processor to act on them, one at a time. Impatient with this limitation, the goal of emergent AI is "pure" computation. Here, the whole system is dynamic, with no distinction between processors and the information they process. Families of neuronlike entities, societies of anthropomorphic subminds, and sub-subminds are in simultaneous interaction. The goal, no less mythic than the creation of a strand of DNA, is the generation of a fragment of mind.

The two AIs, rule-driven and emergent, logical and biological in their aesthetic, fuel very different fantasies of how to build mind from machine. If information-processing AI is captured by the image of the knowledge engineer, hungry for rules, debriefing a human expert in order to embody that expert's methods in algorithms and hardware, emergent AI is captured in the image of the computer scientist, up all night watching the twinkling lights of a computer in the hope that the interaction of "agents" within the machine will create intelligence.

Widely associated with the spirit and substance of the field as a whole (here I have called it the literary stereotype), information processing put AI in a distant relationship to psychoanalysis, whose ideas do not easily translate into rules or algorithms.[8] Indeed, I now turn to how popular notions about AI drawn from information processing suggest that AI is all the things that pyschoanalysis is not. My thesis follows directly: when the stuff of AI is expanded to include not only information but also active and interactive inner agents, there is a starting place for a new dialogue between the psychoanalytic and the computer cultures.

INFORMATION PROCESSING AND PSYCHOANALYSIS

The Freudian slip is a tempting target for psychologists bent on finding computerlike mechanisms behind human behavior. After all, one understands only too well the kinds of errors computers make. What sort of computer would make the kind of error that Sigmund

Freud saw as revealing a very different kind of meaning? In other words, what kind of computers are we?

In *The Psychopathology of Everyday Life,* Freud discusses slips of the tongue and takes as one of his examples a chairman who opens a parliamentary session by declaring it closed. The Freudian interpretation of this slip focuses on the complex feelings that may lie behind. Is the chairman anxious about the session? Does he have reason to believe that nothing good will come of it? Would he rather be at home? The slip is presumed to tell us about real wishes. Its analysis lays bare the concept of ambivalence—in this case, the chairman's mixed emotions about attending the session at all.

How can we see this human slip as an information-processing error? An MIT computer science student had no trouble finding an explanation: "A bit was dropped—the sign bit. There might have been a power surge. No problem." It's interesting that Freud saw a problem precisely because *open* and *closed* are so far apart—their opposite meanings give significance to their substitution. For computer science students, *open* and *closed* are close together. In their conceptual world, it is natural to code opposite concepts as the same root with a different "sign bit" attached (hot = −cold, dry = −wet, open = −closed). So if you think of the human mind as storing information in a computer's memory, substituting *closed* for *open* is easily justified. It might have been a small technical failure due to something as trivial as a power surge. It needs no recourse to the idea of ambivalence, hidden wishes, or emotional conflicts. What was interpreted in terms of sexually charged feelings, as a window onto conflicts, history, and significant relationships, becomes a bit of information lost or a program "derailed." What psychoanalysis would interpret in terms of *meaning,* this computational psychology would see in terms of *mechanism.*[9]

There is another way to look at the difference between the psychoanalytic and the information-processing view of the slip, a perspective that looks at the "width of determinism" in a system of interpretation. As a way of knowing, psychoanalysis has a logic that calls the whole person into play to explain all of his or her actions. This is why an individual can use something as small as a verbal slip to get in touch with the deepest levels of personality. What places the student's saying "There might have been a power surge. No problem" in such radical conflict with psychoanalysis is not so much that power surging is alien to psychoanalytic categories but the idea that any single factor could explain an act of language.

In traditional logic, when you say, "All men are mortal; Socrates is a man; therefore Socrates is mortal," your conclusion is determined by two premises. Change one, and you get a new conclusion. Similarly, with an information-processing computer model, you drop one bit, one piece of information, and you get a new output. The determination is "narrow," like a highway with one lane. Psycho-analysis uses "wide" determination. It is based on another kind of logic, more like the logic that leads you to say that Shakespeare is a great poet. Coming across a bad poem by Shakespeare does not call the statement into question. Nor would the discovery that several of Shakespeare's best poems were written by someone else. So even if the chairman announced that the meeting was closed in the context of his wife being ill, her illness and his desire to be at home would not determine his slip in any simple sense. Psychoanalytic phenomena are as "overdetermined" as judgments of literary merit. Although pop-ular images of a psychoanalytic dream book abound—along with a history of popularizers attempting to write one—there is no such thing as a "look-it-up" dictionary of Freudian symbols. The meaning of a dream can only be deciphered from the complex fabric of a particular dreamer's associations to it.

But computation is not synonymous with the narrow determina-tion of information processing. Emergent AI builds models with broader determination. Whereas information processing gives con-cepts like *closed* and *open* actual symbolic representation in a computer, the building blocks of emergent AI do not have that kind of one-to-one relationship with such ideas. In symbolic representa-tion, knowledge is stored as a static copy of a pattern. In an emergent system, the pattern itself is not stored. What is stored is data about the relationships among agents that would be expected to recreate the pattern. In this kind of system it is not possible for "one bit dropped" or "one rule changed" to make a difference to an outcome. In emergent systems, probabilities take the place of algorithms; statistics take the place of rules.

In a memoir she wrote in 1842, Lady Ada Lovelace, a friend and patroness of Charles Babbage, inventor of the "analytical engine," was the first person to go on record with a variant of the oft-quoted statement "Computers only do what you tell them to do."[10] The

Lovelace model for thinking about computers' strengths and limitations is paradigmatic for information processing. But it does not hold for emergent AI. Here, the point is quite precisely to make computers do more than they were ever told how to. It has become commonplace for people to quote Lovelace to defend against the idea that we are like machines: "People are not computers. They don't follow rules. They learn. They grow." But emergent AI is characterized by "anti-Lovelace" representations of the computer. It breaks down resistance to seeing continuity between computers and people by describing computers that learn and grow, by describing computers whose resonance is biological rather than logical.

EMERGENT AI AND BROAD DETERMINATION

This biological resonance is illustrated by the perceptron, a pattern-recognition machine designed in the late 1950s and a good first example of emergent AI. Information-processing AI is made out of data and rules. Emergent AI is made out of very different stuff, a stuff most easily captured in anthropomorphic language.

Imagine that you have access to the opinions of a thousand simple-minded meteorologists, each of whom has a different unreliable method of weather forecasting. Each bases a judgment on a fragment of evidence that may or may not be related to predicting rain. How do you form a judgment? A narrowly determined method, in an information-processing system, for example, might be autocratic—identifying the meteorologist with the best track record and going with that vote. Another strategy, both more democratic and more broadly determined, would be to let the majority decide. The perceptron refines the democratic strategy by weighing each vote with a number related to the individual meteorologist's past record.

So, for example, to get a perceptron to recognize a triangle, you show it samples of triangles and nontriangles and make the system "guess." Its first guesses are random. But the perceptron is able to take advantage of signals saying whether its guess is right or wrong to create a voting system in which agents who have guessed right get more weight. Perceptrons are not programmed, but learn from the consequences of their actions.

In the narrowly determined method, you would have complete breakdown if the chosen meteorologist went insane. But in the brain, damage seldom leads to complete breakdown. More often it produces a degradation of performance proportional to its extent. In other words, when things go wrong, the system still works, but not as well as before. Information-processing systems lose credibility as models of mind because they lack this feature; the perceptron shows the graceful degradation of performance typical of the brain. Even with some disabled meteorologists on board, the perceptron still produces the best possible decision based on the subset of functioning actors.

In an information-processing model, intelligent behavior follows from fixed rules. In the perceptron there are none. There is no flow-chart, no rule-driven path through the system. Nor are there one-to-one correspondences between information and output. What is important is not what an agent knows but its place in a network, its interactions and connections. The perceptron presents a model of mind as a society in which intelligence grows from the cacophony of competing voices.

In an information-processing model, the concept "rain" would be explicitly represented in the system. In the perceptron the decision "it will rain" is born from interactions among agents, none of whom has a formal concept of rain. Perceptrons show the emergence of what information processing takes as its raw material. Information processing begins with formal symbols. Perceptrons, like Freud's unconscious, operate on a subsymbolic and a subformal level. And most important for the current discussion, perceptrons rely on the interactions of inner agents, objects within the system.

Object theory is a central aspect of emergent AI and forms the link between AI and new directions of psychoanalytic thought. The inner agents in perceptrons make a bridge to the broad determinism of psychoanalysis. But it is only an opening. After perceptrons and the perceptronlike systems of the 1960s, it took another round in the development of computational ideas before inner objects came to occupy center stage. This is the story to which I now turn—the story of a second generation of emergent AI with an emphasis on inner objects and a new pathway for influence on psychoanalysis.

EMERGENT AI AND COMPUTATIONAL OBJECTS

The atmosphere in the AI laboratories of the early 1960s was heady. The work of Norbert Weiner, John von Neumann, and Alan Turing had set off shock waves that were still fresh. The first information-processing programs that emulated fragments of human thought had only recently produced their surprise. Perceptronlike models (and there were many of them, including Oliver Selfridge's "Pandemonium" and Warren McCulloch's "neural nets") led researchers to biologically resonant descriptions of artificial mind. Thoughts were on the ultimate nature of intelligence.

Artificial intelligence researchers saw little reason for a more humble style. On the contrary, AI defined itself as an enterprise of mythic proportions: mind creating mind. In doing so, the field drew a certain kind of person into its culture, not unlike the kind of person drawn into the early circle around Freud. There, too, the enterprise was mythic: the rational understanding the irrational. There, too, it was without precedent or academic security. The first generation of AI researchers, with backgrounds as diverse as mathematics, psychology, economics, and physics, like the first generation of psychoanalysts, had not been trained in "the field" because it did not exist. There was no academic discipline. There were only new worlds to conquer.

In the early 1960s emergent models were as much a part of what seemed exciting in AI as information-processing programs. But for almost a quarter of a century, emergent AI seemed swept aside. In its influence on psychology, AI became almost synonymous with information processing. Newell and Simon developed rule-based systems in purest form—systems that simulated the behavior of people working on a variety of logical problems. Such simulations offered the promise of more—the promise of making artificial mind out of rules. And if you can build mind from rules, then mind can be presumed to have had rules all along. Following this logic, researchers made information-processing models the backbone of cognitive science.

The language of information processing—descriptions of "search," "subroutine," "scripts," and "grammars"—became common currency among psychologists who accepted the idea that "toy programs," little pieces of machine-embodied intelligence, were representative of bigger things to come. Computer programs that could play chess, manipulate blocks, or "converse" with imaginary waiters in imaginary restaurants did more than model small pieces of mental functioning. They supported the idea that the means used to build them, all drawn from the information-processing paradigm, might someday capture the essence of mind. This idea was bolstered by the wordly success of a particular kind of information-processing program—the expert system. In it the AI scientist extracts decision rules from a virtuoso in a field (medical diagnosis, for example) and embeds them in a machine that will then do the diagnosis "for itself."

By the mid-1970s AI was no longer marginal. It had its own academic programs, its own journals, its own conferences. It was well funded because of its value in the marketplace and to the military. Expert systems were used to analyze stock prices, data from oil well drillings, materials from chemical samples. Companies competed to hire AI graduates to start in-house departments. The future of the field became part of a heated discussion about Japanese-American industrial rivalry.

Now AI could promise a more traditional kind of career, much as the medicalization of psychoanalysis paved the way for it to become a professionalized psychiatric specialty. In both psychoanalysis and AI, traditional careers meant new pressure to engage in the kind of work that promised visible results. In psychoanalysis the pressure was to "cure," to work on educational problems, to do "applied psychoanalysis." In AI research the pendulum swung from what had been most mythic about the dreams of the 1950s and early 1960s to what people "knew how to do"—gather rules and code them in computer programs.

But even as the information-processing model reached near-hegemony in the late 1970s, the conditions for something very different were developing. First, there was important technical progress. Computer scientists had long strained against the limitations of the von Neumann computer, in which one processor might manipulate the passive data in a million cells of memory. It had always been obvious that, in principle, the distinction between processor and memory could be abolished by making every cell in the computer an active processor. Doing so, however, had always been prohibitively expensive. But now, projects such as the Connection Machine were realistic enough to be funded. There, the plan is to have a million microprocessors put together to make one computer whose memory and computational power are fully distributed. No longer would there be an operator and the passive material it operated on. Computation was "waking up from the Boolean dream."[11]

Along with hardware that presented fresh possibilities were new ideas about how to program it. The development of programming methodologies with suggestive names like "message passing" and "actor models" created the context for thinking about computational agents in communication. Standard computer programs are lists of instructions in the form of imperatives: "add these numbers," "put the result in memory," "get the content of that memory location." Artificial intelligence programs in LISP or Prolog operate on more abstract data but still consist of instructions for manipulating information. The first quarter of a century of the development of programming was based on a process language for describing how to pass information from one place to another. But researchers now felt the need to deal with a different kind of event: not the *passing* of something but the *making* of something. By a coincidence that turns out to be highly suggestive for the present discussion, computer scientists called their so-far most prominent response "object-oriented programming."

If you want to simulate a line of customers at a post office counter (in order to know, for example, how much longer the average wait would be if the number of clerks were to be reduced by one), you write a program that creates an internal object that "behaves like" a person in a line at the post office. It advances when the person ahead in the line advances; it knows when it has reached the counter and then proceeds to carry out its transaction. The contrast between this object-oriented approach and traditional programming strategies is dramatic. A traditional FORTRAN programmer would assign x's and y's to properties of the customers and write computer code to manipulate the variables. Object-oriented programming refers directly to the inner objects that represent the customers in line: x's and y's do not appear.

In object-oriented programming, the programmer makes new objects that, once created, can be "set free" to interact according to the natures with which they have been endowed. The programmer does not specify what the objects will actually do, but rather "who they are."

If something of the "feel" of an information-processing program is captured by the image of the flow chart, something of the "feel" of object-oriented programming is captured by the pictures of file folders, scissors, and wastebasket that appear on the screens of computers with an iconic interface. The icons are a surface reflection of a programming philosophy in which computers are thought of as "electronic puppet shows" and "there are no important limitations to the kind of plays that can be enacted on their screens, nor to the range of costumes or roles that the actors can assume."[12] For mathematicians, the algebraic manipulations in traditional programming have a compelling reality. But for most nonmathematicians, the object-oriented approach has a more direct appeal, the appeal of actors on a stage.

By the early 1980s the coexistence of new parallel hardware and new ideas about objects in programming set the stage for the pendulum to swing away from information processing. The beginning of the decade saw the first of a growing series of papers from very different origins—engineers eager to build new parallel machines, computer scientists eager to try mathematical ideas that could guide new efforts at parallel programming, psychologists looking for new models that had a biological (indeed, a neurological) resonance. Emergent AI had not so much died as gone underground. It reemerged with a vengeance and with a new label: "connectionism." Once again, there would be no distinction between the processor and what it processed. There would be no specified set of operations. There would only be communities of agents in direct interaction with each other.

But proponents of the new theory of connectionism go beyond earlier stages of emergent AI in the steps they want to take away from Boole. For example, the perceptron could not itself generate new objects or elucidate how new objects could emerge. Its agents were programmed by a human acting from the outside. Today's connectionists hope to go further by bringing together parallel machines, the maturation of ideas about how to program them, and most important, a new sense of the central problem facing the field, something that had scarcely been formulated during the 1960s: How are objects created?

PSYCHOANALYTIC OBJECTS AND SOCIETY MODELS

In the focus on inner objects and their emergence and interaction, AI shares preoccupations that are central to contemporary psychoanalytic theory. As was the case in AI, the development of a psychoanalytic object theory is a later development of the field. It was not where the theory began.

Early psychoanalytic theory was built around the concept of drive, demand that is generated by the body and that provides the energy and goals for all mental activity. But later, when Freud turned his attention to the ego's relations to the external world, the significance and structure of these relations could not easily be framed in drive theory.

By 1917 Freud began to formulate a language to handle these matters. He described a process by which people form inner "objects." In *Mourning and Melancholia,* Freud argued that the sufferings of a melancholic arise from mutual reproaches between the self and an internalized father with whom the self identifies. In this paper Freud described the "taking in" of people (in psychoanalytic parlance, objects, and in this case the father) as part of a pathology, but he later came to the conclusion that this process is part of normal development. Indeed, this is the mechanism for the development of the superego —the taking in, or introjection, of the ideal parent.

According to Freud, we internalize objects because our instincts impel us to. In his work the concept of inner objects needed to coexist with the scaffolding of drive theory. But many psychoanalytic theorists who followed him were less wedded to the drive model. They widened the scope of what Freud meant by "object relations" to the point where we now think of them as a distinctive school. Classical Freudian theory has many overlapping concepts to describe internal objects: memory traces, mental representations, introjects, identifications, and the idea of inner structures such as the superego. The object relations approach is more specific about what we contain. It describes a society of inner agents, or "microminds"—"unconscious suborganizations of the ego capable of generating meaning and experience, i.e. capable of thought, feeling and perception."[13] Relationships with people, "brought inside" as inner entities, are the fundamental building blocks of mental life.

Whereas Freud focused his attention on a single internalized object, the superego, object relations theorists described a richly populated inner world. Psychoanalyst Melanie Klein went so far as to characterize the people that the child brings inside (as well as the representations of parts of the body) as having psychological features, personalities. They can be seen as loving, hating, greedy, envious. Psychoanalyst W. R. D. Fairbairn even reframed the basic Freudian motor for personality development in object relations terms. For

Fairbairn, the human organism is not moved forward by Freud's pleasure principle, the desire to reduce drive tension, but rather by its need to form relationships. This constitutes a profound recasting of the psychoanalytic view of the self: people are not fundamentally pleasure-seeking, but object-seeking.

The language that psychoanalysts need to talk about objects—how they are formed, how they interact—is very different from the language they need to talk about drives. In his "Project for a Scientific Psychology," Freud tried to use informationlike terms derived from the description of the reflex arc—the pain fiber carries information to the brain, the motor fiber carries information to the muscle—to talk about memory, instincts, and the flow of psychic energy. But information metaphors break down completely when you use them to talk about inner objects. As in object-oriented programming in computer science, so it is in psychoanalysis. When one talks about objects, the natural metaphors have to do with making something, not carrying something.

In classical psychoanalytic theory a few powerful inner structures—the superego, for example—act on memories, thoughts, and wishes. Object relations theory posits a dynamic system in which the distinction between processor and processed breaks down. The parallel with computation is clear: in both cases there is movement away from a situation in which a few inner structures act on a more passive stuff. Fairbairn replaced the Freudian dichotomies of ego and id, structure and energy with independent agencies within the mind that think, wish, and generate meaning in interaction with each other, much as emergent AI sets free autonomous agents within a computer system.

The development of object relations theory has led psychoanalysts to ask if allegiance to Freud depends on accepting his drive model. Some have tried to preserve Freud's original drive language but to use it in a way that accommodates a new emphasis on object relations— for example, by assigning objects a role in relation to the discharge of drive: they may inhibit, discharge, facilitate, or serve as drive's target. But this reworking of language is less a solution than an attempt to gloss over the problem. It only works if inner objects do not have elaborate properties or if their creation is seen as an occasional event.

But when objects become central to one's understanding of the psyche there is greater pressure to move away from drive theory.

Although drive theory has become increasingly sophisticated and open to the discussion of inner objects, the split between a drive approach and an object relations approach is a central division in psychoanalysis today.[14] The division is parallel to the split between information processing and emergent AI. To use Thomas Kuhn's language, object relations theorists are saying that psychoanalysis can no longer proceed as "normal science,"[15] growing by the assimilation of new data into the old theory. For them, object relations is a paradigm shift within psychoanalysis, much as the hypothesis of emergence—that intelligence grows out of the interaction of multiple agents (it is not what you know but who and where you are)—represents a paradigm shift in AI.

Artificial intelligence theorists Marvin Minsky and Seymour Papert have built a computational model that evokes Fairbairn's object relations theory. Their model takes the mind as a society of interacting agents. These agents are anthropomorphized, discussed in the terms one usually reserves for a whole person, but they do not have the complexity of people. Indeed, their model is based (as was the perceptron concept) on these agents being "dumb." Each knows one thing and one thing only. And, like the "voting agents" in the perceptron, their narrowness of vision leads them to very different opinions. The complex structure of behavior or emotion or thought emerges from the conflict of their opposing views.

The most elaborate presentation of this theory, Minsky's book *The Society of Mind,* describes a vast array of agents: censor agents, recognition agents, and anger agents, to name only a few.[16] Not surprisingly, Minsky recognizes Freud, who also wrote extensively about censor agents, as a colleague in "society" modeling. More surprisingly, Minsky sees censors as key actors, not only for modeling human thought but also for making intelligent machines.

Minsky's idea of the censor is a dramatic example of the developing resonance between psychoanalysis and emergent AI. Freud's censor protects people from painful thoughts. The extension of this idea to cognitive functioning and to the "thoughts" in a machine does not depend on the assumption that the agents or the system as a whole feels pain. To function coherently, according to Minsky, an intelligent system must develop a certain inattention to its contradictory agent voices. Minsky's formulation is that there cannot be intelligence, artificial or otherwise, without repression. Allen Newell has talked about the necessity for censors in large and complex information-processing systems. But with clear, unambiguous rules stated in advance, an information-processing computer can also do without them. Censors may turn out to be practical, but they are not theoretical necessities in the information-processing paradigm. In the case of society theory, however, censors are intrinsic. Since there cannot be intelligence without contradiction and conflict, only the presence of censors allows intelligence to emerge.

In this, society and Freudian theory join on an important point. Freud did not "discover" the unconscious. His contribution was the elaboration of a *dynamic* unconscious. What is unconscious is not simply forgotten, old, or irrelevant to current functioning. It is repressed. Powerful forces keep it down, and for good reason. Similarly, for Minsky, what is repressed in the computational machine and in what he has called the human "meat machine" *needs* to be repressed.

Freud wrote about the effects of the repression of frightening, emotion-laden experience. Minsky extends Freud's ideas to the cognitive domain. "A thinking child's mind . . . [needs no one] to tell it when some paradox engulfs and whirls it into a cyclone." Paradox, argues Minsky, is as dangerous as the primal scene. The child knows it is in the presence of a threat when it is asked to sketch the nonexistent boundaries between the oceans and the seas or to consider questions about the chicken and the egg, about what came before the start of time, and about where the edge of space is. Minsky adds: "And what of sentences like '*This statement is false,*' which can throw the mind into a spin? I don't know anyone who recalls such incidents as frightening. But then, as Freud might say, this very fact could be a hint that the area is subject to censorship."[17]

Minsky feels that the notions of "cognitive repression" and the "cognitive unconscious" will allow us to go beyond Freud. He uses Freud's discussion of jokes as an example. Freud's 1905 work on jokes explained that inner censors serve as barriers against forbidden thoughts. Most jokes are stories designed to fool the censors. It is a way to enjoy a prohibited wish. This is why so many jokes involve taboos concerning cruelty and sexuality. But it troubled Freud that this theory did not easily account for "nonsense jokes." One of Freud's hypotheses about the power of the nonsense joke was that senselessness reflects "a wish to return to carefree childhood, when one was permitted to think without any compulsion to be logical." The idea of the cognitive unconscious supports this view: paradox and senselessness need to be repressed in the process of developing emergent intelligence, whether in machines or in people. Absurd results of reasoning are taboo, as threatening as sex. The censors work as hard to suppress them; they have no innocence.

SUBVERSION AND NORMALIZATION

Despite their differences, psychoanalysis and AI have always shared theoretical affinities—among these, as we have seen, the challenge to the idea of the autonomous, intentional actor, the need for self-reference in theory building, and the need for objects such as censors to deal with internal conflict. But the affinity became something stronger when the cluster of issues about objects came to occupy center stage for both. This new orientation has made the old common elements more common: agent theories in AI highlight theoretical concerns that echo psychoanalytic ones. These include conflict, internal inconsistency, and perhaps most dramatically, the subversion of the subject, the "decentered" self.

Although both psychoanalysis and AI have always challenged the actor "I," both have theoretical variants that underscore this challenge more than others. The Freudian unconscious undermines the idea of a unified subject, but many of Freud's followers moved toward restoring a sense of there being a mental executive by concentrating their attention on the ego, that part of Freud's divided self that was turned outward toward reality. These "ego psychologists" began to talk about it as an agent capable of integrating the psyche. Anna Freud wrote of its powerful artillery, the mechanisms of defense. Heinz Hartmann argued that the ego had an aspect that was not tied up in the individual's neurosis, a "conflict-free" zone. Hartmann wrote about this unhampered aspect of the ego as though it were free to act and choose, independent of constraints. It almost seemed the seat for a reborn notion of the will, a locus of moral responsibility. Intellectual historian Russell Jacoby, writing of ego psychology's reborn, autonomous "I," went so far as to describe it as the "forgetting of psychoanalysis."[18]

In its subversive form, which splits the ego and undermines the subject, psychoanalysis is hard to take. It flies in the face of common-sense understanding. It is a subversive science. Ego psychology normalizes it. It takes what is most subversive—the decentered self—and softens it. Ego psychology presents the version of the unconscious most acceptable to the conscious.

This pattern of a normalizing response is common to all subversive sciences of mind, including, of course, computational ones. We saw how the very idea of AI calls the self into question through the notion of program. But AI, too, has variants that soften its message about decentering. For example, if you reduce AI to the idea of expert systems, it is a small step to think of the expert system as a resource on which some not clearly specified central executive can call. When you begin with the idea that a computer might have such an executive and such resources, the idea that a human has them too follows directly. It makes an AI model of mind seem less threatening because what needs to be thought of as computational and rule-driven, alienated from intention, is not my "I," but my "expert" in a limited domain—for example, that part of me that can play chess. The self becomes the executive who oversees the expert. So there are versions of both AI and psychoanalysis that defuse the subversive decentering principle by restricting its role to explaining parts of the mind and thus avoid the risk of dissolving the whole.

This strategy for neutralizing subversive theory is less viable in the case of agent and object theories, which are more aggressive in their denial of a unified self. Indeed, these theories define themselves through that denial. They put psychoanalysis and AI in a new and closer relationship with each other and with other intellectual movements that "deconstruct" the humanistic subject.

The strength and the weakness of object theories are the same in both psychoanalysis and AI: the strength is a conceptual framework that offers rich possibilities for models of interactive process; the weakness is that the framework may be *too* rich. The postulated objects may be too powerful: they explain the mind by postulating many minds within it. Object theory confronts both fields with the problem of infinite regress. There is something deeply unsatisfying in a theory that cannot go beyond assuming a homunculus within the human, for how then do we explain the homunculus within without postulating yet another one within it, and so on?

Psychoanalytic theorists struggle with this issue. Within the field much of the criticism of overpowerful inner objects has taken Melanie Klein's work as its target. For example, psychoanalyst Roy Schafer has argued that Klein and the English School of object relations have carried the reification implicit in Freudian metapsychology to a "grotesque extreme": "A multitude of minds is introduced into a single psychic apparatus. . . . The person is being envisaged as a container of innumerable, independent microorganizations that are also microdynamisms."[19] Essentially, Klein's critics feel that her idea of "inner idealized figures protecting the ego against terrifying ones is tantamount to proposing that there are internal friendly and hostile 'demons' operating within the mind."[20]

Kleinians reply that these internal figures are not demons but unconscious fantasies and thoughts. They are the ideas we have about what we contain.[21] But this response hardly settles the question. Psychoanalyst Thomas Ogden puts the problem starkly: How can thoughts behave as agents?

If internal objects are thoughts . . . then they cannot themselves think, perceive, or feel, nor can they protect or attack the ego. Even to the present, Kleinian theorists have not been able to disentangle themselves from the Scylla of demonology and the Charybdis of mixing incompatible levels of abstraction (i.e. active agencies and thoughts).[22]

In computer science, connectionism has not solved the problem of accounting for objects (what they are and how they come into being). Connectionism simply postulates the inner agents it requires, which is why AI scientist Terry Winograd has gone as far as to say that part of its appeal is that "it has a higher percentage of wishful thinking."[23] But the problem of infinite regress (accounting for the entities that are then to account for thought) has a very different cast in AI than in psychoanalysis because computer scientists are used to relying on a controlled form of circular reasoning—"recursion"—as a powerful technical tool.

Most of us learned at school to define x to the power n as x multiplied by itself n times. Power is defined in terms of multiplication. Computer scientists prefer to define x to the power n as x to the power $n-1$ multiplied by x. Power is defined in terms of power. From such simple examples, which are shared with precomputational mathematics, computer science has built a mathematical culture that relies heavily on defining things in terms of themselves.[24]

For the psychoanalyst Ogden, the idea that a thought might think was unthinkable. Information-processing AI also divides thought from thinking. What is closest to a thought is information. What is closest to thinking is its processing. But emergent AI breaks down this distinction. It takes the idea of recursion and turns it into an overarching aesthetic. To put it more sharply, emergent AI provides a way out of the problem of infinite regress by redefining the problem as a source of power. Taking recursion as a scientific aesthetic gives AI a way out of a theoretical hole. It may offer a similar possiblity to psychoanalysis.

What computational memory was to the birth of cognitive science in the 1950s, recursion could be to psychoanalytic studies of the 1990s. One could imagine computer scientists trying to support Kleinian psychoanalysts by building a detailed computer model of Kleinian objects. But one could also imagine computationally sophisticated psychoanalytic theorists finding, in the recursive idea that thoughts might think, a pleasing virtue rather than a devastating vice. One could imagine a psychoanalytic theorist seeing recursive ideas in his or her own work as a source of legitimation rather than a sign of weakness.

There can be no simple prediction about how recursion will help psychoanalysts deal with the infinite regress of object theories, but it seems probable that the kind of influence to look for is psychoanalysis becoming increasingly permeable to recursion as a sustaining myth. This would make the very thing that has been leveled as criticism become a way to support the theory. In the spirit of George Miller's account of computer memory and behaviorism, psychoanalysts might find it embarrassing to deny human thoughts the ability to think, when "computer thoughts" are presumed to do so.

If the central issue in psychoanalytic theory today turned on the nature of the "death instinct," there would be little that is helpful in theories about a machine that was never born. But to the degree that theoretical concerns in psychoanalysis have to do with the structure and functioning of internal objects, it is moving toward AI—to the point where the path to a productive dialogue seems open.

When the dialogue begins, the influence of AI on psychoanalysis will not necessarily be dependent on whether AI offers technical advice but on whether it can offer moral support to beleaguered psychoanalytic object theorists in their debates. Can it serve as sustaining myth? The influence of AI on psychology, psychoanalytic and other, is related not only to the solution of technical problems but also to the growth of psychological cultures.

PSYCHOANALYTIC CULTURE AND COMPUTER CULTURE

Psychological cultures do not exist only in the world of professionals. Artificial intelligence and psychoanalysis set the context in which professional psychologists and the amateur psychologists we all are think about thinking. From a sociological perspective on this wider psychological culture, object theories make ideas in AI and psychoanalysis more "appropriable," easier for people to take up as ways of thinking about themselves, than theories about information or drive. In other words, object theories give psychoanalysis and AI a greater presence as philosophies in everyday life. Fairbairn's dense texts and the mathematical theory of connectionism might not be any more accessible to lay thinking than technical papers on information processing or on psychoanalytic drives. But when object-oriented theories are popularized and move out into the general culture, they have a special appeal. Ideas about objects and agents are more concrete than ideas about drives and flow-charts. They are seductive because it is easy to "play" with them. And they speak to a common problem. We all have the experience of not feeling completely "at one" with ourselves: inner voices offer conflicting advice, reassurance, and chastisement. These experiences are easily and satisfyingly translated into a drama of inner objects.

Freudian ideas about slips of the tongue became well known and gained wide acceptance for reasons that had little to do with positive assessments of their scientific validity. Freudian slips became part of the wider psychological culture because they made it easy to play with what might be hidden behind them. The slips are almost tangible ideas. They are manipulable. Slips are appealing as objects to think with. You can analyze your own slips and those of your friends. The theory of slips provided a way for psychoanalytic ideas to become part of everyday life. They helped to make psychoanalytic theory appropriable.

A Freudian perspective on the appropriability of psychoanalytic ideas might go further to suggest that the theory of significant slips is appealing because it puts us in immediate contact with the taboo. We are afraid of the sexual and aggressive sides of our natures, but we want to be in touch with them as well. Psychoanalytic ideas give us a way to play with what is forbidden. Similarly, we are afraid to think of ourselves as machines, yet we want to find a way to acknowledge this very real, if disturbing, part of our experience. Playing with AI, with the idea of the mind as computer, makes this possible. Now, playing with computational and psychoanalytic theories of objects and agents allows us to go even further. The idea of agents gives us a way to acknowledge the experience of fragmentation. The rational bias in our culture presents consistency and coherency as natural, but feelings of fragmentation abound. Indeed, it has been argued that they are a contemporary cultural malaise.[25] Theories within psychoanalysis and AI that speak simply and dramatically to the experience of a divided self have particular power.

In the past the computer culture and the psychoanalytic culture have been separate. In the main, psychoanalytic ideas for thinking about the self were congenial to people who had little contact with computational ones. If and when members of the psychoanalytic culture met computational models of mind, they were most likely to be information-processing models that seemed out of step with a psychoanalytic outlook. These models described sequences, not associations, and their model of determination was narrow rather than wide. But increasingly, the computational ideas put forward and reported in the popular, as well as the academic, press are not about rules and information but about agents, connections, and societies of mind. These new metaphors have a biological aesthetic—they are the kind of things that could be going on in a brain. They suggest broad determination and dynamic repression. They describe a system in conflict. And, most important, they resonate with the psychoanalytic ideas that are currently abroad, ideas not about drives and their vicissitudes but about objects and their interactions.

When the computer presence relegitimated the idea of memory, it was reinforcing an idea about psychology that predated computation. But ideas about recursion and agents are not precomputational. Dare one speculate what will pass between computation and our psychological culture if AI finds a voice finally divorced from what was static in logic and if psychoanalysis finds a voice finally divorced from the issues of nineteenth-century drive theory?

ENDNOTES

[1] Many of the ideas in this paper emerged in a series of conversations with Seymour Papert, a collaborator in the development of my notion of the role of sustaining myths in the sociology of the sciences of mind.

[2] Cited in Jonathan Miller, *States of Mind* (New York: Pantheon, 1983), 23.

[3] Ibid.

[4] Cited in Sherry Turkle, *The Second Self: Computers and the Human Spirit* (New York: Simon and Schuster, 1984), 256.

[5] Cited in Jeremy Bernstein, *Science Observed* (New York: Basic Books, 1982), 110–11.

[6] Sigmund Freud, "Project for a Scientific Psychology," *The Standard Edition of the Complete Psychological Works of Sigmund Freud*, vol. 1, trans. and ed. James Strachey (London: Hogarth Press, 1960).

[7] George Boole, *The Laws of Thought*, vol. 2 of *His Collected Works* (La Salle, Ill.: Open Court Publishing Company, 1952).

[8] A suggestive effort to construct psychoanalytic algorithms was made by French psychoanalyst Jacques Lacan in his theory of the *mathèmes*. The power of this idea derives from its effort to legitimate systematicity and a closer relationship with science in psychoanalytic studies. See Sherry Turkle, *Psychoanalytic Politics: Freud's French Revolution* (New York: Basic Books, 1978.)

[9] For an example of an information-processing perspective on the Freudian, see Donald Norman, "Post-Freudian Slips," *Psychology Today*, April 1980:41–44ff; Norman, *Slips of the Mind and an Outline of a Theory of Action* (San Diego: Center for Human Information Processing, University of California, November 1979); and Norman, "Categorization of Action Slips," *Psychological Review* 88 (January 1981):1–15.

[10] Lovelace put it like this: "The analytical Engine has no pretensions whatever to originate anything. It can do whatever we know how to order it to perform."

[11] This phrase is borrowed from Douglas R. Hofstadter, who discusses computation and the Boolean aesthetic in "Waking Up From the Boolean Dream, or Subcognition as Computation," in *Metamagical Themas: Questing for the Essence of Mind and Pattern* (New York: Basic Books, 1985).

[12] Alan Kay, "Software's Second Act," *Science 85* (November 1985):122.

[13] Thomas H. Ogden, "The Concept of Internal Object Relations," *The International Journal of Psycho-Analysis* 64 (1983):227.

[14] See Jay R. Greenberg and Stephen A. Mitchell, *Object Relations in Psychoanalytic Theory* (Cambridge: Harvard University Press, 1983).

[15] Thomas Kuhn, *The Structure of Scientific Revolutions*, 2d ed. (Chicago: University of Chicago Press, 1970).

[16] Marvin Minsky, *The Society of Mind* (New York: Simon and Schuster, 1987).

[17] Ibid., 183. Fieldwork with children and computers is rich in examples of the kind of fright that Minsky expects. For example, an incident where it was evoked by a first contact with recursion is reported in Sherry Turkle, *The Second Self*. Interviews with adults on early experiences also reveal many such memories—fear

of prisms, of mirrors reflecting mirrors, fear of questions such as "How far away are the stars?"

[18]Russell Jacoby, *Social Amnesia: A Critique of Contemporary Psychology from Adler to Laing* (Boston: Beacon Press, 1975).

[19]Roy Schafer, *A New Language for Psychoanalysis* (New Haven: Yale University Press, 1976), 3; and Schafer, *Aspects of Internalization* (New York: International University Press, 1968), 62.

[20]Ogden, "Internal Object Relations," 229.

[21]Hannah Segal, *Introduction to the Work of Melanie Klein* (London: Hogarth Press, 1978).

[22]Ogden, "Internal Object Relations," 230.

[23]*Science 86* (May 1986):27.

[24]The computational aesthetic of recursive thought has been expressed in a poetic and accessible form by Douglas R. Hofstadter, who presents recursive phenomena as a source of power in Bach's music and Escher's art as well as in Gödel's mathematics. See *Gödel, Escher, Bach: An Eternal Golden Braid* (New York: Basic Books, 1978).

[25]See, for example, Christopher Lasch, *The Culture of Narcissism* (New York: Norton, 1979).

Hilary Putnam

Much Ado About Not Very Much

THE QUESTION I WANT TO CONTEMPLATE is this: Has artificial intelligence taught us anything of importance about the mind? I am inclined to think that the answer is no. I am also inclined to wonder, What is all the fuss about? Of course, AI may someday teach us something important about how we think, but why are we so exercised now? Perhaps it is this prospect that exercises us, but why do we think now is the time to decide what might in principle be possible? Or am I wrong: Is the "in principle" question really the important one to discuss now? And if it is, have the defenders of AI had anything important to tell us about it?

The computer model of the mind is now associated with AI, but it is not unique to AI (Noam Chomsky is not, as far as I know, optimistic about AI, but he shares the computer model with AI[1]), and the computer model was not invented by AI. If it was invented by anyone, it was invented by Alan Turing. Computer science is not the same thing as AI.

In fact, the idea of the mind as a sort of reckoning machine goes back to the seventeenth century.[2] In the early twentieth century two giants in logic—Kurt Gödel and Jacques Herbrand—first proposed the modern conception of computability (under the name "general recursiveness"[3]). Turing reformulated the Gödel-Herbrand notion of computability in terms that connect directly with digital computers (which were not yet invented, however!) and also suggested his

Hilary Putnam is Walter Beverly Pearson Professor of Modern Mathematics and Mathematical Logic in the department of philosophy at Harvard University.

abstract computers as a model for a mind.[4] Even if Turing's suggestion should prove wrong—even if it should prove in some way more empty than it seems—it would still have been a great contribution to thinking in the way past models of the mind have proved great contributions to thinking—great, even if not finally successful, attempts to understand understanding itself. But AI is not recursion theory, is not the theory of Turing machines, is not the philosophy of Alan Turing, but is something much more specific.

To get to AI, we first have to get to computers. The modern digital computer is a realization of the idea of a universal Turing machine in a particularly effective form—effective in terms of size, cost, speed, and so on. The construction and improvement of computers in terms of both software and hardware is a fact of life. But not everyone concerned with the design of either software or hardware is an AI researcher. However, some of what AI gets credit for—for example, the enormous improvement in the capacities of chess-playing computers—is as much or more due to discoveries of the inventors of hardware as it is to anything that might be called a discovery in AI.

Computer design is a branch of engineering (even when what is designed is software and not hardware), and AI is a subbranch of this branch of engineering. If this is worth saying, it is because AI has become notorious for making exaggerated claims—claims of being a fundamental discipline and even of being "epistemology." The aim of this branch of engineering is to develop software that will enable computers to simulate or duplicate the achievements of what we intuitively recognize as "intelligence."

I take it that this is a noncontroversial characterization of AI. The next statement I expect to be more controversial: AI has so far spun off a good deal that is of real interest to computer science in general, but nothing that sheds any real light on the mind (beyond whatever light may already have been shed by Turing's discussions). I don't propose to spend my pages defending this last claim (Joseph Weizenbaum has already done a good job along these lines[5]). But I will give a couple of illustrations of what I mean.

Many years ago I was at a symposium with one of the most "famous names" in AI. The famous name was being duly "modest" about the achievements of AI. He said offhandedly, "We haven't really achieved so much, but I will say that we now have *machines that understand children's stories.*" I remarked, "I know the program you refer to" (it was one of the earliest language-recognition programs). "What you didn't mention is that the program has to be *revised* for each new children's story." (That is, in case the point hasn't been grasped, the "program" was a program for answering questions about a specific children's story, not a program for understanding children's stories in general.) The famous name dropped the whole issue in a hurry.

Currently the most touted achievement of AI is "expert systems." But these systems (which are, at bottom, just high-speed data-base searchers) are not models for any interesting mental capacities.

Of course, the possibility remains that some idea dreamed up in an AI lab may in the future revolutionize our thinking about some aspect of mentation. (Parallel distributed processing is currently exciting interest as a possible model for at least some mental processes, for example. This is not surprising, however, since the model was suggested in the first place by the work of the neurologist D.O. Hebb.[6]) My point is not to predict the future but just to explain why I am inclined to ask, What's all the fuss about *now?* Why a whole issue of *Dædalus?* Why don't we wait until AI achieves something and *then* have an issue?

"IN PRINCIPLE"/"IN PRACTICE"

Perhaps the issue that interests people *is* whether we can model the mind or brain as a digital computer—in principle as opposed to right now—and perhaps AI gets involved because people do not sharply distinguish the in-principle question from the empirical question, Will AI succeed in so modeling the mind or brain? It may be useful to begin by seeing just how different the two questions are.

In one way the difference seems obvious: we are tempted to say that it might be possible in principle to model the mind or brain as a digital computer with appropriate software, but it might be too difficult in practice to write down the correct software. Or it just looks as if this difference is obvious. I want to say, Tread lightly; things are not so simple: in one sense, any physical system can be modeled as a computer.[7] The claim that the brain can be modeled as a computer is thus, in one way, trivial. Perhaps there is another more meaningful sense in which we can ask, Can the brain be modeled as a computer? At this point, however, all we can say is that the sense of the question has not been made clear.

But the feeling seems to be that not only is it possible in principle to model the mind or brain computationally, but there is a very good chance that we will be able to do it in practice, and philosophers (and defectors from AI like Weizenbaum) are seen as reactionaries who might talk us out of even trying something that promises to be a great intellectual and practical success. If this is how one thinks, then the gap between the two questions (and the vagueness of the in-principle question) may not seem very important in practice. Indeed, it may be of strategic benefit to confuse them.

The reasons for expecting us to succeed in practice are not clear to me, however.[8] If we are digital computers programmed by evolution, then it is important to know how to think about evolution. The great evolutionary biologist François Jacob once compared evolution to a tinker.[9] Evolution should not, Jacob wrote, be thought of as a designer who sits down and produces a lovely blueprint and then constructs organisms according to the blueprint. Evolution should rather be thought of as a tinker with a shop full of spare parts, interesting "junk," etc. Every so often the tinker gets an idea: "I wonder if it would work if I tried using this bicycle wheel in that doohickey?" Many of the tinker's bright ideas fail, but every so often one works. The result is organisms with many arbitrary features as well as serendipitous ones.

Now, imagine that the tinker becomes a programmer. Still thinking like a tinker, he develops "natural intelligence," not by writing a Grand Program and then building a device to realize it but by introducing one device or programming idea after another. (Religious people often reject such a view, for they feel that if it is right, then our nature and history is all "blind chance," but I have never been able to sympathize with this objection. Providence may work through what Kant called "the cunning of Nature.") The net result could be that natural intelligence is not the expression of some *one* program but the expression of billions of bits of "tinkering."

Something like this was, indeed, at one time discussed within the AI community itself. This community has wobbled back and forth between looking for a Master Program (ten or fifteen years ago there was a search for something called inductive logic) and accepting the notion that "artificial intelligence is one damned thing after another."

My point is that if AI is "one damned thing after another," the number of "damned things" the tinker may have thought of could be astronomical.[10] The upshot is pessimistic indeed: if there is no Master Program, then we may never get very far in terms of simulating human intelligence. (Of course, some areas that are relatively closed—for example, theorem proving in pure mathematics—might be amenable. Oddly enough, theorem proving has always been a rather underfunded part of AI research.)

A MASTER PROGRAM?

But why shouldn't there be a Master Program? In the case of deductive logic, we have discovered a set of rules that satisfactorily formalize valid inference. In the case of inductive logic, we have found no such rules, and it is worthwhile pausing to ask why.

In the first place, it is not clear just how large the scope of inductive logic is supposed to be. Some writers consider the "hypothetico-deductive method"—that is, the inference from the success of a theory's predictions to the acceptability of the theory—the most important part of inductive logic, while others regard it as already belonging to a different subject. Of course, if by "induction" we mean any method of valid inference that is not deductive, then the scope of the topic "inductive logic" will be enormous.

If the success of a large number (say, a thousand or ten thousand) of predictions that were not themselves consequences of auxiliary hypotheses alone (and that were unlikely in relation to what background knowledge gives us, Karl Popper would add[11]) always confirmed a theory, then at least the hypothetico-deductive inference would be easy to formalize. But problems arise at once. Some theories are accepted when the number of confirmed predictions is still very small. This was the case with the general theory of relativity, for example. To take care of such cases, we postulate that it is not only the number of confirmed predictions that matters but also the elegance or simplicity of the theory in question. Can such quasi-aesthetic notions as "elegance" and "simplicity" really be formalized? Formal measures have indeed been proposed, but it cannot be said that they shed any light on real-life scientific inference. Moreover, a confirmed theory sometimes fits badly with background knowledge; in some cases we conclude that the theory cannot be true, while in others we conclude that the background knowledge should be modified. Again, apart from imprecise talk about simplicity, it is hard to say what determines whether it is better in a particular case to preserve background knowledge or to modify it. And even a theory that leads to a vast number of successful predictions may not be accepted if someone points out that a much simpler theory would lead to those predictions as well.

In view of these difficulties, some students of inductive logic would confine the scope of the subject to simpler inferences, such as the inference from the statistics for a sample drawn from a population to the statistics for the entire population. When the population consists of objects that exist at different times, including future times, the present sample is never going to be a random selection from the whole population, however, so the key case is this: I have a sample that is a random selection from the members of a population who exist now (or worse, from the ones who exist here, on Earth, in the United States, in the particular place where I have been able to gather samples, or wherever). What can I conclude about the properties of future members of that population (and about the properties of members in other places)?

If the sample is a sample of uranium atoms, and the future members are in the near as opposed to the cosmological future, then we are prepared to believe that the future members will resemble present members, on the average. If the sample is a sample of people, and the future members of the population are not in the very near future, then we are less likely to make this assumption, at least if culturally variable traits are in question. Here we are guided by background knowledge, of course. This sort of example has suggested to some inquirers perhaps all there is to induction is the skillful use of background knowledge—we just "bootstrap" our way from what we know to additional knowledge. But then the cases in which we don't have much background knowledge, as well as the exceptional cases in which what we have to do is precisely question background knowledge, assume great importance; and here, as just remarked, no one has much to say beyond vague talk about simplicity.

The problem of induction is not by any means the only problem confronting anyone who seriously intends to simulate human intelligence. Induction—indeed, all cognition—presupposes the ability to recognize similarities among things; but similarities are by no means just constancies of the physical stimulus or patterns in the input to the sense organs. What makes knives similar, for example, is not that they all look alike (they don't), but that they are all manufactured to cut or stab (I neglect such cases as ceremonial knives here, of course). Thus, any system that can recognize knives as relevantly similar must be able to attribute *purposes* to agents. Humans have no difficulty in doing this. But it is not clear that we do this by unaided induction; we may well have a "hard-wired-in" ability to put ourselves in the shoes of other people that enables us to attribute to them any purposes we are capable of attributing to ourselves—an ability that Evolution the Tinker found it convenient to endow us with and one that helps us to know which of the infinitely many possible inductions we might consider is likely to be successful. Again, to recognize that a Chihuahua and a Great Dane are similar in the sense of belonging to the same species requires the ability to realize that, appearances not withstanding,[12] Chihuahuas can impregnate Great Danes and produce fertile offspring. Thinking in terms of potential for mating and for reproduction is natural for us, but it need not be natural for an artificial intelligence—unless we deliberately simulate this human propensity when we construct the artificial intelligence. Such examples can be multiplied indefinitely.

Similarities expressed by adjectives and verbs rather than by nouns can be even more complex. A nonhuman intelligence might know what "white" is on a color chart, for example, without being able to see why pinkish gray humans are called white, and it might know what it is to open a door without being able to understand why we speak of opening a border or opening trade. There are many words (as Ludwig Wittgenstein pointed out[13]) that apply to things that have only a "family resemblance" to one another; there need not be one thing all *x*'s have in common. For example, we speak of the Canaanite tribal chiefs of the Old Testament as kings although their kingdoms were probably little more than villages, and we speak of George VI as a king, though he did not literally rule England; we even say that in some cases in history, kingship has not been hereditary. Similarly (in Wittgenstein's example), there is no property all games have in common that distinguishes them from all the activities that are not games.

The notional task of artificial intelligence is to simulate intelligence, not to duplicate it. So perhaps one might finesse the problems just mentioned by constructing a system that reasoned in an ideal language[14]—one in which words did not change their extensions in a context-dependent way (a sheet of typing paper might be "white$_1$," and a human being might be "white$_2$" in such a language, where "white$_1$" is color-chart white and "white$_2$" is pinkish gray). Perhaps all family-resemblance words would have to be barred from such a language. (How much of a vocabulary would be left?) But my list of difficulties is not yet finished.

Because the project of symbolic inductive logic appeared to run out of steam after Rudolf Carnap, the thinking among philosophers of science has, as I reported, run in the direction of talking about bootstrapping methods—methods that attribute a great deal to background knowledge. It is instructive to see why philosophers have taken this approach and also to realize how unsatisfactory it is if our aim is to simulate intelligence rather than to describe it.

One huge problem might be described as the existence of conflicting inductions. Here's an example from Nelson Goodman: as far as we know, no one who has ever entered Emerson Hall at Harvard University has been able to speak Inuit (Eskimo). This statement suggests the induction that if any person enters Emerson Hall, then he or she does not speak Inuit.[15] Let Ukuk be an Eskimo in Alaska who speaks Inuit. Shall I predict that if Ukuk enters Emerson Hall, Ukuk will no longer be able to speak Inuit? Obviously not, but what is wrong with this induction?

Goodman answers that what is wrong with the inference is that it conflicts with the "better entrenched," inductively supported law that people do not lose their ability to speak a language upon entering a new place. But how am I supposed to know that this law does have more confirming instances than the regularity that no one who enters Emerson Hall speaks Inuit? Through background knowledge again?

As a matter of fact, I don't believe that as a child I had any idea how often either of the conflicting regularities in the example (conflicting in that one of them must fail if Ukuk enters Emerson Hall) had been confirmed, but I would still have known enough not to make the silly induction that Ukuk would stop being able to speak Inuit if he entered a building (or a country) where no one had spoken Inuit. Again, it is not clear that the knowledge that one doesn't lose a language just like that is really the product of induction; perhaps this is something we have an innate propensity to believe. The question that won't go away is *how much what we call intelligence presupposes the rest of human nature.*

Moreover, if what matters really is "entrenchment" (that is, the number and variety of confirming instances), and if the information that the universal statement "One doesn't lose one's ability to speak a language upon entering a new place" is better entrenched than the universal statement "No one who enters Emerson Hall speaks Inuit" is part of my background knowledge, it isn't clear how that information got there. Perhaps the information is implicit in the way people speak about linguistic abilities; but then one is faced with the question of how one decodes the implicit information conveyed by the utterances one hears.

The problem of conflicting inductions is ubiquitous even if one restricts attention to the simplest inductive inferences. If the solution is really just to give the system more background knowledge, then what are the implications for artificial intelligence?

It is not easy to say, because artificial intelligence as we know it doesn't really try to simulate intelligence at all. Simulating intelligence is only its notional activity; its real activity is writing clever programs for a variety of tasks. But if artificial intelligence existed as a real, rather than notional, research activity, there would be two alternative strategies its practitioners could follow when faced with the problem of background knowledge:

1. They could accept the view of the philosophers of science I have described and simply try to program into a machine all the information a sophisticated human inductive judge has (including implicit information). At the least, this would require generations of researchers to formalize the information (probably it could not be done at all, because of the sheer quantity of information involved), and it is not clear that the result would be more than a gigantic expert system. No one would find this very exciting, and such an "intelligence" would in all likelihood be dreadfully unimaginative, unable to realize that in many cases it is precisely background knowledge that needs to be given up.

2. AI's practitioners could undertake the more exciting and ambitious task of constructing a device that could learn the background

knowledge by interacting with human beings, as a child learns a language and all the cultural information, explicit and implicit, that comes with learning a language by growing up in a human community.

THE NATURAL-LANGUAGE PROBLEM

The second alternative is certainly the project that deserves the name "artificial intelligence." But consider the problems: to figure out what is the information implicit in the things people say, the machine must simulate understanding a human language. Thus, the idea of sticking to an artificial ideal language and ignoring the complexities of natural language has to be abandoned if this strategy is adopted—abandoned because the cost is too high. Too much of the information the machine would need is retrievable only via natural-language processing.

But the natural-language problem presents many of the same difficulties all over again. Chomsky and his school believe that a "template" for natural language, including the "semantic," or conceptual, aspects, is innate—hard-wired-in by Evolution the Tinker.[16] Although this view is taken to extremes by Jerry Fodor, who holds that there is an innate language of thought with primitives adequate for the expression of all concepts that humans are able to learn to express in a natural language,[17] Chomsky himself has hesitated to go this far. What Chomsky seems committed to is the existence of a large number of innate conceptual abilities that give us a propensity to form certain concepts and not others. (In conversation, he has suggested that the difference between postulating innate concepts and postulating innate abilities is not important if the postulated abilities are sufficiently structured.) At the opposite extreme there is the view of classical behaviorism, which explains language learning as a special case of the application of general rules for acquiring "habits"—that is, as just one more bundle of inductions. (An in-between position is, of course, possible: Why should language learning not depend partly on special-purpose heuristics and partly on general learning strategies, both developed by evolution?)

Consider the view that language learning is not really learning but rather the maturation of an innate ability in a particular environment (somewhat like the acquisition of a birdcall by the young of a species of bird that has to hear the call from adult birds of the species to acquire it but that also has an innate propensity to acquire that sort of call). In its extreme form, this view leads to pessimism about the likelihood that the human use of natural language can be successfully simulated on a computer. This is why Chomsky is pessimistic about projects for natural-language computer processing, although he shares the computer model of the mind, or at least of the "language organ," with AI researchers. Notice that this pessimistic view about language learning parallels the pessimistic view that induction is not a single ability but rather a manifestation of a complex human nature whose computer simulation would require a vast system of subroutines—so vast that generations of researchers would be required to formalize even a small part of the system.

Similarly, the optimistic view that there is an algorithm of manageable size for inductive logic is paralleled by the optimistic view of language learning. This is the idea that there is a more or less topic-neutral heuristic for learning and that this heuristic suffices (without the aid of an unmanageably large stock of hard-wired-in background knowledge or topic-specific conceptual abilities) for learning one's natural language as well as for making inductive inferences. Perhaps the optimistic view is right, but I do not see anyone on the scene, in either artificial intelligence or inductive logic, who has any interesting ideas about how the topic-neutral learning strategy works. When someone does appear with such an idea, that will be the time for *Dædalus* to publish an issue on AI.

ENDNOTES

[1] Noam Chomsky, *Modular Approaches to the Study of the Mind* (San Diego, Calif.: San Diego State University Press, 1983).

[2] This is well described in Justin Webb's *Mechanism, Mentalism, and Metamathematics* (Dordrecht: Reidel, 1980).

[3] The Gödel-Herbrand conception of recursiveness was further developed by Stephen Kleene, Alonzo Church, Emil Post, and Alan Turing. The identification of recursiveness with effective computability was suggested (albeit obliquely) by Kurt Gödel in "On Formally Undecidable Propositions of *Principia Mathematica* and Related Systems I." The German original of this was published in the *Monatshefte für Mathematik und Physik* 38 (1931):173–98; the English translation is in *The Undecidable: Basic Papers on Undecidable Propositions, Undecidable Problems, and Computable Functions*, ed. Martin Davis (Hewlett, N.Y.: Raven Press, 1965), 5–38. The idea was then explicitly put forward by Church in

his classic paper on the undecidability of arithmetic, "A Note on the Entschei-dungsproblem," *Journal of Symbolic Logic* 1 (1) (March 1936):40–41; correc-tion, ibid. (3) (September 1936):101–102; reprinted in Davis, *The Undecidable*, 110–15.

⁴Alan Turing and Michael Woodger, *The Automatic Computing Machine: Papers by Alan Turing and Michael Woodger* (Cambridge: MIT Press, 1985).

⁵Joseph Weizenbaum, *Computer Power and Human Reason: From Judgment to Calculation* (San Francisco: Freeman, 1976).

⁶See David E. Rummelhart and James L. McClelland and the PDP Research Group, eds., *Parallel Distributed Processing: Explorations in the Microstructure of Cognition*, vols. 1 and 2 (Cambridge: MIT Press, 1986); and D. O. Hebb, *Essay on Mind* (Hillsdale, N.J.: Lawrence Erlbaum Associates, 1980).

⁷More precisely, if we are interested in the behavior of a physical system that is finite in space and time and we wish to predict that behavior only up to some specified level of accuracy, then (assuming that the laws of motion are themselves continuous functions) it is trivial to show that a step function will give the prediction to the specified level of accuracy. If the possible values of the boundary parameters are restricted to a finite range, then a finite set of such step functions will give the behavior of the system under all possible conditions in the specified range to within the desired accuracy. But if that is the case, the behavior of the system is described by a recursive function and hence the system can be simulated by an automaton.

⁸In his reply to this paper (in this very issue), Daniel Dennett accuses me of offering an "a priori" argument that success is impossible. I have not changed the text of the paper at all in the light of his reply, and I invite the reader to observe that no such "a priori proof of impossibility" claim is advanced by me here or elsewhere! Although Dennett says that he is going to explain what AI has taught us about the mind, what he in fact does is to repeat the insults that AI researchers hurl at philosophers ("We are experimenters, and you are armchair thinkers!"). On other occasions, when Dennett is not talking like a spokesman for AI but doing what he does best, which is philosophy, he is, of course, well aware that I and, for that matter, other philosophers he respects are by no means engaged in a priori reasoning, and that the fact that we do not perform "experiments" does not mean that we are not engaged—as he is—in thinking about the real world in the light of the best knowledge available.

⁹François Jacob, "Evolution and Tinkering," *Science* 196 (1977):1161–66.

¹⁰That the number of times our design has been modified by evolution may be astronomical does not mean that the successful modifications are not (partially) hierarchically organized, nor does it mean that there are not a great many principles that explain the functioning together of the various components. To describe the alternative to the success of AI as "the mind as chaos," as Dennett does, is nonsense. If it turns out that the mind is chaos when modeled as a computer, that will only show that the computer formalism is not a perspicuous formalism for describing the brain, not that the brain is chaos.

¹¹Karl Popper, *The Logic of Scientific Discovery* (London: Hutchinson, 1959).

¹²Note that if we had only appearances to go by, it would be quite natural to regard Great Danes and Chihuahuas as animals of different species!

¹³See Ludwig Wittgenstein, *Philosophical Investigations* (Oxford: Basil Blackwell, 1958), sec. 66–71.

[14]Note that this idea was one of the foundation stones of logical positivism. Although the positivists' goal was to reconstruct scientific reasoning rather than to mechanize it, they ran into every one of the problems mentioned here; in many ways the history of artificial intelligence is a repeat of the history of logical positivism (the second time perhaps as farce).

[15]Nelson Goodman, *Fact, Fiction, and Forecast,* 4th ed. (Cambridge: Harvard University Press, 1983).

[16]Chomsky speaks of "a subsystem [for language] which has a specific integrated character and which is in effect the genetic program for a specific organ" in the discussion with Seymour Papert, Jean Piaget, et al. reprinted in *Language and Learning,* ed. Massimo Piatelli (Cambridge: Harvard University Press, 1980). See also Noam Chomsky, *Language and Problems of Knowledge, The Managua Lectures* (Cambridge: MIT Press, 1987).

[17]Jerry A. Fodor, *The Language of Thought* (New York: Thomas Y. Crowell, 1975).

Daniel C. Dennett

When Philosophers Encounter Artificial Intelligence

H OW IS IT POSSIBLE for a physical thing—a person, an animal, a robot—to extract knowledge of the world from perception and then exploit that knowledge in the guidance of successful action? That is a question with which philosophers have grappled for generations, but it could also be taken to be one of the defining questions of artificial intelligence. AI is, in large measure, philosophy. It is often directly concerned with instantly recognizable philosophical questions: What is mind? What is meaning? What is reasoning and rationality? What are the necessary conditions for the recognition of objects in perception? How are decisions made and justified?

Some philosophers have appreciated this aspect of AI, and a few have even cheerfully switched fields to pursue their philosophical quarries through thickets of LISP.* In general, however, philosophers have not welcomed this new style of philosophy with much enthusiasm. One might suppose that this is because they have seen through it. Some philosophers have indeed concluded, after cursory inspection of the field, that in spite of the breathtaking pretension of some of its publicists, artificial intelligence has nothing new to offer philosophers beyond the spectacle of ancient, well-drubbed errors replayed in a glitzy new medium. And other philosophers are so sure

Daniel C. Dennett is distinguished arts and sciences professor and professor of philosophy at Tufts University. He is director of the Center for Cognitive Studies and codirector of the Curricular Software Studio, both at Tufts.

*The programming language LISP, created by John McCarthy, is the lingua franca of AI.

this must be so that they haven't bothered conducting the cursory inspection. They are sure the field is dismissable on "general principles."

Philosophers have been dreaming about AI for centuries. Hobbes and Leibniz, in very different ways, tried to explore the implications of the idea of breaking down the mind into small, ultimately mechanical, operations. Descartes even anticipated the Turing test (Alan Turing's much-discussed proposal of an audition of sorts for computers, in which the computer's task is to convince the judges that they are conversing with a human being[1]) and did not hesitate to issue a confident prediction of its inevitable result:

It is indeed conceivable that a machine could be made so that it would utter words, and even words appropriate to the presence of physical acts or objects which cause some change in its organs; as, for example, if it was touched in some spot that it would ask what you wanted to say to it; if in another, that it would cry that it was hurt, and so on for similar things. But it could never modify its phrases to reply to the sense of whatever was said in its presence, as even the most stupid men can do.[2]

The appreciation Descartes had for the powers of mechanism was colored by his acquaintance with the marvelous clockwork automata of his day. He could see very clearly and distinctly, no doubt, the limitations of that technology. Not even a thousand tiny gears—not even ten thousand—would permit an automaton to respond gracefully and rationally! Perhaps Hobbes or Leibniz would have been less confident of this point, but surely none of them would have bothered wondering about the a priori limits on a million tiny gears spinning millions of times a second. That was simply not a thinkable thought for them. It was unthinkable then, not in the familiar philosophical sense of appearing self-contradictory ("repugnant to reason") or entirely outside their conceptual scheme (like the concept of a neutrino), but in the more workaday, yet equally limiting, sense of being an idea they would have had no way to take seriously. When philosophers set out to scout large conceptual domains, they are as inhibited in the paths they take by their sense of silliness as by their insight into logical necessity. And there is something about AI that many philosophers find off-putting—if not repugnant to reason, then repugnant to their aesthetic sense.

This clash of vision was memorably displayed in a historic debate at Tufts University in March of 1978, staged, appropriately, by the Society for Philosophy and Psychology. Nominally a panel discussion on the foundations and prospects of artificial intelligence, it turned into a tag-team rhetorical wrestling match between four heavyweight ideologues: Noam Chomsky and Jerry Fodor attacking AI, and Roger Schank and Terry Winograd defending it. Schank was working at the time on programs for natural-language comprehension, and the critics focused on his scheme for representing (in a computer) the higgledy-piggledy collection of trivia we all know and somehow rely on when deciphering ordinary speech acts, allusive and truncated as they are. Chomsky and Fodor heaped scorn on this enterprise, but the grounds of their attack gradually shifted in the course of the match. It began as a straightforward, "first principles" condemnation of conceptual error—Schank was on one fool's errand or another—but it ended with a striking concession from Chomsky: it just might turn out, as Schank thought, that the human capacity to comprehend conversation (and more generally, to think) was to be explained in terms of the interaction of hundreds or thousands of jerry-built gizmos—pseudorepresentations, one might call them but that would be a shame, for then psychology would prove in the end not to be "interesting." There were only two interesting possibilities, in Chomsky's mind: psychology could turn out to be "like physics"—its regularities explainable as the consequences of a few deep, elegant, inexorable laws—or psychology could turn out to be utterly lacking in laws—in which case the only way to study or expound psychology would be the novelist's way (and he much preferred Jane Austen to Roger Schank, if that were the enterprise).

A vigorous debate ensued among the panelists and audience, capped by an observation from Chomsky's colleague at the Massachusetts Institute of Technology, Marvin Minsky, one of the founding fathers of AI and founder of MIT's Artificial Intelligence Laboratory: "I think only a humanities professor at MIT could be so oblivious to the third interesting possibility: psychology could turn out to be like engineering."

Minsky had put his finger on it. There is something about the prospect of an engineering approach to the mind that is deeply repugnant to a certain sort of humanist, and it has little or nothing to do with a distaste for materialism or science. Witness Chomsky's physics worship, an attitude he shares with many philosophers. The days of Berkeleyan idealism and Cartesian dualism are over (if one can judge from the current materialistic consensus among philosophers and scientists), but in their place there is a widespread acceptance of what we might call Chomsky's fork: there are only two appealing ("interesting") alternatives.

On the one hand, there is the dignity and purity of the Crystalline Mind. Recall Aristotle's prejudice against extending earthly physics to the heavens, which ought, he thought, to be bound by a higher and purer order. This was his one pernicious legacy, but now that the heavens have been stormed, we appreciate the beauty of universal physics and can hope that the mind will be among its chosen "natural kinds," not a mere gerrymandering of bits and pieces.

On the other hand, there is the dignity of ultimate mystery, the Inexplicable Mind. If our minds can't be fundamental, then let them be anomalous. A very influential view among philosophers in recent years has been Donald Davidson's "anomalous monism," the view that while the mind is the brain, there are no lawlike regularities aligning mental facts with physical facts.[3] John Searle, Davidson's colleague at Berkeley, has made a different sort of mystery of the mind: the brain, thanks to some unspecified feature of its biochemistry, has some terribly important—but unspecified—"bottom-up causal powers" that are entirely distinct from the mere "control powers" studied in AI.

One feature shared by these otherwise drastically different forms of mind-body materialism is a resistance to Minsky's tertium quid: in between the mind as crystal and the mind as chaos lies the mind as gadget, an object that one should not expect to be governed by "deep" mathematical laws, but nevertheless a *designed* object, analyzable in functional terms: ends and means, costs and benefits, elegant solutions on the one hand, and on the other, shortcuts, jury rigs, and cheap *ad hoc* fixes.

This vision of the mind is resisted by many philosophers despite its being a straightforward implication of the current view among scientists and science-minded humanists of our place in nature: we are biological entities designed by natural selection, which is a tinker, not an ideal engineer. Computer programmers call an *ad hoc* fix a "kludge" (it rhymes with *Scrooge*), and the mixture of disdain and begrudged admiration reserved for kludges parallels the biologists' bemusement with "the panda's thumb" and other fascinating examples of *bricolage,* to use François Jacob's term.[4] The finest inadvertent spoonerism I ever heard was uttered by the linguist Barbara Partee in heated criticism of an acknowledged kludge in an AI natural-language parser: "That's so odd hack!" Nature is full of odd hacks, many of them perversely brilliant. Although this fact is widely appreciated, its implications for the study of the mind are often repugnant to philosophers, since their traditional aprioristic methods of investigating the mind give them little power to explore phenomena that might be contrived of odd hacks. There is really only one way to study such possibilities: with the more empirical mind-set of "reverse engineering."

The resistance is clearly manifested in Hilary Putnam's essay in this issue of *Dædalus,* which can serve as a convenient (if not particularly florid) case of the syndrome I wish to discuss. Chomsky's fork, the mind as crystal or as chaos, is transformed by Putnam into a pendulum swing he thinks he observes within AI itself. He claims that AI has "wobbled" over the years between looking for the Master Program and accepting the notion that "artificial intelligence is one damned thing after another." I have not myself observed any such wobble in the field over the years, but I think I know what he is getting at. Here, then, is a different perspective on the same issue.

Among the many divisions of opinion within AI there is a faction (sometimes called the logicists) whose aspirations suggest to me that they are Putnam's searchers for the Master Progam. They were more aptly caricatured recently by a researcher in AI as searchers for "Maxwell's equations of thought." Several somewhat incompatible enterprises within the field can be lumped together under this rubric. Roughly, what they have in common is the idea not that there must be a Master Program but that there must be something more like a master programming language, a single, logically sound system of explicit representation for all the knowledge residing in an agent (natural or artificial). Attached to this library of represented facts (which can be treated as axioms, in effect) and operating upon it computationally will be one sort or another of "inference engine," capable of deducing the relevant implications of the relevant axioms and eventually spewing up by this inference process the imperatives or decisions that will forthwith be implemented.

For instance, suppose perception yields the urgent new premise (couched in the master programming language) that the edge of a precipice is fast approaching; this should provoke the inference engine to call up from memory the appropriate stored facts about cliffs, gravity, acceleration, impact, damage, the paramount undesirability of such damage, and the likely effects of putting on the brakes or continuing apace. Forthwith, one hopes, the engine will deduce a theorem to the effect that halting is called for, and straightaway it will halt.

The hard part is designing a system of this sort that will actually work well in real time, even allowing for millions of operations per second in the inference engine. Everyone recognizes this problem of real-time adroitness; what sets the logicists apart is their conviction that the way to solve it is to find a truly perspicuous vocabulary and logical form for the master language. Modern logic has proven to be a powerful means of exploring and representing the stately universe of mathematics; the not unreasonable hope of the logicists is that the same systems of logic can be harnessed to capture the hectic universe of agents making their way in the protean macroscopic world. If you get the axioms and the inference system just right, they believe, the rest should be easy. The problems they encounter have to do with keeping the number of axioms down for the sake of generality (which is a must), while not requiring the system to waste time rededucing crucial intermediate-level facts every time it sees a cliff.

This idea of axiomatizing everyday reality is surely a philosophical one. Spinoza would have loved it, and many contemporary philosophers working in philosophical logic and the semantics of natural language share at least the goal of devising a rigorous logical system in which every statement, every thought, every hunch and wonder can be unequivocally expressed. The idea wasn't reinvented by AI; it was a gift from the philosophers who created modern mathematical logic: George Boole, Gottlob Frege, Alfred North Whitehead, Bertrand Russell, Alfred Tarski, and Alonzo Church. Douglas Hofstadter calls this theme in AI the Boolean dream.[5] It has always had its adherents and critics, with many variations.

Putnam's rendering of this theme as the search for the Master Program is clear enough, but when he describes the opposite pole, he elides our two remaining prospects: the mind as gadget and the mind as chaos. As he puts it, "If AI is 'one damned thing after another,' the number of 'damned things' the tinker may have thought of could be astronomical. The upshot is pessimistic indeed: if there is no Master Program, then we may never get very far in terms of simulating human intelligence." Here Putnam elevates a worst-case possibility (the gadget will be totally, "astronomically" *ad hoc*) as the only likely alternative to the Master Program. Why does he do this? What does he have against exploring the vast space of engineering possibilities between Crystal and Chaos? Biological wisdom, far from favoring his pessimism, holds out hope that the mix of elegance and Rube Goldberg found elsewhere in nature (in the biochemistry of reproduction, for instance) will be discernible in the mind as well.

There is, in fact, a variety of very different approaches being pursued in AI by those who hope the mind will turn out to be some sort of gadget or collection of partially integrated gadgets. All of these favor austerity, logic, and order in some aspects of their systems and yet exploit the peculiar utility of profligacy, inconsistency, and disorder in other aspects. It is not that Putnam's two themes don't exist in AI, but that by describing them as exclusive alternatives, he imposes a procrustean taxonomy on the field that makes it hard to discern the interesting issues that actually drive the field.

Most AI projects are explorations of *ways things might be done* and as such are more like thought experiments than empirical experiments. They differ from philosophical thought experiments not primarily in their content but in their methodology: they replace some—not all—of the "intuitive," "plausible," hand-waving background assumptions of philosophical thought experiments by constraints dictated by the demand that the model be made to run on the computer. These constraints of time and space and the exigencies of specification can be traded off against each other in practically limitless ways, so that new "virtual machines" or "virtual architectures" are imposed on the underlying serial architecture of the digital computer. Some choices of trade-off are better motivated, more realistic, or more plausible than others, of course, but in every case the constraints imposed serve to discipline the imagination—and hence the claims—of the thought experimenter. There is very little chance that a philosopher will be surprised (or more exactly, disappointed) by the results of his own thought experiment, but this happens all the time in AI.

A philosopher looking closely at these projects will find abundant grounds for skepticism. Many seem to be based on forlorn hopes or misbegotten enthusiasm for one architectural or information-handling feature or another, and if we extrapolate from the brief history of the field, we can be sure that most of the skepticism will be vindicated sooner or later. What makes AI an improvement on earlier philosophers' efforts at model sketching, however, is the manner in which skepticism is vindicated: by the actual failure of the system in question. Like philosophers, researchers in AI greet each new proposal with intuitive judgments about its prospects, backed up by more or less a priori arguments about why a certain feature has to be there or can't be made to work. But unlike philosophers, these researchers are not content with their arguments and intuitions; they leave themselves some room to be surprised by the results, a surprise that could only be provoked by the demonstrated, unexpected power of the actually contrived system in action.

Putnam surveys a panoply of problems facing AI: the problems of induction, of discerning relevant similarity, of learning, of modeling background knowledge. These are all widely recognized problems in AI, and the points he makes about them have all been made before by people in AI, who have then gone on to try to address the problems with various relatively concrete proposals. The devilish difficulties he sees facing traditional accounts of the process of induction, for example, are even more trenchantly catalogued by John Holland, Keith Holyoak, Richard Nisbett, and Paul Thagard in their recent book *Induction*,[6] but their diagnosis of these ills is the preamble for sketches of AI models designed to overcome them. Models addressed to the problems of discerning similarity and mechanisms for learning can be found in abundance. The SOAR project of John Laird, Allen Newell, and Paul Rosenbloom[7] is an estimable example. And the theme of the importance—and difficulty—of modeling background knowledge has been ubiquitous in recent years, with many suggestions for solutions under investigation. Now perhaps they are all hopeless, as Putnam is inclined to believe, but one simply cannot tell without actually building the models and testing them.

This last statement is not strictly true, of course. When an a priori refutation of an idea is sound, the doubting empirical model builder who persists despite the refutation will sooner or later have to face a chorus shouting "We told you so!" That is one of the occupational hazards of AI. The rub is how to tell the genuine a priori proofs of impossibility from mere failures of imagination. The philosophers' traditional answer is, More a priori analysis and argument. The AI researchers' answer is, Build it and see.

Putnam offers us a striking instance of this difference in his survey of possibilities for tackling the problem of background knowledge. Like Descartes, he manages to imagine a thought-experiment fiction that is now becoming real, and like Descartes, he is prepared to dismiss it in advance. One could, Putnam says,

simply try to program into a machine all the information a sophisticated human inductive judge has (including implicit information). At the least, this would require generations of researchers to formalize the information (probably it could not be done at all, because of the sheer quantity of information involved); and it is not clear that the result would be more than a gigantic expert system. No one would find this very exciting; and such an "intelligence" would in all likelihood be dreadfully unimaginative. . . .

This almost perfectly describes Douglas Lenat's enormous CYC project.[8] One might say that Lenat is attempting to create the proverbial walking encyclopedia: a mind-ful of commonsense knowledge in the form of a single data base containing all the facts expressed—or tacitly presupposed—in an encyclopedia! This involves handcrafting millions of representations in a single language (which must eventually be unified—no small task), from which the inference engine is expected to be able to deduce whatever it needs as it encounters novelty in its world: for instance, the fact that people in general prefer not to have their feet cut off or the fact that sunbathers are rare on Cape Cod in February.

Most of the opinion setters in AI share Putnam's jaundiced view of this project: it is not clear, as Putnam says, that the project will do anything that teaches us anything about the mind; in all likelihood, as he says, it will be dreadfully unimaginative. And many would go further and insist that its prospects are so forlorn and its cost so great that it should be abandoned in favor of more promising avenues. (The current estimate is measured in person-*centuries* of work, a figure that Putnam may not have bothered to imagine in detail.) But the project is funded, and we shall see.

What we have here is a clash of quite fundamental methodological assumptions. Philosophers are inclined to view AI projects with the patronizing disdain one reserves for those persistent fools who keep trying to square the circle or trisect the angle with compass and straightedge: we have *proved* that it cannot be done, so drop it! But the proofs are not geometric; they are ringed with assumptions about "plausible" boundary conditions and replete with idealizations that may prove as irrelevant here as in the notorious aerodynamicists' proofs that bumblebees cannot fly.

But still one may well inquire, echoing Putnam's challenge, whether AI has taught philosophers anything of importance about the mind *yet*. Putnam thinks it has not and supports his view with a rhetorically curious indictment: AI has utterly failed, over a quarter century, to solve problems that philosophy has utterly failed to solve over two millennia. He is right, I guess, but I am not impressed.[9] It is as if a philosopher were to conclude a dismissal of contemporary biology by saying that the biologists have not so much as asked the question, What is Life? Indeed, they have not; they have asked better questions that ought to dissolve or redirect the philosopher's curiosity.

Moreover, philosophers (of all people) should appreciate that solutions to problems are not the only good gift; tough new problems are just as good! Matching Putnam's rhetorical curiosity, I offer as AI's best contribution to philosophy a deep, new, unsolved epistemological problem ignored by generations of philosophers: the frame problem. Plato almost saw it. In the *Theaetetus*, he briefly explored the implications of a wonderful analogy:

Socrates: Now consider whether knowledge is a thing you can possess in that way without having it about you, like a man who has caught some wild birds—pigeons or what not—and keeps them in an aviary he has made for them at home. In a sense, of course, we might say he "has" them all the time inasmuch as he possesses them, mightn't we?

Theaetetus: Yes.

Socrates: But in another sense he "has" none of them, though he has got control of them, now that he has made them captive in an enclosure of his own; he can take and have hold of them whenever he likes by catching any bird he chooses, and let them go again; and it is open to him to do that as often as he pleases.[10]

Plato saw that merely possessing knowledge (like birds in an aviary) is not enough; one must be able to command what one possesses. To perform well, one must be able to get the right bit of knowledge to fly to the edge at the right time (in real time, as the engineers say). But he underestimated the difficulty of this trick and hence underestimated the sort of theory one would have to give of the organization of knowledge in order to explain our bird-charming talents. Neither Plato nor any subsequent philosopher, so far as I can see, saw this as in itself a deep problem of epistemology, since the demands of efficiency and robustness paled into invisibility when compared with the philosophical demand for certainty, but so it has emerged in the hands of AI.[11]

Just as important to philosophy as new problems and new solutions, however, is new raw material, and this AI has provided in abundance. It has provided a bounty of objects to think about—individual systems in all their particularity that are much more vivid and quirky than the systems I (for one) could dream up in a thought experiment. This is not a trivial harvest. Compare philosophy of mind (the analytic study of the limits, opportunities, and implications of possible theories of the mind) with the literary theory of the novel (the analytic study of the limits, opportunities, and implications of possible novels). One could in principle write excellent literary theory in the absence of novels as exemplars. Aristotle, for instance, could in principle have written a treatise on the anticipated strengths and weaknesses, powers and problems, of the various possible types of novels. Today's literary theorist is not required to examine the existing exemplars, but they are, to say the least, a useful crutch. They extend the imaginative range and the surefootedness of even the most brilliant theoretician and provide bracing checks on enthusiastic generalizations and conclusions. The minitheories, sketches, and models of AI may not be great novels, but they are the best we have to date, and just as mediocre novels are often a boon to literary theorists—they wear their deficiencies on their sleeves—so bad theories, failed models, and hopelessly confused hunches in AI are a boon to philosophers of mind. But you have to read them to get the benefit.

Perhaps the best current example of this benefit is the wave of enthusiasm for connectionist models. For years philosophers of mind have been vaguely and hopefully waving their hands in the direction of these models—utterly unable to conceive them in detail but sure in their bones that some such thing had to be possible. (My own first book, *Content and Consciousness,* is a good example of such vague theorizing.[12]) Other philosophers have been just as sure that all such approaches were doomed (Jerry Fodor is a good example). Now, at last, we will be able to examine a host of objects in this anticipated class and find out whose hunches were correct. In principle, no doubt, it could be worked out without the crutches, but in practice, such disagreements between philosophers tend to degenerate into hardened positions defended by increasingly strained arguments, redefinitions of terms, and tendentious morals drawn from other quarters.

Putnam suggests that since AI is first and foremost a subbranch of engineering, it cannot be philosophy. He is especially insistent that we should dismiss its claim of being epistemology. I find this suggestion curious. Surely Hobbes and Leibniz and Descartes were doing philosophy, even epistemology, when they waved their hands and spoke very abstractly about the limits of mechanism. So was Kant, when he claimed to be investigating the conditions under which experience was possible. Philosophers have traditionally tried to figure out the combinatorial powers and inherent limitations of "impressions and ideas," of "petites perceptions," "intuitions," and "schemata." Researchers in AI have asked similar questions about various sorts of "data structures" and "procedural representations" and "frames" and "links" and yes, "schemata," now rather more rigorously defined. So far as I can see, these are fundamentally the same investigations, but in AI they are conducted under additional (and generally well-motivated) constraints and with the aid of a host of more specific concepts.

Putnam sees engineering and epistemology as incompatible. I see at most a trade-off: to the extent that a speculative exploration in AI is more abstract, more idealized, less mechanistically constrained, it is "more philosophical"—but that does not mean it is thereby necessarily of more interest or value to a philosopher! On the contrary, it is probably because philosophers have been too philosophical—too abstract, idealized, and unconstrained by empirically plausible mechanistic assumptions—that they have failed for so long to make much sense of the mind. AI has not yet solved any of our ancient riddles about the mind, but it has provided us with new ways of disciplining and extending philosophical imagination that we have only begun to exploit.

ENDNOTES

[1] Alan Turing, "Computing Machinery and Intelligence," *Mind* 59 (236) (1950): 433, reprinted in Douglas Hofstadter and Daniel Dennett, eds., *The Mind's I* (New York: Basic Books, 1981), 54–67.

[2] René Descartes, *Discourse on Method* (1637), trans. Laurence J. LaFleur, 3d ed. (New York: Bobbs-Merrill, 1960), 41–42.

[3] Donald Davidson, "Mental Events," in L. Foster and J. W. Swanson, eds., *Experience and Theory* (Amherst: University of Massachusetts Press, 1970), 79–101.

[4] François Jacob, "Evolution and Tinkering," *Science* 196 (1977):1161–66.

[5] Douglas Hofstadter, "Waking Up from the Boolean Dream, or Subcognition as Computation," chap. 26, in *Metamagical Themas* (New York: Basic Books, 1985), 631–65.

[6] John H. Holland, Keith J. Holyoak, Richard E. Nisbett, and Paul R. Thagard, *Induction: Processes of Inference, Learning and Discovery* (Cambridge: MIT Press, 1986).

[7] John E. Laird, Allen Newell and Paul S. Rosenbloom, "SOAR: An Architecture for General Intelligence," *Artificial Intelligence* 33 (September 1987):1–64.

[8] Douglas Lenat, Mayank Prakash, and May Shepherd, "CYC: Using Commonsense Knowledge to Overcome Brittleness and Knowledge Acquisition Bottlenecks," *AI Magazine* 6 (4) (1986):65–85.

[9] In "Artificial Intelligence as Philosophy and as Psychology," in *Philosophical Perspectives in Artificial Intelligence*, ed. Martin Ringle (Atlantic Highlands, N.J.: Humanities Press International, 1979), and in *Brainstorms: Philosophical Essays on Mind and Psychology* (Cambridge: MIT Press, 1978), I have argued that AI has solved what I have called Hume's Problem—the problem of breaking the threatened infinite regress of homunculi consulting (and understanding) internal representations such as Hume's impressions and ideas. I suspect Putnam would claim, with some justice, that it was computer science in general, not AI in particular, that showed philosophy the way to break this regress.

[10] *Plato's Theaetetus*, trans. Francis M. Cornford (New York: Macmillan, 1957), 197 C–D.

[11] Daniel C. Dennett, "Cognitive Wheels: The Frame Problem of AI" in *Minds, Machines and Evolution: Philosophical Studies*, ed. Christopher Hookway (Cambridge: Cambridge University Press, 1985), reprinted in the new anthology *The Robot's Dilemma: The Frame Problem in Artificial Intelligence*, ed. Zenon W. Pylyshyn (Norwood, N.J.: Ablex, 1987). In this introduction to the frame problem, I explain why it is an epistemological problem and why philosophers didn't notice it.

[12] Daniel C. Dennett, *Content and Consciousness* (Atlantic Highlands, N.J.: Humanities Press International, 1969).

John McCarthy

Mathematical Logic in Artificial Intelligence

HIS ARTICLE concerns computer programs that represent information about their problem domains in mathematical logical languages and use logical inference to decide what actions are appropriate to achieve their goals.

Mathematical logic is not a single language. There are many kinds of mathematical logic, and even choosing a kind does not specify the language. The language is determined by declaring what nonlogical symbols will be used and what sentences will be taken as axioms. The nonlogical symbols are those that concern the concrete subject matter to be stored in a computer's data base—for example, information about objects and their locations and motions.

Whatever the choice of symbols, all kinds of mathematical logic share two ideas. First, it must be mathematically definite what strings of symbols are considered formulas of the logic. Second, it must be mathematically definite what inferences of new formulas from old ones are allowed. These ideas permit the writing of computer programs that decide what combinations of symbols are sentences and what inferences are allowed in a particular logical language.

Mathematical logic has become an important branch of mathematics, and most logicians work on problems arising from the internal development of the subject. Mathematical logic has also been applied to studying the foundations of mathematics, and there it has had its greatest success. Its founders, Aristotle, Leibniz, Boole, and

John McCarthy is professor of computer science and Charles M. Pigott Professor of Engineering at Stanford University.

Frege, also wished to apply it to making reasoning about human affairs more rigorous. Indeed, Leibniz was explicit about his goal of replacing argument with calculation. However, expressing knowledge and reasoning about the commonsense world in mathematical logic has entailed difficulties that seem to require extensions of the basic concepts of logic, and these extensions are only beginning to develop.

If a computer is to store facts about the world and reason with them, it needs a precise language. The program must be based on a precise idea of what reasoning is allowed—that is, how new formulas may be derived from old. It was natural in the beginning to try to use mathematical logical language to express what an intelligent computer program "knows" that is relevant to the problems we want it to solve and to make the program use logical inference in order to decide what to do. The first proposal to use logic in artificial intelligence for expressing what a program knows and how it should reason was in a paper I wrote in 1960. The problem of proving logical formulas as a domain for AI had already been studied. In this paper I said:

The *advice taker* is a proposed program for solving problems by manipulating sentences in formal languages. The main difference between it and other programs or proposed programs for manipulating formal languages (the *Logic Theory Machine* of Newell, Simon and Shaw and the Geometry Program of Herbert Gelernter) is that in the previous programs the formal system was the subject matter but the heuristics were all embodied in the program. In this program the procedures will be described as much as possible in the language itself and, in particular, the heuristics are all so described.

The main advantage we expect the *advice taker* to have is that its behavior will be improvable merely by making statements to it, telling it about its symbolic environment and what is wanted from it. To make these statements will require little if any knowledge of the program or the previous knowledge of the *advice taker*. One will be able to assume that the *advice taker* will have available to it a fairly wide class of immediate logical consequences of anything it is told and its previous knowledge. This property is expected to have much in common with what makes us describe certain humans as having *common sense*. We shall therefore say that *a program has common sense if it automatically deduces for itself a sufficiently wide class of immediate consequences of anything it is told and what it already knows.*[1]

The advice taker prospectus, ambitious in 1960, would be considered ambitious even today and is still far from being immediately realizable. Mathematical logic is especially far from the goal of expressing the heuristics in the same language in which are expressed the facts the heuristics must act on. Yet the main reasons for using logical sentences extensively in AI are better understood by researchers today than in 1960. Expressing information in declarative sentences is far more flexible than expressing it in segments of computer program or in tables. Sentences can be true in much wider contexts than specific programs can be useful. The supplier of a fact does not have to understand much about how the receiver functions or about how or whether the receiver will use it. The same fact can be used for many purposes; the logical consequences of collections of facts can be made available.

Existing computer programs come more or less close to this goal, depending on the extent to which they use the formalisms of logic. I shall begin by describing four levels of their use.

1. A machine on the lowest level uses no logical sentences. It merely executes the commands of its program. All its "beliefs" are implicit in its state. Nevertheless, it is often appropriate to ascribe beliefs and goals to the program. A missile may believe its target is friendly and abandon the goal of hitting it. One can often usefully say that a certain machine does what it thinks will achieve its goals. Daniel Dennett, Allen Newell, and I have all discussed ascription of mental qualities to machines.[2] The intent of the machine's designers and the way it can be expected to behave may be more readily described in terms of intention than with a purely physical description.

The relation between the physical and the intentional descriptions of a machine is most easy to understand in simple systems that admit readily understandable descriptions of both kinds. Take a thermostat as an example. We might say that when it believes the temperature is too hot, it turns on the cooling system in order to achieve its goal of getting the right temperature. Some finicky philosophers object to such ascription. Unless a system has a full human mind, they contend, it should not be regarded as having any mental qualities at all. This restriction is like omitting zero and one from the number system on the grounds that numbers are not required to count sets with no elements or with one element. Of course, ascribing beliefs to machines (and people) is more important when our physical knowledge is inadequate to explain or predict behavior. Much more can be said about ascribing mental qualities to machines, but that is not what AI is mainly concerned with today.

2. The next level of logic use involves computer programs that put sentences in machine memory to represent their beliefs but use rules other than ordinary logical inference to reach conclusions. New sentences are often obtained from the old ones by *ad hoc* programs. Moreover, the sentences that appear in memory are from a program-dependent subset of the logical language being used. Adding certain true sentences in the language may even spoil the functioning of the program. Logic is used at this second level in "expert systems," programs that consist of knowledge bases (e.g., lists of disease symptoms in medical expert systems) and inference engines (which contain rules, in the form of explicit instructions to the machine, on how to manipulate the information in the knowledge base). In comparison with the languages of first-order logic, languages used at this level are often rather unexpressive. For example, they may not admit quantified sentences (i.e., sentences including "for all" or "there exists"), and they may represent general rules in a separate notation. Often, rules cannot be consequences of a program's action; they must all be put in by a "knowledge engineer." Sometimes the reason programs have this form is just ignorance, but the usual reason for the restriction is the practical one of making the program run fast and deduce just the kinds of conclusions its designer anticipates. Most often, the rules are implications used in just one direction (in other words, the contrapositive of an implication is not used). I believe the need for such specialized inference will turn out to be temporary and will be reduced or eliminated by improved ways of controlling general inference—for example, by allowing the heuristic rules to be expressed also as sentences, as advocated in the preceding extract from my 1960 paper.

3. The third level uses first-order logic as well as logical deduction. Usually the sentences are represented as clauses, and the deduction methods are based on J. Allen Robinson's method of resolution.[3] A fact in one such program's data base might be:

$$(\text{for all } (x) \text{ (if (and (inst } x \text{ vegetable) (color } x \text{ purple))}$$
$$(\text{inst } x \text{ eggplant)))}$$

Translated into more common language, the fact reads: "All purple vegetables are eggplants." Its structure is typical of if-then clauses in logical data bases: given any x, if x satisfies the stated conditions, then x ensures a certain result—(for all (x) (if (conditions) then (result))).

In the example, x must satisfy two conditions: (inst x vegetable) and (color x purple). The first condition means that x must be a specific instance of the class of vegetables, and the second means that the color of x must be purple. The result, (inst x eggplant), means that x is an instance of an eggplant. Armed with this fact, the program might seem ready to take on this task:

$$\text{(inst Gertrude vegetable)}$$
$$\text{(color Gertrude purple)}$$
$$\text{(SHOW: (inst Gertrude eggplant))}$$

Translated, the task is: Given the fact that Gertrude is a purple vegetable, show that Gertrude is an eggplant. But with just the logical fact, the program can do nothing with the task. It needs a method for reasoning from general statements about nondescript x's to specific statements about Gertrude. The reasoning of Robinson's resolution method prescribes a way to substitute Gertrude for x and thereby unify the clauses in the data base with those in the task.

Examples of such programs used commercially are "expert system shells" (ART, KEE, OPS-5)—computer programs that create generic expert systems. You tell the program what facts you want in the data base; the program converts the facts into logical statements and then follows the heuristics in its own inference engine to create an inference engine tailored to the facts you put into the program.

The third level of logic is less used for practical purposes than is level two because techniques for controlling the reasoning are still insufficiently developed and it is common for a program to generate many useless conclusions before it reaches a desired solution. Indeed, unsuccessful experience with this method[4] has led to more restricted uses of logic (for example, the STRIPS system of Richard Fikes and Nils Nilsson[5]).

In this connection it is important to mention logic programming, first introduced in Microplanner[6] and approached from different points of view by Robert Kowalski and Alain Colmerauer in the 1970s.[7] Microplanner was a rather unsystematic collection of tools, unlike Prolog, a computer language that relies almost entirely on one mathematically tractable kind of logic programming,[8] but the main idea is the same. If one uses a restricted class of sentences, the so-called Horn clauses, then it is possible to use a restricted form of logical deduction. This eases the control problem and makes it possible for the programmer to anticipate the course the deduction will take. The problem is that only certain kinds of facts are conveniently expressed as Horn clauses. Nevertheless, expressibility in Horn clauses is an important property of a set of facts, and logic programming has been successfully used for many applications (although it seems unlikely to dominate AI programming, as certain of its advocates hope).

Although they express both facts and rules as logical sentences, third-level systems are still rather specialized. The axioms with which the programs begin are not general truths about the world but sentences whose meaning and truth are limited to the narrow domain in which the program has to act. For this reason, the facts of one program usually cannot be used in a data base for other programs.

4. The fourth level is still a goal. It involves representing general facts about the world as logical sentences. Once put in a data base, the facts can be used by any program. The facts would have the neutrality of purpose characteristic of much human information. The supplier of information would not have to understand the goals of the potential user or how his mind works. The present ways of "teaching" computer programs amount to education by brain surgery.

A major difficulty is that fourth-level systems require extensions to mathematical logic. One kind of extension is nonmonotonic reasoning, first proposed in the late 1970s.[9] Traditional logic is monotonic in the following sense. If a sentence p is inferred from a collection A of sentences, and if B is a more inclusive set of sentences, then p can be inferred from B. For example, let collection A be these sentences: All bachelors are unmarried; John is a bachelor. Let collection B be these sentences: All bachelors are unmarried; John has no girlfriends; John is a bachelor. From both sets of questions, you can infer sentence p: John is unmarried. The set of sentences A is a model of the set: All x are y; w is x. If "w is y" is true in all models of this general set, then it will be true in all models of the general form of set B. So we see that the monotonic character of traditional logic does not depend on the details of the logical system, but is quite fundamental.

While much human reasoning corresponds to that of traditional logic, some important human commonsense reasoning is not monotonic. We reach conclusions from certain premises that we would not reach if certain other sentences were included in our premises. For example, learning that I own a car, you conclude that it is appropriate on a certain occasion to ask me for a ride; but when you learn the further fact that the car is in the garage being fixed, you no longer draw that conclusion. Some people think it is possible to try to save monotonicity by saying that what was in your mind was not a general rule about asking for a ride from car owners but a probabilistic rule—something like "On 70 percent of occasions it is appropriate for you to ask for a ride if I own a car." So far it has not proved possible to work out the detailed epistemology of this approach—that is, to determine exactly what probabilistic sentences should be used. Instead, AI has moved to directly formalizing nonmonotonic logical reasoning.

Formalized nonmonotonic reasoning is under rapid development, and many kinds of systems have been proposed. I shall concentrate on an approach called "circumscription" because I know it, and because it has met with wide acceptance and is perhaps the most actively pursued approach at present. The idea is to single out, from among the models of the collection of sentences being assumed, some "preferred," or "standard," models. The preferred models are those that satisfy a certain minimum principle. What is to be minimized is not yet decided in complete generality, but many domains that have been studied yield quite general theories using minimizations of abnormality or of the set of some kind of entity. The idea is not entirely unfamiliar. For example, Occam's razor, "Do not multiply entities beyond necessity," is such a minimum principle.

Minimization in logic is another example of an area of mathematics being discovered in connection with applications rather than through the normal internal development of mathematics. Of course, the reverse is happening on an even larger scale; many logical concepts developed for purely mathematical reasons turn out to have importance for AI.

As a more concrete example of nonmonotonic reasoning, consider the conditions under which a boat may be used to cross a river. Now consider things that might be wrong with a boat. It might have a leak. It might have no oars, no motor, or no sails, depending on what kind of a boat it is. It would be reasonably convenient to list some of these things in a set of axioms. However, besides those obstacles that we can expect to list in advance, human reasoning will admit still others should they arise, but it cannot be expected to think of them all in advance (e.g., a fence down the middle of the river). One can handle this difficulty by using circumscription to minimize the set of things that prevent the boat from crossing the river—that is, the set of obstacles to be overcome. If the reasoner knows of none in a particular case, he will conjecture that the boat can be used, but if he learns of one, he will get a different result when he minimizes.

This illustration shows that nonmonotonic reasoning is conjectural rather than rigorous. Indeed, it has been shown that certain mathematical logical systems cannot be rigorously extended, that they have a certain kind of completeness.

It is as misleading to conduct a discussion of this kind entirely without formulas as it would be to discuss the foundations of physics without formulas. Unfortunately, many people are unable to follow the mathematics. So I discuss instead a formalization by Vladimir Lifschitz of a simple example called "the Yale shooting problem."[10] Drew McDermott, who has become discouraged about the use of logic in AI and especially about nonmonotonic formalisms, devised the problem as a challenge.[11] Lifschitz's method works well here, but I think it will require further modification.

In this problem there is initially an unloaded gun and a person, Fred. The gun is then loaded. There is a wait, and then the gun is pointed at Fred and fired. The desired conclusion is that Fred dies. Informally, the rules are (1) that a living person remains alive until something happens to him, (2) that loading causes a gun to become loaded, (3) that a loaded gun remains loaded until something unloads it, (4) that shooting unloads a gun, and (5) that shooting a loaded gun at a person kills him. We are intended to reason as follows: Fred will remain alive until the gun is fired because nothing can be inferred to happen to him; the gun will remain loaded until it is fired because nothing can be inferred to happen to it; Fred will then die when the gun is fired. The nonmonotonic part of the reasoning is minimizing the things that happen or assuming that nothing happens without a reason.

The logical sentences are intended to express these five premises, but they do not explicitly say that no other phenomenon occurs. For example, there is no assertion that Fred is not wearing a bulletproof vest, nor are any properties of bulletproof vests mentioned. Nevertheless, a person will conclude that unless some unmentioned aspect of the situation is present to prevent Fred's death, he will die. The difficulty is that the sentences admit an "unintended minimal model," to use the terminology of mathematical logic. Namely, it may happen that for some unspecified reason the gun becomes unloaded during the wait, so that Fred remains alive. The way nonmonotonic formalisms (e.g., circumscription and R. A. Reiter's logic of defaults) were used to formulate the problem, minimizing "abnormality" results in two possibilities, not one. The unintended possibility is that the gun mysteriously becomes unloaded.

It seems likely that introducing nonmonotonic reasoning will not be the only modification of logic that will be required in order to give machines human capability for commonsense reasoning. To make programs that reason about their own knowledge and belief (i.e., programs that have even rudimentary consciousness), it is necessary to formalize many intensional notions (e.g., knowledge and belief). One can formalize some of them in first-order logic by introducing propositions and concepts as individuals.[12] Complicating such efforts are the paradoxes discovered by Richard Montague.[13] To avoid them, it will be necessary to weaken the axioms suitably, but a good way of doing so has yet to be found. It also seems necessary to formalize the notion of context, but this is in a very preliminary state of investigation.[14]

AI AND PHILOSOPHY

Artificial intelligence cannot avoid philosophy. If a computer program is to behave intelligently in the real world, it must be provided with some kind of framework into which to fit particular facts it is told or discovers. This amounts to at least a fragment of some kind of philosophy, however naive. Here I agree with philosophers who advocate the study of philosophy and claim that one who purports to ignore it is merely condemning himself to a naive philosophy.

Because it is still far behind the intellectual performance of people who are philosophically naive, AI could probably make do with a naive philosophy for a long time. Unfortunately, it has not been possible to say what a naive philosophy is, and philosophers offer little guidance.

The next plausible alternative might be to build our programs to seek and represent knowledge in accordance with the tenets of one of the philosophies that have been proposed by philosophers. This also has not been possible. Either no one in AI (including retreaded philosophers) understands philosophical theories well enough to program a computer in accordance with their tenets, or the philosophers have not even come close to the required precision. Actually, some of the empiricist philosophies appear to be precise enough, but they turn out to be inadequate when one attempts to use them in the most modest of computer programs. Therefore, we AI researchers have found ourselves on our own when it comes to providing a program with a basic intellectual structure. Here is some of what we think this would require:

Ontology. I adopt Willard Quine's idea that our ontology is defined by the range of bound variables.[15] With this idea, we need to specify what kinds of entities are to be assumed, that is, what the robot's beliefs are to be about. His nominalism would further suggest, it seems to me, that variables take only material objects as values. This theory promptly proves inadequate because, for example, it doesn't permit the robot's designer to inform it about what properties of objects are preserved when certain kinds of events take place.

Quine tells us that "there is no place in science for ideas," and argues for this view with examples of the difficulty of defining what it means for two people to have the same idea.[16] However, if a program is to search for a good idea by generating lots of ideas and then testing them, it needs some criteria for deciding when it has already tested a certain idea. Thus, ideas as objects seem to be required, but how to avoid the difficulty Quine cites has not yet been discovered. Present AI systems cannot enumerate ideas.

Free will. The robots we plan to build are entirely deterministic systems. However, a sophisticated robot must decide what to do by considering the various things it *can* do and choosing which has the best consequences in view of the goals it has been given. To do so, it must be able to represent "I can do A and I can do B, but B seems better, so while I can do A, I won't." What does it mean for a robot to believe "I can, but I won't"? It is a deterministic system, so either it will do A or it won't. Patrick J. Hayes and I have offered some proposals for resolving the problem of free will for robots.[17]

Nonmonotonic reasoning. AI programs require ways of jumping to conclusions on the basis of insufficient evidence.

AI researchers' attempts to determine an intellectual framework precise enough for programming AI systems have already led to certain philosophical views—both to taking sides in some ancient philosophical controversies and to proposals that we regard as new. I will discuss two points:

1. *Incrementalism, or modesty.* The facts about the effects of actions and other events that have been put into the data bases of AI programs are not very general. They are not even as general as what questioning would elicit from naive people, let alone general enough to satisfy people familiar with the philosophical literature. However, they suffice in certain cases to determine the appropriate action to achieve a goal. Observing the limitations of these cases leads to further advance. This is a useful methodology even when the objectives are philosophical. One can design formalisms that can be used in working systems and improve them when their defects become apparent.

The philosopher might claim that the working systems are too trivial to be of interest to him. He would be wrong, because it turns out that the philosophical investigations of action have missed important phenomena that arise as soon as one tries to design systems that plan actions. Here are two examples. First, the ideas on association, dating at least from Mill and going through the behaviorists, are too vague to be programmed at all. Second, philosophers have missed most of the nonmonotonic character of the reasoning involved in everyday decision making. For AI it is important not only that the researcher be able to revise his ideas, but also that the program be able to improve its behavior incrementally, either by accepting advice from the user or by learning from experience, and such improvement requires new languages for expressing knowledge. For example, a baby first considers the word *mother* a proper name, then a general name for adult women, and still later a designation of a relation. I think that before we can have computer programs with the general intelligence and linguistic flexibility of a human child, AI researchers must develop languages with "elaboration tolerance." For example, such a language would allow the usage of the word *mother* to develop as described above without losing older information. Elaboration tolerance is a current AI research topic.

2. *Objectivity*. Regardless of one's ultimate view of reality, in designing robots we need to make the robot view the world as an external reality about which it has and can obtain only partial knowledge. We will not be successful if we design the robot to regard the world as merely a structure built on the robot's sensory information. There needs to be a theory (it could be called metaepistemology) relating the structure of a world, a knowledge-seeker in that world, the interaction channel between the knowledge-seeker and the rest of the world, the knowledge-seeker's rules for deciding what assertions about the world are meaningful, and the knowledge-seeker's rules for accepting evidence about the world and what the knowledge-seeker can discover. If the rules are too restrictive (as perhaps they are in some operationalist philosophies of science), the knowledge-seeker, regarding the assertions as insufficiently operational to be meaningful, will be unable to discover basic facts about the world.

REMARKS

Much of what I want to say involves stating a position on issues that are controversial even within AI.

I believe, for example, that artificial intelligence is best regarded as a branch of computer science rather than as a branch of psychology. AI is concerned with methods of achieving goals in situations in which the information available has a certain complex character. The methods that have to be used are related to the problem presented by the situation and are similar whether the problem solver is human, a Martian, or a computer program.

Initially, some people were overoptimistic about how long it would take to achieve human-level intelligence. Optimism was natural because only a few of the difficulties had been identified. Enough difficulties have been identified by now to establish AI as one of the more difficult sciences. Maybe it will take five years to achieve human-level intelligence, and maybe it will take five hundred.

It is still not clear how to characterize situations in which intelligence is required. Evidently, they are open-ended. Even in a game like chess, where the rules are fixed, the methods for deciding on a move are open-ended in character—new ways of thinking about chess positions are invented all the time.

AI has so far identified certain methods of pattern matching, heuristic searching of trees of possibilities, and representation of information by rules and learning. Other methods are still to be characterized, especially methods of representing problems as collections of subproblems that can be examined separately to get results that can then be used in studying their interactions.

Approaching AI through logic is not the only strategy that may lead to success. For example, approaches more closely tied to biology may succeed eventually, even though most of the biology-motivated approaches that have been tried since the 1950s have dried up.

Much controversy surrounds AI's implications for philosophy, a subject about which there are strong views. AI tends to support rationalist and realist views of philosophical problems rather than empiricist, phenomenological, or idealist views. It encourages a piecemeal approach to the philosophy of mind, in which mental qualities are considered separately rather than as part of a grand package. This is because some systems have important, but rather limited, mental qualities.

There are many problems in formalizing common sense, and many approaches to solving them await exploration. Two thousand years of philosophy have only limited relevance in this regard. In my opinion, the proper discussion of these problems is unavoidably mostly technical, involving the actual logical formalisms being used. The situation calculus used has important known limitations. The *result* (e, s) formalism, used in AI to express the consequences of actions and other events, has to be modified to handle continuous time. A quite different formalism is needed to express facts about concurrent events. Robert Kowalski and Mark Sergot's "event calculus" is a candidate for meeting both of these requirements.[18]

The study of AI may lead to a mathematical metaepistemology analogous to metamathematics—to a study of the relation between a knower's rules for accepting evidence and a world in which he is embedded. This study could result in mathematical theorems about whether certain intellectual strategies can lead to the discovery of certain facts about the world. I think this possibility will eventually revolutionize philosophy.

ENDNOTES

[1] John McCarthy, "Programs with Common Sense," in *Proceedings of the Teddington Conference on the Mechanization of Thought Processes* (London: Her Majesty's Stationery Office, 1960), 77–84.

[2] Daniel C. Dennett, "Intentional Systems," *Journal of Philosophy* 68 (4) (25 February 1971):25; Allen Newell, "The Knowledge Level," *AI Magazine* 2 (2) (1981):87–106; and John McCarthy, "Ascribing Mental Qualities to Machines," in *Philosophical Perspectives in Artificial Intelligence,* ed. Martin Ringle (Brighton, Sussex: Harvester Press, 1979), 1–20.

[3] J. Allen Robinson, "A Machine-oriented Logic Based on the Resolution Principle," *Journal of the Association for Computing Machinery* 12 (1) (1965):23–41.

[4] Cordell Green, "Application of Theorem Proving to Problem Solving," *International Joint Conference on Artificial Intelligence* 1 (1969):219–39.

[5] Richard Fikes and Nils Nilsson, "STRIPS: A New Approach to the Application of Theorem Proving to Problem Solving," *Artificial Intelligence* 2 (3,4) (January 1971):189–208.

[6] Gerald J. Sussman, Terry Winograd, and Eugene Charniak, "Micro-planner Reference Manual," Report AIM–203A (Cambridge: Artificial Intelligence Laboratory, Massachusetts Institute of Technology, 1971).

[7] Robert Kowalski, *Logic for Problem Solving* (Amsterdam: North-Holland, 1979); the first implementation of Prolog was developed by Alain Colmerauer of the University of Marseilles in 1971, but this is described only in the internal documents of his group.

[8] A recent text on logic programming is Leon Sterling and Ehud Shapiro, *The Art of Prolog* (Cambridge: MIT Press, 1986).

[9] John McCarthy, "Epistemological Problems of Artificial Intelligence," in *Proceedings of the Fifth International Joint Conference on Artificial Intelligence* (Cambridge: Massachusetts Institute of Technology, 1977); McCarthy, "Circumscription—A Form of Non-Monotonic Reasoning," *Artificial Intelligence* 13 (1,2) (1980):27–39; McCarthy, "Applications of Circumscription to Formalizing Common Sense Knowledge," *Artificial Intelligence* 28 (1) (1986):89–116. See also Raymond A. Reiter, "A Logic for Default Reasoning," *Artificial Intelligence* 13 (1,2) (1980):81–132; and Drew McDermott and Jon Doyle, "Non-Monotonic Logic I," *Artificial Intelligence* 13 (1) (1980):41–72.

[10] Vladimir Lifschitz, "Formal Theories of Action," a preliminary report in vol. 2 of *Proceedings of the International Joint Conference on Artificial Intelligence* (Los Altos, Calif.: Morgan-Kaufmann, 1977), 966–72.

[11]Drew McDermott, "A Critique of Pure Reason," *Computational Intelligence* (forthcoming, 1988).

[12]John McCarthy, "First Order Theories of Individual Concepts and Propositions," in *Machine Intelligence 9,* ed. Donald Michie (Edinburgh: University of Edinburgh Press, 1979), 129–48.

[13]Richard Montague, "Syntactical Treatments of Modality, with Corollaries on Reflexion Principles and Finite Axiomatizability," *Acta Philosophica Fennica* 16(1963):153–67, reprinted in Richard Montague, *Formal Philosophy* (New Haven: Yale University Press, 1974).

[14]Michael Genesereth and Nils Nilsson have written the best general text on the logic approach to AI, *The Logical Foundations of Artificial Intelligence* (Los Altos, Calif.: Morgan-Kaufmann, 1987).

[15]Willard V. Quine, *Quiddities* (Cambridge: Harvard University Press, 1987).

[16]Ibid.

[17]John McCarthy and Patrick J. Hayes, "Some Philosophical Problems from the Standpoint of Artificial Intelligence," in *Machine Intelligence 4,* ed. Donald Michie (New York: American Elsevier, 1969).

[18]Robert Kowalski and Sergot Marek, *A Logic-based Calculus of Events* (London: Department of Computing, Imperial College, 1985).